Miss Lucy of the CIO

The Life and Times

of Lucy Randolph Mason,

1882–1959

Miss Lucy
of the CIO

The Life and Times
of Lucy Randolph Mason,
1882–1959

John A. Salmond

The University of Georgia Press

Athens and London

© 1988 by the University of Georgia Press
Athens, Georgia 30602
All rights reserved
Designed by Kathi L. Dailey
Set in 10 on 13 Mergenthaler Caledonia with Radiant display
The paper in this book meets the guidelines for
permanence and durability of the Committee on
Production Guidelines for Book Longevity of the
Council on Library Resources.

Printed in the United States of America

92 91 90 89 88   5 4 3 2 1

Library of Congress Cataloging in Publication Data

Salmond, John A.
Miss Lucy of the CIO.

Bibliography: p.
Includes index.
1. Mason, Lucy Randolph, 1882–1959. 2. Trade-unions—
United States—Officials and employees—Biography.
3. Congress of Industrial Organizations (U.S.)—Biography.
4. Feminists—United States—Biography. I. Title.
HD6509.M375S25   1988   331.88'33'0924 [B]   87-5822
ISBN 0-8203-0956-7 (alk. paper)

British Library Cataloging in Publication Data available.

All photographs in this book are from the Manuscript Department of the
William R. Perkins Library, Duke University.

The publication of this book is supported by a grant from the
Publications Committee of La Trobe University,
Melbourne, Australia.

To the Claytons, to the Cells,
and to my children

Contents

Preface

In 1946, responding to a reporter's question, Lucy Randolph Mason tried to explain why she had joined the organized labor movement. The reason, she said, had to do with her deep religious belief. She was, after all, the daughter and granddaughter of Episcopal clergymen. Had she been born a man, she would have followed her father into the church. Because she had been born a woman, which she was glad to be, she had had to find other ways of serving the Lord. "I have spent my life working religion out in social action," she explained to the young reporter. "Church people ought to do something to bring about the Kingdom of God on earth. That's why I am in the labor movement." For this reason, too, she had worked for the Richmond YWCA, first as its industrial secretary and then its general secretary. For the same reason, in 1932, she had left her home town to become general secretary of the National Consumers League in New York. Her public life had always had as its unifying principle the extension of God's Kingdom in this world, in line with the exhortation to Moses: "Thou shalt love thy neighbor as thyself."[1]

Lucy Mason rarely disclosed as directly as she did in that interview just how deeply and directly she had been influenced by the message of the social gospel. Yet as her life unfolded, there could be no doubt that its primary purpose was to work toward the earthly extension of God's Kingdom. This goal took her, as she said, into the labor movement as public relations representative for the Congress of Industrial Organizations (CIO) in the South, where, if she had not been present and active, hundreds of local organizers, often working in difficult and dangerous circumstances, would have found their lives even more precarious. She is best remembered, and deservedly so, for this work.

Concern for labor, however, was but one of three interconnected themes, though perhaps the most important, to which she brought her social gospel concerns and which, through them, helped shape her life.

The other two were feminism and the South; her allegiance to the region included a passion to eliminate its worst inequities and injustices. Throughout her life, Lucy Mason closely identified herself with the long and unfinished struggle to enable women to participate fully and equally in American life, and she never vacillated on the issue. As for the South, her love for her state and her region was total. Her dedication was hardly surprising, given the nature of Lucy Mason's lineage. The blood of a constellation of Virginia heroes who included George Mason, John Marshall, and Robert E. Lee flowed in her veins; she came from a background steeped in history and tradition. Her social gospel beliefs, however, meant that she could not uncritically accept every aspect of southern life and belief. In particular, she deeply abhorred the notion of racial superiority and the constricting effect that racist policies had had on southern blacks. God's Kingdom, she fervently believed, included his black children as well as his white ones. These themes gave Lucy Mason's life its unity, as I hope the pages of the present book will demonstrate.

In my research and writing I was fortunate enough to have an avalanche of assistance. First, I feel lucky to have enjoyed the aid and interest of a score or more of librarians and archivists throughout the United States, without whom I could not have written this book at all. The fact that I cannot acknowledge them all by name in no way diminishes the debt I owe them. My research was made possible by the financial support of the Australian Research Grants Scheme and La Trobe University. Duke University in 1981 housed me as a research associate during a most rewarding period of leave from La Trobe University. Virginia Durr discussed Lucy Mason with me, while Mason's nephew, Taylor Burke, generously made available his private papers. I express my gratitude to these institutions and individuals.

For permission to use and to quote from materials in their possession I thank: the Manuscript Department at the William R. Perkins Library, Duke University; the Southern Historical Collection, University of North Carolina at Chapel Hill; the Manuscripts Department at the University of Virginia Library (Virginius Dabney Papers); the Special Collections and Archives Department, James Branch Cabell Library, Virginia Commonwealth University (Adele Clark Collection); the Franklin D. Roosevelt Library; the Southern Labor Archives at Georgia State University; the Special Collections Department at Emory University (Julian Harris Papers);

the State Historical Society of Wisconsin (Carl and Anne Braden Papers); and the Hollis Burke Frissell Library, Tuskegee University (Southern Conference for Human Welfare Papers).

The support of colleagues at La Trobe University and elsewhere made the task of research, thinking, and writing a pleasure rather than a burden. My mentor at Duke University, Richard L. Watson, Jr., was as usual a source of strength and inspiration. Bruce Clayton of Allegheny College and William J. Breen of La Trobe University in their several ways exerted a decisive influence on my ideas as well as sustaining the friendship that had begun in our graduate school days at Duke University. Alan Frost and Erik Olssen both discussed with me the problems of biography. Kerrie Newell generously shared with me her research on the National Consumers League. Susan Poynton, Johanna Breen, and Diane Kirkby read the manuscript and improved it through their suggestions, and Marcia Brubeck refined it significantly in her copyediting. Barbara Sayers typed it with her usual skill and good humor. The Cell family, of Chapel Hill, North Carolina, provided me with encouragement, friendship, and sharp scholarly criticism to a degree which makes this book partly their property. I humbly thank all these people.

Friends and colleagues made the effort seem worthwhile: the La Trobe University history department; my sister, Anne Malcolm; Peter Tomory; Derick and Anne Marsh; Isobel Moutinho; Tony and Hilary Barta; Carrah Clayton; Grant Wason; Michael and Judith Bassett; Lucy Frost; David Jolley; and Karin Liedke. All of them shared in this undertaking. The errors and deficiencies that undoubtedly remain in this book are my responsibility alone.

John Salmond

Melbourne 1986

Miss Lucy of the CIO

The Life and Times

of Lucy Randolph Mason,

1882–1959

1

A Virginia Girlhood

In her later years, Lucy Randolph Mason was often to dispute the assertion that she had been born with a silver spoon in her mouth. There was, she observed, little wealth in the stipend of a small-town Episcopal minister in the South in the late nineteenth century. This statement was probably true. Her lineage, however, could not be denied. In her veins flowed the blood of some of Virginia's most illustrious sons. She was born on July 26, 1882, in Clarens, an elegant old two-story dwelling on Seminary Hill about two miles from Alexandria, Virginia, with a fine view of the Potomac River. This very house had been the home of James Murray Mason, her great-grandfather on her mother's side, who had once been a United States senator and during the Civil War had served as a Confederate ambassador to Great Britain. He had also come to public attention in the Mason-Slidell affair, when the Confederacy's commissioners, bound for London on a British ship, were removed by Union sailors and briefly imprisoned. The matter threatened to provoke hostilities between the Union and the British, and the situation was defused only by the release of the prisoners and their safe passage to England.[1]

James Murray Mason was only one of Miss Lucy's many distinguished relatives. The first Virginia Mason, Colonel George, arrived in the colony in 1651 and soon became a member of the House of Burgesses. There he acquired a reputation as a defender of the rights of the less privileged. Her mother's colonial antecedents included the Randolphs, one of the most powerful of the great eighteenth-century families. Both lines came together in George Mason, signatory to the Declaration of Independence

1

and author of the Virginia Bill of Rights, which became the basis for the Bill of Rights of the United States Constitution. George Mason was a friend of George Washington and Thomas Jefferson and was a man whose thought permeated much of the legal fabric of American life. Mason, like some of the other giants in the revolutionary generation, saw in the rupture with Great Britain a chance to bring justice to the oppressed in the new land. In 1775, for example, he urged his fellow patriots to abolish slavery, prophetically arguing, "Providence punishes national sins by national calamities." He was one of the few members of the Constitutional Convention of 1787 who refused to sign the document, partly because it failed to abolish slavery. George Mason was Miss Lucy's great-great-grandfather on her father's side and her great-great-great-grandfather on her mother's. In her family tree he rubbed shoulders with John Marshall, the first chief justice of the Supreme Court and her mother's great-great-uncle. Perhaps most significant, her father's second cousin was Robert E. Lee. As Ralph McGill once wrote of Lucy Mason, "When it came to ancestors she made all the others seem parvenus."[2]

Lucy Mason's father, Landon Randolph Mason, was born in Fairfax County, Virginia, in February 1841, the son of Dr. Richard Chichester Mason and Lucy Randolph. He was educated at the Episcopal High School of Virginia in Alexandria and was expected to take holy orders but left school in 1861 in order to enlist in the army commanded by his famous relative. He served first with the Seventeenth Virginia Infantry and later with Mosby's Raiders. Toward the end of the war he was captured and imprisoned at Fort Warren. Through her father, then, Lucy Mason could claim membership in the United Daughters of the Confederacy as well as membership in the Daughters of the American Revolution, to which she was entitled by virtue of both parents.

Largely because of his imprisonment, Landon Mason developed a chronic lung complaint. In the hope that sea air would alleviate this condition, and lacking anything better to do at war's end, he enlisted in the United States Navy and served for a brief period as a midshipman on the USS *Monongahela*. The church still called, however, and he returned to the Alexandria Episcopal Theological Seminary, from which he graduated in 1873. He married shortly thereafter, in 1875. His bride, Lucy Ambler, born in 1848, was his third cousin and the daughter of a minister, the Reverend John Cary Ambler. Her mother was Anne Maria Mason.

Together they began the life of a country parson and wife, first at Drakes Branch, in southern Virginia, and then in Shepherdstown, West Virginia, which was his parish at the time that Lucy was born. Lucy's mother went home to Clarens, where she had spent her girlhood, to have the baby, as she had done for the birth of her three older children, Anna, Randolph Fitzhugh, and John Ambler, and as she was to do for the two younger offspring, Landon Randolph and Ida Oswald. Lucy Mason was to grow up in a large and evenly balanced family, although her elder sister, Anna, died of diphtheria when she was just three.

Lucy Mason later described both her parents as "deeply good, sincerely spiritual and most humanly kind," with a theology that "included social ethics." Her father once carried a sack of coal through heavy snow to the home of a poor widow, not even one of his parishioners, who lacked fuel for heating and cooking. Miss Lucy cited the incident as an example of his concern to try "to supply the needs of others." Yet Lucy's mother seemed the more concerned of the two with social reform and attempted to channel her Christian impulses to serve social ends. She was, her older daughter wrote much later, "a born social worker, without benefit of study for that profession. In addition to helping countless individuals, she frequently turned her attention to remedying evil institutions."[3]

One of her strongest convictions related to the need for prison reform. She had once spent a night in jail, comforting a hysterical young woman who had been charged with infanticide, and the conditions of the prison had shocked her profoundly. She publicized these in the local papers and through pamphlets. She was a constant visitor at the state penitentiary in Richmond, where she taught a Sunday school class for some years. She also appeared often before the state legislature on behalf of the prison reform movement. Indeed, authorities in the state penitentiary, in an attempt to curb her criticisms, once created a smallpox scare in order, as the superintendent put it, to "keep those damned old women out." The movement for prison reform eventually had some success in Virginia largely because of Lucy Ambler Mason and women like her. Lucy Ambler Mason befriended many of the convicts she taught, or tried to help. Indeed, the Mason home in Richmond became an unofficial halfway house for recently released convicts. Lucy recalled, "After my brothers went off to the University and the room next to mine on the third floor was available for guests, many a newly-released convict spent days or weeks with us until a way was found to get him back on his feet. Nearly all of these men," she said, "kept up with Mother afterwards and became good citizens—and mostly good Christians."

In addition to working constantly for the poor and desperate in the city of Richmond, Lucy Ambler Mason served as president of the Richmond branch of the Mission to Lepers. Under her leadership thousands of dollars were raised to combat leprosy. Nearly forty years later, the Reverend Sam Higginbotham, who had known her at the time, wrote to her daughter: "Her frail body and her active mind always made me think of a ship whose engine was too powerful for the frame, that the vibrations would shake it to pieces. Yet she was kindly and gracious, observed all the niceties of Southern hospitality, made one feel at ease and at home in her presence. Her great passion," he said, "was to carry out her Lords [sic] Command to cleanse the leper." Indeed, in 1909, when the total income of the Mission to Lepers in the United States was $700, Mrs. Mason had personally raised $400 of this amount. She gave the members of the board of the American leper mission no peace, he said, always "prodding them to do more." More than any other person, she was responsible for whatever success the mission had at that time. "So," he concluded, "you can see what cause we had for thanksgiving to God for sending Mrs. Mason into our lives."[4]

In the breadth of her social concerns and in her activism, Lucy Ambler Mason was representative of one particular strain of southern womanhood in the late nineteenth century. There were many women like her who were upper or middle class in social origin, with close church affiliations, and who, in the changing economic and social climate, began to concern themselves actively with matters outside the home and went to work for social reform in their various communities. Their efforts represented an important way station in the journey from the "Pedestal to Politics," to use Anne Scott's phrase.[5]

John P. McDowell, who discussed the convictions and the work of such women in his important monograph *The Social Gospel in the South*, concluded that the lives of women such as Lucy Ambler Mason require us to reassess the notion that the social gospel had little influence in the South. On the contrary, he asserts, the "hope of extending God's Kingdom on earth"—the advocacy of a Christian message which addressed itself to the social, physical, and economic needs of people as well as to their spiritual well-being—was very much part of southern Protestantism, starting in the last years of the nineteenth century. Lucy Ambler Mason held this perspective on the Christian message, and her daughter came very much to share it.[6]

Both her parents, according to Lucy Mason, took seriously the command "love thy neighbour as thyself." They taught her "that religion includes both one's relationship to God and to man" and were in large part the reason, as she was to claim half a century later, that she, a churchwoman, participated in the labor movement.[7]

Lucy Mason grew up in a loving Christian family. Though her father's annual salary in Shepherdstown was only $1,500, her mother was a good manager, and the family had a large cow, a large garden, and, of course, the usual gifts from parishioners. Her mother once claimed that her husband's salary seemed to be paid "mostly in bacon and black eyed peas." The children were all healthy. Miss Lucy ascribed their good health to her mother's dictum that "what goes into them in food and ideas is more important than what goes on them in clothes and ornaments." Lucy Mason's remembrances of childhood in Shepherdstown were happy ones. She recalled that her father made his parochial calls on a powerful bay horse named Lucifer, of "a fiery temper and intractable disposition." She remembered frequent and prized visits from her maternal grandfather, then an Episcopal missionary to the people of the West Virginia mountains, and she recalled the love she felt for Kitty Brim, the family's black cook. "She lightened my mother's load," she said, "and spoiled each one of us five children."[8]

Lucy Mason recalled, too, the intensely religious atmosphere in which she grew up and in which she was to remain. Sitting on the stone step of her father's study, at the age of five, she was enjoying the spring sun when suddenly "a chill of fear smote me." Where would she go when she died? she wondered. She knew her parents would go to heaven. Unless she went there too, she "would be a lonely waif in eternity." She had, she said, no fear of hell in itself but was "mortally afraid" of being separated from her parents. Pondering the problem, she decided that the only way to be sure of getting to heaven was to live a good life. "There and then," she recollected," I decided once and for all where I wanted to go." On another occasion, Lucy's great-aunt Jeannie, who lived with the family, came across her tiny niece "praying for the devil." When asked why, the child responded, "He is so bad he must be very unhappy, and I want to ask God to make him good." From Miss Lucy's earliest years, God was central to every aspect of her existence.[9]

In 1890, the family left Shepherdstown so that her father could answer a call to Marietta, Georgia. Lucy cried herself to sleep for nights before their departure, swallowing her sobs as she lay in her trundle bed so that her father and mother would not hear. On the day of their departure, Kitty Brim swept Lucy up in her arms and kissed her. "My first tears over leaving a friend were shed," she later wrote, "when I parted forever from Kitty Brim." They were to remain in Marietta less than a year. Aunt Jeannie taught Landon and Lucy at home, but Lucy's elder brothers went to the public school. Public education in Georgia in 1890, after years of cost cutting by economy-minded administrations, was in a deplorable state. For this reason, and also because his salary of $1,500 was proving inadequate for a growing family, Reverend Mason decided to move back to Virginia in 1891 when Grace Church, in Richmond, offered him a salary of $2,500. He was to remain in Richmond until his retirement in 1917. The three-story red brick rectory would be Lucy Mason's home for the next twenty-five years, and Richmond was the city that formed her.[10]

In concluding his superb study of Richmond in the three decades after the Civil War, Michael B. Chesson describes the city as being in decline, inheriting "the worst of both the Old and the New South." The "racism and the conservatism of life before the war," he said, was still present and had indeed intensified. A narrow materialism, according to novelist Ellen Glasgow, supplanted the graciousness and the relative lack of concern for money that had characterized the prewar city. It had become, she said, a superficial city. The notions of progress central to the creed of the New South had not extended into the area of municipal services. The city even lacked a public library in the 1890s.[11]

Richmond's three main industries—flour milling and the processing of iron and tobacco products—had all been steadily declining since the early 1880s despite the boosters' proud boast that the city was enjoying "roaring progress." Population growth was steady though slower than in other, comparable southern cities, especially Norfolk, which presented Richmond with increasingly stiff competition. Indeed, the black population declined in absolute numbers in these decades, a reflection, perhaps, not only of shrinking economic opportunity for blacks but also of the increasingly rigid segregation.[12]

Richmond's working class—skilled and unskilled, male and female, black and white—lived at the turn of the century with growing insecurity and want. Wage rates had fallen well below the national average, seasonal layoffs were increasingly frequent, and the general quality of life was steadily deteriorating. As Peter Rachleff has observed, "Stability, let alone security, continued to escape Richmond's workers." The trade union movement, in other cities a means of achieving economic advancement, was, again in Rachleff's phrase, "exceedingly limited and ineffectual." Craft-based, male dominated, and racially exclusionist, it scarcely touched the lives of most of the city's workers. In 1899 there were only 1,436 union members in the whole state of Virginia, stark testimony to labor's moribund state. [13]

Such had not always been the case. Both Rachleff and Leon Fink have recently demonstrated that a strain of labor activism in post–Civil War Richmond culminated in the formation of a working-class political movement in the 1880s under the aegis of the Knights of Labor. The high point was the capture, in May 1886, of the Richmond City Council by a Workingmen's Reform party, a popular movement which crossed racial lines, as Richmond's black voters gave it overwhelming support. The triumph was, however, a brief one. The political movement, and the Richmond branch of the Knights of Labor itself, had virtually ceased to exist by the end of the year, unable in the end to bridge the gulf between espoused egalitarianism and actual racism. The Richmond labor movement very quickly entered a long period of decline. The principal victims were the working men and women of the city. [14] There was much poverty in the city among blacks and whites, as Ellen Glasgow was to learn when, at seventeen, she worked for a winter with the City Mission. The squalor, she said, horrified her. [15]

Still, there remained some areas of grace and charm, with leafy streets and handsome houses. Lucy Mason lived in such a home in one of Richmond's most attractive neighborhoods. Less than three blocks away lived Nancy Langhorne, who as Lady Astor was to become the first woman elected to the British House of Commons and was a Tory M.P. for many years. The two women grew up together and were to stay in contact off and on throughout their lives. [16]

Little information survives regarding Lucy Mason's later childhood and adolescence. Like her brothers and Ida, she was educated in private schools. She attended the exclusive Powell's School for Girls in Rich-

mond, but unlike the boys, all of whom matriculated at the University of
Virginia, she did not attend college. Indeed, neither she nor Ida was even
able to complete high school. There was simply not enough money.
Though she dreamed of becoming a foreign missionary, circumstances
dictated otherwise. At the age of twenty-two she "rented a typewriter,
brought a short hand manual," and taught herself stenography so that she
could seek employment at home.

Her social conscience had already been aroused. At the age of eighteen
she began teaching a Sunday school class in a mission church in one of
Richmond's working-class districts. Her pupils were predominantly working girls from the nearby tobacco factories. Later, she organized industrial
clubs for the same girls and through them was able to glimpse the bleak-
ness of their lives. "I had occasion then to see at first hand what was
happening to the working class," she later said. "I saw girls of 14 working
10 hours a day for less than a living wage, as a matter of course. I saw
women who had worked under those conditions from 14 to 25. They
looked like women of 50." This experience, she explained, together with
her realization that individual action was unavailing against such evils,
first drew her to the cause of organized labor and to the advocacy of protective legislation for women and children. "I couldn't do much alone
though," she said. "Neither could the ministers, working singly or in little
groups. They had no organization." But perhaps labor unions could. Her
social consciousness led her very early to a commitment that would become the dominant force in her life.[17]

In her early commitment to the cause of organized labor, Lucy Mason
had taken a path along which many women reformers in the first two
decades of this century came to tread. As Nancy Schrom Dye argues in
her study of the Women's Trade Union League of New York (WTUL),
middle- and upper-class women became interested in labor unions as a
means of bridging class differences and improving the conditions of working women everywhere. "The WTUL," Dye writes, "was founded in the
faith that women could overcome social class differences and work together for a common cause." The WTUL and other reformist organizations with a predominantly female membership such as the National Consumers League, whose general secretary Mason would later become,
always worked closely with labor unions in their endeavors to secure protective legislation and to raise the quality of working women's lives. The

women reformers believed themselves to be both feminists and trade unionists. In the unfolding of her own life, Lucy Mason never lost sight of these twin considerations.[18]

Lucy's social conscience was further developed by her reading and by her experiences when she first became employed. The theologians of the social gospel, so important in helping explain the social justice aspect of Progressivism, naturally attracted her. In particular Walter Rauschenbush, with his emphasis on the need to relate religion and social action, struck a responsive chord in her and in many other reform-minded women. In responding positively to his insistence that Christians must be socially active, aiming to bring earthly society in "harmony with the will of God," Lucy Mason reacted as did many young women of her generation, her background, and her region.[19] She was in her early twenties when she first heard Florence Simms, industrial secretary of the national YWCA, speak. The message, "that personal goodness is not enough. There must be a passion for social justice," had a similar effect upon her. Such social gospel notions, acquired early in Lucy Mason's life, were to stay with her until her death and informed every goal she strove to accomplish.[20]

In 1906, she obtained a position as a stenographer in the Richmond office of Braxton and Eggleston, one of Virginia's largest and most respected law firms, where she was to work for the next eight years. The firm's senior partner was Allen Caperton Braxton, like Mason a scion of one of Virginia's oldest and most prominent families. His great-grandfather, Carter Braxton, had signed the Declaration of Independence, and his family included Carters, Lees, and Washingtons. Braxton was also a leading exponent of Virginia's variety of Progressivism and was deeply suspicious of the increasingly direct influence of corporations in Virginia politics. Though no evidence survives of a direct connection between the Mason and Braxton families, it is reasonable to infer that they knew each other and that the social connection helped Lucy land the job.[21]

The firm of Braxton and Eggleston often represented casualty insurance companies in industrial accident suits. As Lucy Mason typed the details of many such cases, she was horrified by both the prevalence of injuries and the relative helplessness of the injured workers and their families in the face of corporate might. In one case, the family of a factory employee who had been ground to death while cleaning a machine received no compensation; the court accepted the company's contention that the accident was due to the worker's own negligence. The case which stuck most firmly in Lucy's mind, however, involved a seventeen-year-old girl who might have been one of Miss Lucy's Sunday school pupils. The girl, an employee of a local bookbindery, had lost most of her right hand in a bookbinding machine. A young lawyer from Braxton and Eggleston prevailed on her to accept seventy-five dollars as compensation. Lucy Mason was appalled. "That is what I mean when I talk about the indifference of most of us to what happens to the rest of us," she said nearly thirty years later. "How could that young lawyer have stood by and seen a girl of 17 get $75 for her right hand. . . . how could he have taken the case? She was poor, her wages probably didn't bring in a living; the loss of her right hand meant that she was unfit for work in a factory and that was all she knew how to do. . . . I can never forget her. All my life she has followed me."[22]

The experience of that girl and of many others like her fed Lucy Mason's growing conviction that a strong labor movement would press for protective legislation and adequate industrial compensation laws so that such horrible occurrences could become a thing of the past. As her support for organized labor developed, she became active in the Richmond branch of the Union Labor League and a firm believer that industrial action was often justified. Hers was not always a popular view in the South during the early twentieth century. As early as 1903, during a two-month strike by Richmond's streetcar operators which so bitterly divided the city that the state militia had to be called out to keep order, Mason resolutely refused to ride the trolleys still being operated by company officials and their business allies. Instead she walked to her destination through the summer heat. She lobbied the state legislature constantly on labor issues, in particular to institute the eight-hour working day.[23]

After office hours, Miss Lucy's volunteer work consumed much of her time. She continued her activities with the girls from Richmond's factories increasingly through her involvement with the YWCA. Moreover, her concern for the plight of women, and her growing consciousness of her position as a woman in a male-dominated society, inevitably drew her into the quickening drive for women's suffrage, soon to be one of the United States' most powerful reform currents.

The spearhead of the suffrage battle was the National American Woman Suffrage Association (NAWSA). Founded in 1890, it had, under the successive presidencies of Elizabeth Cady Stanton, Susan B. Anthony, Carrie Chapman Catt, and Anna Howard Shaw, become a powerful though relentlessly middle-class pressure group with thriving branches in every state and hundreds of active local associations. The Virginia Equal Suffrage League was founded in November 1909, at the Richmond home of Mrs. Dabney Crenshaw. Those attending the meeting included Ellen Glasgow. Lucy Mason was apparently not present but joined the organization soon thereafter. Her membership marked the beginning of her commitment to this most important of causes.[24]

Lucy Mason soon became one of the most effective local publicists for the cause. She wrote a series of newspaper articles and pamphlets under the name Lucy Cary in order to avoid causing more embarrassment than necessary to her father, who bitterly disapproved of her involvement. In these pieces she attempted to show that the suffrage movement and social Christianity were inextricably linked. "There is in the suffrage movement a religious element, a deep strain of spirituality and altruism, which gives it a peculiar moral significance," she remarked, "and fully justifies faith in its ultimate vindication." It was because of the "hardness of men's hearts" and "the dullness of their understanding, that they have not long ago learned that there can be no separation of duty to God and duty to men." With regard to the great changes occurring in American society, she argued:

> In this social revolution nothing is more obvious and inevitable than the consequent change in the status of women. As a natural result, the growth within women of new conceptions of justice, truth, duty, privilege and opportunity, under conditions which bind and hamper them at every turn, leads to a revolt against things as they were which is generally misunderstood and attributed to a mere desire to be mannish and shake off feminine shackles. But it is not a fad—it is a fight for life, for a fuller, free, more blessed, because more useful life.

Women, she said, must become a factor in government in order to humanize it. The condition of female industrial workers particularly aroused her. She asked whether women were so indifferent to the wrongs of young girls that "these conditions will not be bettered when the more humane self of our nation is possessed of political power." Equal suffrage she viewed not as a universal panacea but as only one important phase of a greater movement, "which may be termed the awakening of women."

"The leaders of the leisure classes," by which she meant people like herself, should provide leadership for this movement because of the time and energy at their disposal. "Let us awake to the needs of the world about us," she concluded, "to a sense of our individual responsibility in meeting those needs, and to an opportunity for serving God and man."[25]

We may never know the precise cause of Lucy Mason's own particular "awakening." Clearly, however, her growing feminist principles were already sufficiently entrenched to arouse the wrath of her father, to whom she was otherwise so strongly attached. Though the record is silent regarding her mother's attitude toward the suffrage movement, the elder Lucy's encouragement and support may have been important factors in enabling her daughter to take this position. Moreover, there was always a close connection in the South between church activism of the social gospel type that Lucy Mason was coming to exemplify and the woman suffrage movement. As McDowell has noted, women such as Miss Lucy were inevitably drawn to the cause from a realization that the Kingdom of God could not be extended on earth without the framing of good laws. They were excluded from a vital part in the lawmaking process, namely the choosing of lawmakers. Political action directed at ending this situation, McDowell writes, was therefore "integral to the women's transformed understanding of their Christian mission." Women had to win the vote in order to achieve the social ends they desired so strongly. In embracing the cause of female suffrage with such fervor, Lucy Mason was very much following the southern social gospel pattern.[26]

The notion that Christian witness and social reform were bound together was further developed in *The Divine Discontent*, a pamphlet that Miss Lucy wrote in 1912 under her own name. She argued that, though "the woman suffrage movement is an expression of discontent," it was discontent of a sufficiently noble nature to be labeled "The Divine Discontent," thus distinguishing it from mere dissatisfaction or disquiet. "Divine Discontent," she claimed, "has been responsible for every reformation accomplished in the history of our race. It has furnished the incentive for progress and development. It has led to the purifying of religion, politics and all social institutions." The equal suffrage movement stood firmly in this tradition. It was "distinctly a product of Christian and civilized nations. The mentally and spiritually torpid women of Mahometan countries are the last to ask for political recognition; and in Christian lands this demand invariably comes from highly intelligent and moral women. The most effective way to fight woman suffrage, would be by stunting the minds and deadening the spiritual perceptions of women." Women, she said, were filled "with a divine discontent" at the glaring inequalities of life—the placid acceptance of the double standard of morals "that the sinning father goes free, while the sinning mother must endure the shame." They were possessed with a sense of obligation to relieve those who were oppressed and abused, and that sense was the justification of the suffrage movement; it was "part of the upward trend of human nature."[27]

In "Expediency or Right," an article written the following year, Lucy appealed specifically to Christians who agreed with equal suffrage but had not yet allied themselves with the Equal Suffrage League to do so forthwith. "Every name counts in the total summing up," she claimed, and noted that the "doctrine of individual responsibility is essentially a Christian doctrine, and to just the extent that we are really Christians, we will not plead lack of personal influence as an excuse for staying outside any righteous movement." The equal suffrage movement *was* unmistakably a righteous one. "No good woman," she said, had found her influence in church work or her effectiveness in social or philanthropic organizations lessened or injured by the fact that she was a suffragist. "As usual the lion vacates the path as soon as we set our feet firmly upon it." Her conclusion was that compromise with one's conscience on the suffrage issue was not consistent with Christianity.[28]

In such pamphlets and articles Miss Lucy undoubtedly expressed many of the beliefs and prejudices of her class and her time. She also expressed with clarity and vigor a view of Christian witness that provided the basic justification for her whole life. To be a true Christian, she believed, was to be a social reformer. Her pamphlets required her to cast aside the cloak of anonymity. In 1912 she accepted election to the board of the Richmond branch of the Equal Suffrage League and the following year was a Richmond delegate to the league's state conference. This activism distressed her father greatly, and indeed some of his parishioners avoided contact with her for a time. Eventually, however, the rift healed, and the Reverend Mason even put in a good word for women's suffrage from the pulpit. Father and daughter were always very close. When, in 1908, the Commonwealth Club in Richmond decided to give Reverend Mason a holiday in England in appreciation of his ministry, he asked Lucy to accompany him. She went, using her savings to do so. It was the first of only two trips she was to make abroad.[29]

Lucy Mason would probably have continued working for Braxton and Eggleston indefinitely, developing her social concerns through voluntary work, concentrating in particular on the twin and intertwined issues of protective labor legislation and women's rights, had it not been for the death in 1914 of the firm's senior partner, Allen Caperton Braxton. For a number of reasons, it was decided to dissolve the firm, and Lucy Mason was therefore out of a job. Fortunately, a number of alternative positions were available, and the one she accepted would enable her to develop and deepen the social gospel notions and the general social concerns that had already become the driving force in her life. In 1914 she became industrial secretary of the Richmond YWCA.[30]

2

Social Work and Suffrage

The Industrial Department of the YWCA was developed on a national level by the energetic and committed Florence Simms, who became the first YWCA national industrial secretary in 1904. Believing that Christians could transform individual lives by transforming the social and economic environment, she began her long fight to develop autonomous industrial departments—at first known as "extension" departments or "industrial clubs"—within the local YWCAs, developing programs specifically geared to the needs of working-class young women. These were the people whom Lucy Mason had already met through her volunteer activities and whose working conditions she had deplored and resolved to change. By 1914 some 375 such clubs were in existence, and many local YWCAs had already appointed industrial or extension secretaries to create programs for working-class young women, often with the acute misgivings of the firmly middle-class, conservative YWCA boards.

As Mary Frederickson has written,

> For middle-class women the YWCA Industrial Department provided a structured national network for spreading the idea of trade union organization, and served as a conduit into more extensive work within the labor movement. For working-class women, the Industrial Department offered a form of collective support in communities with few women's organizations, and the opportunity of leadership training rarely available even for female trade unionists. [1]

According to Katharine Lumpkin, industrial secretaries tended to be more radical and more committed than the general YWCA employees, and the Industrial Department became a focal point of advocacy for labor legislation for women. Indeed, there was growing tension between the Industrial Department and other departments in the YWCA. The national body had close links to Protestant churches. Church membership was in fact a prerequisite for association membership, and many members believed that the YWCA should be providing lunchtime evangelism for working girls, not raising questions of economic and social reform. Nevertheless, as Mary Frederickson has noted, "under Simms's leadership, the Industrial Department moved in new directions; it hired staff members trained in the social sciences, maintained independence from employers wherever possible, and assisted industrial women in raising questions about working conditions." Industrial secretaries, she said, came to form "a cohesive group, a network of reform-minded women."[2]

Katharine Lumpkin, who worked closely with the Industrial Department for some years, believed that, in the largely unorganized South, industrial secretaries "aimed at helping working class girls to express themselves, to consider their own lives, their own conditions and to work for changing them." According to Frederickson, "Southern YWCA work in the industrial sphere hardly went beyond welfare work in the mill communities." Certainly, it was an uphill struggle, and the rewards were slow in coming. Yet it remains true that the contribution of the YWCA's Industrial Department was crucial in setting an agenda for labor legislation affecting southern working women, in revising the consciousness of thousands of these women, and in training a battalion of dedicated field workers who would promote a range of women's issues. Many of the southern women who later became prominent as labor organizers, as advocates of a range of reform programs, and as members of the southern strand of the "women's network" which Susan B. Ware has identified as crucially important in bringing women's issues to the fore in the New Deal era, had gotten a start as progressives within the industrial division of the YWCA.[3]

Such developments lay in the future when Lucy Mason became Richmond's extension secretary in 1914 and incidentally the first woman to be appointed to such a position in the South. She was always inclined to downplay her success in the job. "I think I made more of a contribution as a General Secretary than I did when Industrial Secretary," she later wrote, "as I was feeling my way through the first period and had not then developed as much of an understanding of industrial problems as I did later."[4] In her autobiography she dismissed the period in a single sentence. Certainly little record remains of her time there. Scrapbooks recording various activities of the Richmond YWCA at that time mention her as having organized in 1915 a series of "Come-over lunches" at the YWCA building, the main purpose being to enable factory workers and office workers to meet, as they would almost certainly not otherwise, given Richmond's rigid social stratification.

In 1917 Simms spent some time in Petersburg with Lucy in order to establish an industrial club there. Mason herself returned to the city on several occasions and reported to Simms on the progress of the work. Growth was extremely slow. There were two tobacco factories in Petersburg, one employing 100 girls, the other 500. In September 1917 Mason visited both places and found the girls friendly and receptive to her message, but only two came to a meeting that she had scheduled at the new industrial club.

Lucy Mason was saddened but hardly surprised. "In this part of the world," she reported to Miss Simms, "girls are so ashamed of working in factories at all, that to get them out in public places in groups is almost impossible without years of preparatory work." They were most anxious "not to be identified with their working companions"; until this attitude altered, the industrial movement in the South could not expect spectacular growth. The situation in Petersburg, too, was complicated by the fact that the local YWCA secretary had little understanding of the need to reach out beyond the middle class to influence the lives of these working girls. Still, Miss Lucy said, she would continue to visit the city regularly and would offer what help she could.[5]

Lucy Mason later commented that she had used her position as industrial secretary to continue her struggle for legislation regulating women's working conditions. She had lobbied in particular for the eight-hour day and for the restriction of night work. Certainly, the few records remaining from her tenure in the office show a deepening involvement in industrial matters and concern with the need to build labor unions in the South. "I got involved in a strike of the only women's trade union in the entire South," she told Miss Simms in October 1917. In her capacity as chairman for the Committee of Women in Industry, she had attempted conciliation and had failed completely. The particular company had "failed to recognize the human element now coming into industrial relations," she said.

Only the presence of strong labor unions would effect a change in attitude or bring about ameliorative legislation.[6]

One of Lucy Mason's concerns during this period was to communicate to women of her own class something of the grim reality of the working girl's existence. She was a frequent speaker before women's groups in the Richmond area, where she vigorously combatted the common middle-class notion that "people are hungry because they deserve to be hungry." Often the attitudes of women of her own background exasperated her. Years later she recalled an instance when, after giving before a women's club a lecture entitled "The Humanness of the Poor," one of the audience came up to her and said, "I simply get so exasperated with poor people. They are so unreasonable. Just the other day I went into the home of a woman who had nothing to eat in the house, but who had lace curtains on the windows." Another woman said it "peeved her because factory girls who couldn't really afford such things wore silk stockings on the street." Mason replied tersely to both of these complaints. She asked the first woman if she really wanted to "take away the last vestige of front to the world that the poor women had left." To the second she asked where girls would wear silk hose if not in the street. In the factories, she said, "they must wear gingham aprons and dresses, and when they came home at night it was to put on another gingham apron and dress." Why on earth begrudge them a few minutes' glamor? In speaking to both these ladies, Miss Lucy made a point which she was to repeat throughout her life. The poor, the deprived, were not a class, they were people—individuals—and should be treated as such.[7]

She continued to speak and write of the changing industrial conditions in the South and their effect on the lives of southern women. In one article, written for a YWCA magazine in 1917, she spoke of thousands of "our girls who have been drawn into the web of modern industry," a trend exacerbated by the increased demand for labor occasioned by World War I. In putting women to industrial work, the United States was simply following precedents already firmly established in Europe, where the "woman power of the warring nations is responding until millions of women are doing what had been considered men's work" but not at men's wages. This "appalling situation" must not be replicated in America. Women workers should be paid the same rates as men for equal work. It was up to middle-class women to see that they were. "Setting other

women free from woman's immemorial task of manufacture in the home,"
she argued,

> bearing the burdens of modern industry . . . , giving their young lives to
> industrial progress, these girls are providing leisure and opportunity for
> those of us who are set free from the production of life's necessities to follow
> other paths. Do we owe them nothing? . . . Are we going to let their young
> shoulders bear the full weight of our industrial life, or shall we get under,
> carrying some of their load and solving some of their difficulties. Sisters of
> ours they are—are we going to shut our eyes to their needs, or are we going
> to help create new and higher standards for industry so that it may not bear
> so heavily on slender shoulders?[8]

The expression of such sympathies first drew Lucy Mason into the national arena. In October 1917, Samuel Gompers, president of the American Federation of Labor, appointed her Virginia chairman of the Committee of Women in Industry of the National Advisory Committee on Labor,
one of the bodies in the complex structure of voluntary organizations set
up to assist the domestic war effort and coordinated by the Council of
National Defense. Such a position would normally have been held by a
union representative. It was awarded to Miss Lucy in recognition of her
concern for issues affecting women workers. It was, she said, also her first
"union appointment."[9] She was pleased to be given the job. Between
October and December 1917 she traveled extensively throughout the
state, speaking to local women's groups—to the detriment, she feared, of
her work in Richmond. Still, she enjoyed the change of pace, though she
found the bulk of the women she spoke to, all of whom were thoroughly
middle class, completely ignorant of industrial conditions in their own
communities. They "cheerfully write me that conditions in their community are ideal for working women," she complained to Simms, when the
reality was disturbingly different. "I bombard them with literature from
the Trade Union League bearing on war problems and other pertinent
information and hope that somewhere seeds will sprout." Such hope
seemed forlorn indeed.[10]

Her professional work ceased abruptly, however, the following year,
and her voluntary work was to be severely curtailed. In January 1918, her
mother died suddenly of a heart attack. Her father, who had retired in
1917, was then seventy-six, half blind and with severe hearing difficulties.

Someone had to care for him. Lucy had two brothers fighting in Europe and a third (John) living in Baltimore; her sister, Ida, had recently married and moved to Alexandria. Lucy scarcely had a choice. She resigned from the YWCA and, partly supported by her brother John, who was doing well as an industrial engineer, she devoted the next five and a half years to her father's increasing needs. During this time, she said with some exaggeration, she rarely spent a night away from home.[11]

Lucy's brother Landon, unable to wait for the United States to enter the war, had joined up in New Zealand. He fought with the ANZACs in their most symbolic of encounters, on Gallipoli, where he was severely wounded and later decorated for "conspicuous bravery." Evacuated to England, he convalesced for a time at the home of his sister's friend and fellow Virginian Lady Astor. He then reentered the British army on the French front, where again he was wounded. Once more he recovered, and was sent, having attained the rank of major, to Palestine with General Allenby. In the skirmishes along the Dead Sea, he again sustained a severe wound. Armistice came before he could return to the front.

Lucy's eldest brother, Randolph, was thirty-nine years old when the United States entered the war but became convinced that it was his duty to volunteer. Lucy remembered sitting up with him one evening, talking about the decision. Once he had made up his mind, she later wrote, "he constantly volunteered for whatever took him into the war by the shortest route." He refused a captaincy, became a machine gunner, and was killed while on a reconnoitering mission near Belleau Wood in the summer of 1918. So popular was he that when, upon his failure to return, his captain called for volunteers to search for him, "every man jumped to his feet and offered to answer the captain's call."[12]

The family was devastated by Randolph's death and none more so than Lucy. Of all her siblings, he was the one closest to her in nature and in social concerns. More than twenty years later she still spoke of the "deep regret" she felt that she had encouraged him to volunteer. Certainly this personal loss was one of the reasons for her embracing the cause of pacifism. In the days after she received the news of his death, she displayed what was already a conviction and one which she was to demonstrate time and again throughout her life, that death was just part of a continuum of life, that the spirit did live on, that existence continued beyond the grave. "Ranny is surely happier now than ever before," she wrote her stricken sister, Ida, "and I think he is finding an even greater service beyond than he found here. He and mother must have had a wonderful reunion—and some day we will all share it. I am so glad that she was there to meet him—so glad she was not here to lose him." Her beliefs in this area enabled her throughout her life to cope personally with the death of family and friends and to assist others less able to do so.[13]

Though Lucy had to give up her job because of her domestic obligations, she continued with volunteer work. That she was able to do so was partly due to the assistance of her two good friends, Hermine and Carrie Moore, who lived with her and helped her care for her increasingly dependent father. She continued working for the cause of equal suffrage and in 1919 was elected president of the Richmond branch of the Equal Suffrage League when Mrs. B. B. Valentine decided to step down from the post for health reasons. In her acceptance speech, she asserted that suffrage for women had passed from an unpopular stage to a popular one and stressed her already familiar theme that it was the duty of progressive middle-class women—"who believe that the very spirit of God is moving among mankind and stirring and lifting them to better forms of life"—to agitate for social reform, especially reforms of benefit to their less fortunate sisters, women industrial workers.[14]

As the suffrage campaign drew to its culmination in the constitutional amendment giving votes to women, Lucy Mason continued to defend the cause publicly. In the *Richmond News Leader,* she wrote, "Surely the time has come to stop treating women as a peculiar class of human beings not entitled to any argument that holds good for men. . . . We hold it to be unjust that the vast number of Southern women who are qualified to vote, who want to vote, who have a distinct and valuable contribution to make to our public life, should have to wait indefinitely for political freedom." She ridiculed the argument that to give women the vote would endanger "the Southern way of life" through a consequent increase in the number of black voters. That notion was "a scarecrow unworthy of serious consideration." She was, in short, an articulate and committed defender of a cause whose hour had come, a fact that the NAWSA explicitly recognized when, in February 1920, she was officially placed on the association's honor roll.[15]

With the passage of the constitutional amendment, the role of the NAWSA and its associated bodies was in one sense over. Yet the momentum built up during the long campaign could scarcely be dissipated overnight. Moreover, few doubted the need for women to remain mobilized to ensure that the hard-won vote would be wisely used. Women, it was argued, would need education for citizenship. Those who had campaigned hardest for the vote had a duty to lead the way in the forthcoming new era, to provide this education, to assist the newly franchised women to use the vote to promote social and economic justice and, in particular, justice for their sex. The NAWSA therefore transformed itself during 1919 and 1920 into the National League of Women Voters (LWV), one of the most important of the "social feminist" agencies which in the 1920s battled for protective legislation for women, for child labor legislation, for the continuation of Progressive reform. It also battled against the more militant feminists of the National Woman's party (NWP) and associated groups, who regarded protective legislation as restricting opportunities for women and who saw in a constitutional amendment prohibiting any discrimination on sexual grounds the surest avenue for the advancement of their sex to full equality. The battle became a bitter one, and Lucy Mason soon joined the ranks of the social feminists. Her growing conviction that the lot of working women and their children in the industrializing South could be ameliorated only through protective legislation almost certainly determined which position she would adopt.[16]

Mason's opposition to the Equal Rights Amendment because of her concern to maintain and extend the drive for protective legislation therefore placed her firmly in the social feminist camp. In so declaring herself, she made common cause with a group of women of otherwise widely divergent political beliefs. Some, like Belle Sherwin of the League of Women Voters, could be described as conservative Democrats; others, most notably Florence Kelley of the National Consumers League (NCL), considered themselves socialists. There was thus a wide spectrum of opinion among social feminists. Miss Lucy herself came somewhere in the middle of the continuum. Although she was certainly no socialist, she nevertheless had an abiding belief in the need for state action to redress the imbalances and inequalities in American life and to curb the excesses of unbridled private economic power—in short, "to extend God's Kingdom on earth." She was, like many of her contemporaries, to find her political home eventually in Franklin Roosevelt's New Deal.

Moreover, again like other social feminists, Mason was not initially opposed to the proposition that protective legislation should apply to all workers, men and women alike. After the National Woman's party decided to press for its amendment and the debate became more heated, however, people like Florence Kelley, increasingly fearful that recently won gains might be lost if the amendment was passed, concentrated on advocating the cause of their sex rather than that of all workers. Their opposition to the amendment therefore became more vehement and less open to any compromise. Miss Lucy certainly followed this trend. By 1923 her opposition to the Equal Rights Amendment had become both vociferous and total.[17]

The Richmond Equal Suffrage League followed the national body in transforming itself. The first meeting of the Richmond League of Women Voters was held in December 1920. Mrs. G. T. W. Kern was elected temporary chairman, but Lucy Mason took over the office in the spring of 1921 and held it for the next two years. She also became Virginia Chairman of the Women in Industry Committee of the national League of Women Voters. She used both these offices whenever she could to press for protective legislation and to argue the case for the greater involvement of women in politics. By the end of 1922, for example, the Virginia Women in Industry Committee had sponsored a number of bills before the Virginia General Assembly, including child welfare legislation, a measure advocating a nine-hour day and a fifty-hour week for women in industry, the creation of a women's and children's division in the state Bureau of Labor, and the appointment of a commission aimed at simplifying the state's administrative structure. Lucy Mason spent long hours at the state capitol lobbying on behalf of these and other measures, most often unsuccessfully. Yet she believed that some progress had been made. "In criticizing this session of the legislature," she reported to members of the Richmond league in 1922, "for the failure to enact certain measures deemed necessary, the fact should not be overlooked that it has been one of the most interesting sessions in recent years and will go down in history as having enacted more progressive legislation relating to women and children than has been enacted in any preceding session." Women, she thought, were already raising the tone of government.[18]

Despite the restrictions placed on her movements by her father's failing health, she was able to travel from time to time on league business. Indeed, in November 1920, even before the Virginia League of Women

Voters had been formally formed, she had been speaking throughout the state, urging women to register to vote, persuading them of the need to continue the work of the Equal Suffrage League in some way. In the summer of 1922, she spent nearly two months on the road, with her father in tow and driving her own car, on a speaking tour of small Virginia towns, talking about the League of Women Voters, publicizing its program especially as it applied to working women, and seeking support for it. The pace was brisk, and she sometimes complained about it. "The League is knocking the spots off me in a way," she wrote Adele Clark in early August, "but it is such a healthy vigorous child it demands a lot of attention." Still, she was clearly enjoying herself thoroughly. Despite her complaints, Lucy Mason was never happier and never more fulfilled than when she was on the road, speaking to diverse groups, answering their queries and allaying their doubts, being a propagandist for causes in which she deeply believed. She played this role with consummate skill later for the National Consumers League and for the CIO.[19]

Miss Lucy always grasped with both hands any opportunity to state her social concerns publicly. She was delighted, for example, when in 1921 she was invited to write a column for the *Warrenton* (Virginia) *Times* for several weeks during the absence of the regular columnist. "I will start with the anti-war propaganda," she exulted, "then think it will be the Childrens Code or women in industry." No chance to advance the cause should ever be passed up, she believed.[20]

As president of Women in Industry, Lucy Mason had organized a statewide program of educational work involving a network of local committees, each doing in-depth research on specific problems relating to women workers. She herself produced a widely distributed pamphlet, *The Shorter Day and Women Workers,* as a background for legislative activity. It argued the case for restricting the hours of work for women and prompted Edward Costigan, then the United States commissioner for tariffs, to write congratulating Miss Lucy on the "balance, restraint and comprehensiveness of your treatment."[21]

Indeed, Lucy Mason had caught the attention of the national league officers. She was subsequently offered the chair of the National Committee on Women in Industry. She was thrilled to be asked. "I think if I had money and could choose my career at this moment," she told Adele Clark, "I would take that Chairmanship and run for the next legislature." Unfortunately, family obligations stood in the way. When she refused the position, citing as a reason her inability to travel, the league's vice president, Belle Sherwin, urged her to change her mind. "If the necessity of being at home with your Father is the determining factor in your decision," she wrote,

> I have wondered whether you might think it possible to form a National Committee, among whose members might be one or two persons who could travel for you in those States where the Committee agreed it might be particularly necessary for its Representative to spend some time speaking or helping on a legislative campaign. . . . Please do not think me rude or importunate, but only extremely anxious that the League may have the service of your clear head and sound information, and special knowledge of particular localities.

Reluctantly, Lucy Mason again refused.[22]

Early in 1923, Miss Lucy became one of eleven state chairmen who were invited to a conference on women industrial workers that was called by the United States Department of Labor. Clearly she was acquiring a reputation as an expert on the issues. She later described this conference to the Richmond league as marking "an epoch in the ability of women to get together on a common basis, regardless of religious creed, social position, occupation, wealth or poverty," to move toward solutions to the problems of the working woman. At a later gathering she said that the "most inspiring" feature of the conference was the way "the women got together in understanding the needs of the women at the bottom of the economic ladder." Later that year she became further involved in the league's national affairs. A *New York Evening Post* story, identifying her as "a young leader of the South," announced her appointment to a new national committee of the league, on international cooperation to end war.[23]

As president of the Richmond league, Miss Lucy had as a prime concern the education of women for their new role as voters. Under her auspices, the Richmond league arranged a series of breakfasts and lunches at which women could hear guest speakers discuss various problems relating to the workings of the city's government. Such meetings, she believed, would be beneficial in creating "the intelligent public opinion," which would advance Richmond's progress. Richmond was a beautiful city, she wrote on one occasion, but it needed much improvement. "Those of us who love Richmond most," she said, "dream of a city in which there shall be no slums, no vast areas of drab and ugly streets, but that dream will be long in its realization. Meantime, much can be done to enrich and beautify those crowded sections where a great number of our citizens live, but through which one does not take the tourist." Educated and committed women voters, she believed, maintaining pressure on local officials, could assist in achieving the parks and playgrounds which would give every Richmond child, "white and colored . . . , a safe and wholesome recreation place."[24]

Certainly the city needed the pressure of people like Lucy Mason, for in the first decades of this century, the areas "through which one does not take a tourist" had grown steadily. Richmond in the 1920s was becoming, in Silver's words, a city characterized by "blighted inner-city neighborhoods," where the poor of both races dwelled in increasingly deprived conditions. In drawing attention to the deterioration in the quality of the Richmond environment, Miss Lucy was addressing no imaginary need.[25]

Lucy used her presidential office constantly to urge women to participate in local affairs. In 1923, chiding women for failing to register to vote, she asserted that "if the mass of women were as indifferent to their own housekeeping as they are to their community and state housekeeping what a muddle homes would be in all the time." Women had the capacity, she believed, "for humanizing government." The LWV should rouse them to a greater sense of their personal responsibility. Lucy Mason's 1923 presidential address reiterated this theme. "You have the latent capacity for the highest and most unselfish kind of service," she reminded her audience,

> but it is latent, it will always remain latent unless you develop it, and believe me, it is a long task to develop that kind of spirit. Individual fulfillment is found only in service, only in right relations of the individual with society. Love is the great dynamic. You do not know what love is unless you have felt its outward urge. I am not speaking of love for your near and dear, I am speaking of love for your kind; wide human love. You cannot have that kind of love without being impelled to serve and serve generously.

Lucy Mason took her message of service and the particular role of women within the political structure wider than the city's white middle-class community. Adele Clark, first president of the Virginia LWV, reported that, almost alone among the local league officers, Miss Lucy made contact with Negro women, visiting "Negro Clubs and all," talking to their members about civic affairs.[26]

Lucy Mason very rarely spoke specifically about race, yet during her public life from these Richmond days onward she sought to bring economic and social justice to all of the South's citizens, black as well as white. During her CIO years she was considered to be someone remarkably free from the racism characteristic of most southerners. Though CIO policy sometimes meant that she had to subordinate personal belief in the interests of local custom, the beliefs themselves were never in doubt. In 1932, when she was leaving Richmond, the city's black community paid her a remarkable tribute when, at a church service held in her honor, speaker after speaker noted her fairness, her commitment to racial justice, and her ability to relate to people in a way that made their skin color irrelevant. Responding to these plaudits, Miss Mason addressed the question of race directly, as she seldom did in her life, making clear in her response the depth of her admiration for the Negro people. "When the history of America is written, say two hundred years from now," she claimed, "the virtues, the struggles, the triumphs and the courage of the minority race will form one of the most thrilling epics in that history." If there was such a thing as reincarnation, she declared, she would not mind coming back to earth as a black woman. Even allowing for the emotion of the moment, her perspective was remarkable for a southern white woman in 1932 and particularly her public acknowledgment of it. Even in the Richmond years, her views on race clearly diverged from those of the southern mainstream.[27]

How and why Lucy Mason came to this position cannot be known, for her own record is silent on the matter, but a few generalizations may help. In taking a different road from that of most southerners, she was walking in company with other women of her region. As McDowell and Jacqueline Hall have both observed, women like Miss Lucy, imbued with social gospel ideas, could not evade the race issue. The extension of the Kingdom on earth had to include God's black children. Increasingly, such women began to meet with black women in interracial discussion groups and began to press for improvements in the conditions of black life—for better black schools, recreational facilities, and living conditions. Such women of course also backed the drive to rid the South of the scourge of lynching. Their views, as McDowell points out, were often heavily environmental.

Blacks were the victims of deplorable social conditions, and if they were to advance, these conditions had to be improved. Initially, such women approached blacks with a strong sense of noblesse oblige, but as they met and talked with Negro women—as they gained some knowledge of Negro communities and Negro life—this attitude frequently gave way to a new respect for black people as human beings and as citizens. Not everyone went as far as Lucy Mason; most would never have dreamed of even thinking about being reborn black. Yet in her thinking Miss Lucy was nevertheless part of a general inclination among some southern women to extend their social gospel concerns to the South's black citizens.[28]

Lucy Mason's connection with the YWCA possibly deepened her commitment to social justice. In an excellent study, Frances Taylor has recently discussed the importance of the student YWCA in the South in attempting to change the consciousness of its members regarding race by its consistent advocacy of racial equality and integration. Hall, too, has shown the importance of the YWCA in creating a climate of opinion and cooperation such that interracial discussion could take place. Mason was never a member of the student YWCA, of course, but as an industrial and later a general secretary, she would certainly have known its officers, would have attended some of its meetings, and would have been familiar with its program. Given her own social gospel convictions, it would have been odd had she not shared this particular aspect of its vision. However she acquired them, Lucy Mason's views on race were firm and consistent, and she came to them early.[29]

As Richmond president of the LWV, Lucy Mason was particularly concerned that Richmond women understand the dangers of adopting the National Woman's party approach to women's issues and, in particular, of supporting the proposed Equal Rights Amendment. At a special meeting in 1922, she and the state league president, Adele Clark, discussed the deficiencies of the amendment, noting that it would negate recent advances made in the protection of women and would destroy the standards established in industry for their welfare. In 1923, she prevailed on the redoubtable Florence Kelley, founder and executive secretary of the National Consumers League, to speak to the Richmond league on the amendment and to explain why she opposed it so vigorously. It was the first time that Miss Lucy had met Mrs. Kelley, whose successor she was eventually to become. Lucy Mason consistently opposed the Equal Rights

Amendment. Like many others, she saw it as a pernicious device which would bring the exploitation of women, not their emancipation.[30]

The highlight of her period as president of the Richmond league, however, is perhaps best described as a social event rather than a political one. In 1922 Lady Astor returned to the city in which she had grown up, and the local LWV was deeply involved in planning the civic festivities for her. The occasion was a tumultuous affair, of the kind normally reserved for royalty, with breathless media coverage. There were bands, massed choirs, an official welcome in the civic auditorium, where "God Save the King," "The Star Spangled Banner," and "Dixie" were all sung. A Negro choir contributed "Roll Jordan Roll," completing the eclectic effect. Part of the gallery, in fact, had been reserved for the "colored mammies" whom Lady Astor claimed to miss in her new home. "I loved my black mammy," she reminisced, "better than I could have loved any white mammy in the world." Lucy Mason had a place of honor beside the visitor at all the festivities and undoubtedly enjoyed the whole extravaganza. It provided some relief from the burden of domestic duties and the generally serious nature of her volunteer work.[31]

There were some joys even in domesticity, however. She delighted in her sister Ida's children and visited them in Alexandria whenever she could. Like other childless women, she found surrogates in her nieces and nephews. "Our baby is delectable and very happy and healthy," she wrote in 1922 of Ida's latest. Throughout her life she was to be a pillar of support for her sister and her family. Through them, she herself experienced some of the delights and occasionally the sadnesses, of close family life.[32]

Miss Lucy's presidency of the Richmond LWV ceased abruptly the following year. Her father died rather suddenly in June of acute appendicitis. He had, she later wrote, "never recovered from the deaths of his beloved wife and eldest son. Confidently anticipating reunion with them, his going was a consummation." His daughter Lucy was therefore free to seek professional work once more, and she decided that it would be incompatible with her LWV duties. A suitable position was soon available. The controversial general secretary of the Richmond YWCA, Emma Zanzinger, resigned to take a position in New York, and Lucy was asked to succeed her. She accepted the offer, something which distressed Florence Kelley, who had also offered her a post as southern secretary of the

National Consumers League. "I consider it a calamity of national dimen-
sion," she wrote her,

> that at this moment you are bending your best energies to the work of a local
> organization of *any* kind, instead of sharing the vast opportunity to modern-
> ize the Supreme Court and the US Constitution. . . . I note with some feel-
> ing of consolation for this lost year, the ray of hope you hold out that, after a
> year, some arrangement different from the present one might be possible for
> you. And I hasten to point out that I waited nine years for Miss Dewson, and
> on one occasion four years for Pauline Goldmark, and in the end both came
> into this office.
>
> So, I am girding on the armour of patience for a year, trusting that the
> situation will then be such that you will consent to become Secretary for the
> southern states, or to assume any title that may be more to your taste than
> this.

In the end, Miss Lucy was to come as well but not for nine more years. In
the meantime, she was back with the YWCA. Feeling the need to devote
all her energies to the new job, she therefore resigned both her LWV
offices. Her period of greatest involvement in the league's activities was
over. [33]

3

At the Richmond YWCA

The first group to call itself the YWCA was formed in Boston in 1866. Its purpose was to assist young women and girls coming to work in the city from rural areas of New England. The following year similar organizations were formed in three other cities. The movement grew steadily until at the turn of the century there were nearly 600 local organizations in existence. In 1906 these local groups formed a loose national association, and in 1908 a training school for YWCA secretaries and administrators was established. The women who attended this school and moved into the ranks of local and national administrators were predominantly exemplars of the social feminist impulse. Like Lucy Mason they were imbued with social gospel notions and believed that Christians could, in Mary Frederickson's words, "transform individual lives by transforming the social and economic environment."[1]

The reformist thrust of the bulk of the YWCA's salaried employees often led to considerable tensions between them and the conservative, middle-class boards of directors to whom they were responsible and who provided the money. The tensions manifested themselves at both the local and the national levels. Progress in developing a reformist commitment was necessarily slow, but it came nonetheless. "Gradually," writes Frederickson, "YWCA staff members . . . moved beyond the YWCA's philosophy regarding a limited commitment to organized labor and a carefully guarded allegiance to business and manufacturing interests." The YWCA, said Stanley Lemons, "courageously adopted an industrial action program in the face of threats from conservative businessmen to refuse donations.

It came after a most bitter internal fight which led to the resignation of several members of the national board. By the time Lucy Mason returned full time to the institution, however, the YWCA stood firmly for such progressive causes as the eight-hour day and forty-hour week, collective bargaining and the ban on night work for women, and the prohibition of child labor. The YWCA had become, then, part of the social feminist phalanx. [2]

Southern YWCAs tended to follow the national trend. In the absence of a strong labor tradition, and because of the paternalist atmosphere in which industrial development had occurred, YWCA workers were usually in the progressive forefront in the 1920s. As such they often lived in a continual state of strife with their predominantly conservative boards, whose membership often reflected social prominence rather than social concern. There was certainly strife in Richmond, where Miss Lucy's predecessor, Emma Zanzinger, a brisk, tough New Yorker, and her board were constantly at loggerheads. Miss Zanzinger was "a *thorough* German in *every* sense of the word," complained Mrs. Allene Y. Stokes, the Richmond YWCA president in 1921 to the president of the national board; she was "autocratic, domineering, with no idea or desire to co-operate, utterly lacking in a spirit of compromise." The relationship did not improve in the next two years, and Miss Zanzinger's sudden resignation was greeted with unalloyed joy throughout the Richmond YWCA. Her abrupt New York manner had been quite alien to the middle-class southern ladies who controlled the organization. They determined that her successor should be one of their own. Lucy Mason fitted this particular bill admirably. Brownie Lee Jones, who was industrial secretary at the Richmond YWCA during part of Lucy Mason's term as general secretary, called her "the real social force" in the institution and said that the board supported her all the way. "You see they wouldn't have kept Lucy if they hadn't been supporting Lucy, too," she said, and this certainly made Lucy's job easier. [3]

Brownie Lee Jones, commenting on Lucy's style as an administrator, said that she was easy to work with and that she worked very hard, but "she didn't know too much about doing any discipline of staff or anything, you know. Everybody just went their own way, but we all had our own ideas, and they seemed to merge pretty well." Lucy was "very creative," she further asserted, and could overcome opposition in what she described as "a remarkably typical Southern way." Lucy was not assertive or

aggressive, just quietly and politely persuasive, and was, according to
Brownie Lee Jones, very well regarded at the YWCA.[4]

Many of the duties of the general secretary were routine. The finances
had to be attended to, the residences to be maintained, the cafeterias to
be staffed, the daily activities to be planned. The records of the Richmond
YWCA show that Lucy Mason was continually engaged in such administrative tasks. In 1924, for example, she spent a considerable amount of
time negotiating the mortgages on YWCA property. In 1927, she conducted a major overhaul of the branch's administrative structure, while
much of 1929 she spent redrafting the Richmond branch's constitution,
bringing it more into line with developments elsewhere. This side of her
job she enjoyed least; at times she confessed to being "fearfully tired" of
the routine. She very much preferred the public relations aspect, the
speechmaking in support of the YWCA ideal. She constantly visited wom-
en's clubs and similar organizations, explaining the purpose of the YWCA
and discussing aspects of her work. Thus on October 16, 1925, she gave in
Richmond a speech entitled "Present Day Activities in the Association"
and less than a week later was on the public platform again, this time to
talk on selling the YWCA idea. She became, in short, an effective publicist for her institution. A reporter for the *Richmond Times Dispatch*,
having heard one of her speeches, observed, "It is a real treat to hear
Lucy Mason talk. It is doubly a treat to listen when she is telling of things
that are so near to her heart in which she is really wrapped up. That is
why she kept that bunch of noisy Kiwanians on their mettle Monday night
when she told them in that sweet lisping Victorian voice of hers all about
the splendid work of the YWCA."[5]

From time to time Miss Lucy upheld the YWCA's views in discussions
with representatives of its fraternal organization, the Young Men's Christian Association. There was often friction between the two institutions;
the men were less concerned than the women about the social aspects of
their work. Mason was particularly irritated by this difference. In September 1928, writing to the national board about a forthcoming conference with local YMCA officials, she spoke feelingly of the male organization's lack of any conception "of the meaning and purpose of the YWCA
in the 'woman movement,' or that a 'woman movement' exists at all. This
being one of my favorite topics of discussion, I am really rather glad to talk
with the brethren." Talk she certainly did. Indeed the transcript of the

discussion shows that she dominated the conference, constantly stressing that, as the YWCA was more progressive than its male counterpart and emphasized education rather than recreation, the work of the two bodies should always be regarded as complementary rather than competitive. She thought the discussion went well enough. "Some of the men were really fine," she admitted; some accepted her general views, though others were "masculine" and believed that the YWCA had a perfect right to work with girls as well as boys if it wanted to. In the main, however, she thought she had communicated the women's perspective and "given this bunch more to think about than they ever had in a meeting before." Miss Lucy was always uncompromising in her adherence to social feminist views and stressed them in all situations. It was one of the consistent themes, not only of her time with the YWCA, but also of her public life.[6]

From her earliest involvement with the suffrage movement, Lucy Mason identified herself closely with the struggle to enable women to participate more fully and equally in the public life of the United States while at the same time protecting them, where necessary, from exploitation in a male-dominated world. In one of her earliest pamphlets, *The Divine Discontent*, she claimed that women had been in subjection since the dawning of history, that "they have never yet had the freedom essential to their best development and this suppression has been harmful to the whole race." It was, she said, against such a status that women in the United States were rebelling in 1912. For the rest of her life, Lucy Mason kept the faith. She fought for votes for women and for including working girls in the activities of the middle-class YWCA. She participated in the Southern Summer School, urging protective legislation on often reluctant male legislators, and argued for fuller participation for women with equally reluctant male union officials. Whatever she was doing, Lucy Mason invariably endeavored to answer the question she had posed at the conclusion of her 1912 pamphlet. "Am I my sister's keeper?" she had written then. It was a question, she said, "which should burn into the brain and heart of the sheltered woman." Throughout her life, in her advocacy of women's issues, in her determination to secure protection for women less fortunate than she, and in her insistence on participating equally with men in her public world, she answered her own question positively.[7]

Her feminism nevertheless had its limits. She was never a supporter of the National Woman's party or of those who believed that the best route to securing equality was to amend the constitution, removing all mention of sexual differentiation. Her opposition stemmed only partly from the effect that such a change would have on the cause of protective legislation. It was also because she had little use for the stridency of the more extreme feminists or for their often harsh antimale attitudes. Lucy Mason liked men. She always had men friends, more to the point, and unlike many of the feminists whom she opposed, she was always able to work well and easily with them. Her world was always inhabited by decent, committed, like-minded men with whom she sometimes fought but who, more often than not, fought alongside her. Her opposition to the extreme feminist perspective, then, as much reflected her positive experience with men as her fears of the consequences of abandoning protective legislation.

Miss Lucy also often produced articles and pamphlets about her job and why she had come to it. She loved her work, she said in one pamphlet, and she believed the YWCA "to be one of the most valuable of our social institutions. Its program combines activities which meet the immediate needs and desires of women and girls and at the same time it has a social program which builds for progress and in its humble way is one of the factors for making the Kingdom of God a reality on earth."[8] One of her articles was reprinted and distributed widely within the YWCA organization. Entitled "Is the Secretary a Dweller or a Sojourner in her Community?" it was an attempt to set down her conception of how a good general secretary should approach the job. In it she argued that such a person must get to know the community in which she worked. She must "understand its history and its backgrounds, its social, cultural and religious traditions, its racial groups, its economic and industrial conditions, its likes and dislikes: "Crude snap judgements," of a town, or a situation, effectively prevented her [a secretary] from making a real contribution. The good secretary must make deep social and community contacts, and church attendance was particularly important. "The average community," she argued, "looks with some suspicion upon the social worker or the Association secretary who seems to think herself independent of church membership." A secretary must involve herself deeply in community work, she said, and must place her vision, judgment, and idealism at the community's service. Moreover, she should plan to stay in the community for a lengthy spell and not simply use it as a stepping-stone to bigger and better things. If these rules were followed, she concluded, the secretary would become a "dweller" in her community in the truest sense and not simply a "sojourner" there, without real involvement in it. Miss Lucy clearly dwelled in the community of Richmond. Certainly the YWCA's national office thought so. An evaluation of the Richmond program made in 1930 stressed the excellence of the relationship between the YWCA and the community, for which, the report stated, Miss Lucy was largely responsible. "Richmond still is outstanding in much that it is accomplishing," concluded the evaluation.[9]

Probably the aspect of the job that she enjoyed most, however, was the ability it gave her to pursue again her particular social goals in the professional context. She was a constant presence at conferences for industrial secretaries, often as a featured speaker. She attended many other conferences, not necessarily sponsored by the YWCA, which had to do with the issues of women in industry or women's rights generally. She attended the Bryn Mawr summer school for women workers in 1926, for example, where she first met Frank Graham of the University of North Carolina and Mary Anderson, head of the Woman's Bureau. They both became long-term friends and colleagues with whom she would later work closely on a variety of matters. In 1929 she attended the social service conference of the Women's Missionary Council of the Methodist Episcopal Church, South, where she gave a speech entitled "Home and Women Workers." She became involved in adult education and in 1926 attended a conference on trends in American adult education sponsored by the Carnegie Foundation. She was one of only fifteen invited delegates selected from the nation at large. She also became interested in international relations and especially the peace movement. The international relations section of the YWCA's national board had a strong pacifist bent, scarcely unusual in the aftermath of World War I. It sponsored peace research and organized annual conferences on "the cause and cure of war." Miss Lucy regularly attended these conferences and at this time was a committed pacifist. One of the most important benefits of a three-month vacation that she took in Europe in 1929 was the opportunity it gave her to meet and talk with leaders of the peace movement abroad. Her pacifism was an important sustaining force for her. She lost it only slowly and painfully during the 1930s, in the wake of Hitler's aggression.[10]

Lawrence Wittner, in the introductory chapter to his brilliant survey of the American peace movement between 1941 and 1960, speaks of the

extraordinary growth of the pacifist ideal following the disillusioning experience of World War I. He shows that women were unusually prominent within the movement's widening constituency, especially Protestant
social-gospel-oriented women. Women's organizations such as the YWCA
were always in the vanguard of the movement, supporting the mainstream bodies like the National Council for the Prevention of War and
developing, through their international network, their own plans for out-
lawing militarism. Moreover, one of the most important antiwar bodies
was the Women's International League for Peace and Freedom, founded
by women reformers who considered the causes of social justice and
world peace to be intertwined.[11]

The link between the peace movement and social reformers had been
obvious even before the outbreak of the First World War, and the bond
had strengthened since 1914. C. Roland Marchand has discussed the
woman suffrage movement in connection with the peace cause. The
women most closely identified with social reform in the United States had
by 1914 also joined the peace movement. Jane Addams, after all, having
toured the capitals of Europe on behalf of the women of the world, founded
the United States branch of the Women's International League for Peace
and Freedom. The connection between social gospel, social reform, and
the cause of peace was thus well established even before the postwar
growth in pacifist support.[12]

The link held as much for the South as for the rest of the nation. As John
McDowell has shown, southern women who supported the social gospel
also supported the pacifist ideal. In the wake of the experience of war, the
connections were strengthened. Some feminist reformers had come to
favor American entry into the conflict and believed that a lasting peace
might come in the end. Now, however, following the selfishness of the
victors and America's failure to join the League of Nations, the reformers
knew they had been wrong. Peace could never be achieved through war,
and their pacifism developed accordingly. "The Kingdom the women
were extending was a kingdom of peace," McDowell writes. In making
her own commitment to pacifism, Lucy Mason, like many other women,
could feel guided by the loss of a beloved member of her immediate
family. She was also, however, as in most aspects of her life, following a
cause that she shared with other women of her region, her religion, and
her cast of belief.[13]

Lucy Mason's interest in international affairs had been heightened through her developing relationship with a woman who was to influence her life crucially. Katherine Gerwick of Zanesville, Ohio, joined the national board of the YWCA after studying literature and drama at Columbia University and eventually became international secretary of the Department of Educational Research in the World Fellowship Department. Later she was known as the secretary for international education. She was attractive, vivacious, and highly intelligent. Part of her job was to visit local YWCA branches, explaining the national board's policy on various international issues and especially on the YWCA's efforts to promote world peace. Probably during such a journey to Richmond, she met Lucy Mason, sometime in 1924. She was to return to Richmond frequently. The two women were the same age, felt the same Christian social commitment, and were immediately attracted to one another. On the occasion of her death, one of Katherine Gerwick's associates wrote of "her staunch, intrepid feminism, never assertive, always persistent," which "held inviolable the dignity and importance of half the human family and admitted no decision as final into which that consideration had not entered." In this level-headed, committed woman, with her dislike of cant and insincerity, Lucy Mason clearly recognized a soulmate.[14]

By 1925 they had become firm friends and spent as much time as possible together. The *Richmond Times Dispatch* reported in September:

> Miss Lucy Mason, general secretary of the YWCA is back at her desk after a months vacation spent in Michigan. Miss Mason attended, unofficially, the international relations section of the Fellowship for a Christian Social Order Conference, which was held at Oliver College, Michigan. She was accompanied by Miss Katherine Gerwick, secretary for international relations from the national board of the YWCA who is well known in Richmond, where she has often spoken. Following this conference, Miss Mason and Miss Gerwick spent several weeks camping near Frankfort, Michigan.

Katherine was to continue to visit Richmond frequently, while Lucy sometimes went to Zanesville at times when Katherine was there with her family.[15]

As Susan Ware has pointed out, intense and long-term relationships, sometimes physical, sometimes not, were not uncommon between single professional women of Lucy Mason's generation. Molly Dewson, to take one example, maintained such a relationship with Polly Porter for more than fifty years, from which came her "primary emotional fulfillment." There was also the friendship of Lillian Smith and Paula Snelling. It was, Ware reminds us, easier in many ways for such women to spend their lives together then than it would be the case later. "Throughout the nineteenth century and into the early twentieth," she says, "women looked to other women for their closest and most intimate friendships." Many of the settlement houses were predominantly all-female communities. Moreover, it was common and socially acceptable for one single woman to live with another, especially for upper-middle-class professional and educated women. Such arrangements were popularly known as "Boston marriages." Though Katherine and Lucy were never able to live together permanently, their relationship very much followed the pattern.[16]

Sadly, the friendship was to be short-lived. In May 1927, not long before Katherine's projected departure for a conference in Honolulu on Pacific relations—she was to have been Carrie Chapman Catt's cabin companion on the voyage—she became ill. On May 14, she died after surgery. Lucy was at her bedside, in her family home in Zanesville. Lucy's utter desolation and inability for years to accept the loss powerfully attest to the depth of her love for Katherine. The pain was intense. "She who walked among us yesterday," she wrote later that year,

> we knew as one of earth's great hearts, noble, steadfast, poised, serene, wise, kind, valiant. Today with eyes illumined by Death's awakening fingers, we see with keener vision and discern those more subtle spiritual values that were hers. There was the Madonna heart that made her one with all womankind and in the common daily tasks that served human wants, uniting her thoughts with her toiling sisters everywhere.[17]

Lucy's grief eventually brought on a nervous breakdown, and she was forced in 1929 to take three months' leave of absence from the YWCA. She spent the time in Europe. Eventually her developing involvement in spiritualism, her certainty that life continued beyond the grave, that the dead could be contacted and could act upon the living, brought her partial relief. "Another thing I believe," she wrote in 1930,

> is that, if people on the other side of life have someone, or several people here who love them a lot it helps them to direct energy into our world. Especially if there is one person very, very close, who understands and loves

them tremendously and who believes that love and life can pass the barriers of death, I think they can use that person as a sort of fulcrum to influence other people here. Such a person gives them a sort of power-house or base of energy. It has seemed very real to me since Katherine died—we go on as co-partners on enterprises that are worthwhile, and she can get at lots of other people because she has my brains and heart as a human center.

"But, oh, how well I know the ache of physical missing, the hours when one seems almost defeated," she also wrote at the same time.[18] Lucy "talked with her often," she said, and eventually with her mother, Lucy Ambler, as well. Frequently she wrote Katherine letters, as if she were still a real and vital presence. Their tone and intensity tell much about the nature of her love for her friend. "It has been years, beloved of my heart," ran one such in 1931,

> since you walked the earth clothed in material frame, yet this Sunday morn-ing you are nearer than the air around me, fairer than the sunshine this brilliant day. . . . You remember how we would look into each others eyes those years ago, seeing beyond the shining surface, seeing into the soul that lay beyond the eyes, nothing veiled in me from you, nor in you from me. We saw each other in all that potential best which is spirit animating matter. In you nothing is hid from me, when those clear moments came, and in me you see the scroll unrolled, you read me as I truly am—weak, blind, dull yet aspiring, seeing perceiving the ideal that lies enwrapped within me—within all human souls. No place is strange, for you are there; no task is impossible, for you share it, no defeat is defeat for you help me find the lesson defeat would teach me. . . . Without you, what would life be? I cannot know, for in fact life so far as I can remember has never been without you. Love like that which lies between us can only mean that for endless aeons we have walked hand in hand, thru suffering and joy, thru defeat and victory, forging the bonds that now bind us so close that no power in all the universe can sepa-rate us.

Lucy's mysticism, then, enabled her to believe that the relationship con-tinued. The bond was the most important one of her life, and though she was to become very closely involved with someone else—again a woman—in the 1940s, it was an attachment of a different order and lacked the passion and totality of the earlier one. Katherine remained the most significant influence on Lucy Mason's emotional life.[19]

Miss Lucy did not conceal her belief in the ability to communicate beyond the grave. Indeed she liked to speak of it. "She used to always tell me about talking to her friends, you know," said Brownie Lee Jones, "those that were long gone." Brownie Lee also said the habit didn't bother her. "I would listen and be interested, but that was all. I know that she had one friend, Katherine Gerwick, she was always talking with Katherine."[20]

Though neglected by historians, spiritualism has always had considerable support in the United States. It exerted its greatest influence in the last decades of the nineteenth century. Thereafter, its popularity declined somewhat, though a solid core of adherents remained, a disproportionate number of whom were middle-class, old-stock females. Perhaps Brownie Lee was not bothered by Lucy Mason's beliefs because they were not unheard of.[21]

Lucy's position as YWCA general secretary would have involved her in the more general aspects of Richmond's community life even without her intense commitment to social reform. She was always active in the community. She retained her membership in the Richmond League of Women Voters and became a member of the Council of the National Consumers League and of the Virginia Commission on Interracial Cooperation. Her growing commitment to social justice for Richmond's blacks developed into public opposition to segregation, an unusual position for a middle-class white woman to take in the South in the 1920s. In 1928 she chaired a committee of the Richmond Council of Social Agencies that was charged with surveying the economic status of Richmond's Negro community. The committee's final report revealed a mosaic of discrimination and deprivation—something Negroes already knew, as Raymond Gavin observes, but which whites had been often able to evade. Few blacks earned a decent wage; their children had no recreational facilities and were taught in inadequate schools by poorly paid teachers. Negroes in the city could expect to live fifteen years less than whites, committed three times as many crimes, and were fourteen times as likely to be illiterate as whites. It was a bleak and depressing picture. In the course of the investigation, Lucy Mason became convinced that the blame for the situation confronting most blacks could be laid at the door of Jim Crow. Not until the constriction of economic opportunity inherent in a segregated society was abandoned, she believed, could any progress be made toward social and economic justice.[22]

Her growing commitment to ending segregation she made public in 1929. During the previous two decades the Richmond City Council, determined to restrict black residential mobility in the city, had applied a series of increasingly restrictive residential zoning ordinances. Though the concept of residential segregation was never mentioned directly in any of these documents—the Supreme Court had declared in 1917 that ordinances whose sole purpose was to enforce residential segregation were unconstitutional—everyone understood the implicit meaning of the language. Negro living space in the city was steadily curbed throughout the decade until the situation had become desperate. Certainly Richmond's blacks identified insufficient and inadequate housing as the most serious problem they faced in the city.[23] In 1929 the council resolved to impose its most restrictive ordinance yet, the result of which would have been to confine the city's blacks to a very few run-down areas. Predictably, the measure was bitterly opposed by representatives of the Negro community. It was also opposed by Lucy Randolph Mason. At a public meeting in January 1929 she spoke vigorously against it and was the only white woman to do so. Armed with "a set of figures that indicated the living conditions of the colored people were not of the best," she demanded improvements for schools, streets, and sewerage. If these changes were made, then the pressure on white districts might be relieved. Blacks had a right to a decent environment, she insisted, and should not be prevented by restrictive ordinances from seeking it. Her arguments were not supported, however, and the ordinance was passed by a large majority. Nonetheless, her opposition to it was one further example to the black community that in this small, neat, eminently respectable southern lady they had a true and courageous friend. George B. Harris, a black who had formerly lived in Richmond, expressed the views of many when in a letter he thanked her for "the stand you have taken on behalf of justice and right for the Negro there in Richmond—pay no attention to the disapproval of your stand by some. God has seen you act, and knows your heart."[24]

The most powerful testimony of the esteem in which she was held by Richmond's blacks came, as previously noted, when she prepared to leave the city in 1932. At the church service of appreciation in her honor, speaker after speaker paid tribute to "her courage, her sense of fairness and justice," and her energy. Lucretia W. Jordan, representing black so-

cial workers, called her "a Southern gentlewoman and the embodiment of
the modern, progressive ideal of social work—helping others to help
themselves." Dr. W. L. Ransome, on behalf of the black ministers, recalled the occasion when "she spoke on behalf of justice" against the segregation ordinance and asserted that "she works for people . . . . she
wears no air of complex superiority, she does not talk down to people, but
with people, whether they be white or black." Gordon B. Hancock, professor of sociology at the black Virginia Union University, one of Richmond's leading Negro citizens and the organizer of the gathering, spoke of
"the spirit of a New South which is embodied in the life and labors of this
Christian-hearted white woman." In all, 124 of Richmond's black citizens
spoke or recorded their appreciation in a testimonial volume which was
presented to her. [25]

In response, Miss Lucy disclaimed any great merit of her own. "Many
white people of this city believe as I do," she said, "and do the things that
I do, but they are not quite so spectacular as I am." She expressed surprise at the ignorance of those who arrogantly laid claim to racial superiority. She knew nothing about superior races, she said, but she did know
some superior people. One of these was clearly Dr. Hancock, whom she
described as "the most perfect gentleman, under all circumstances," she
had ever known. "The white race is on test," she said, "and the future will
be influenced to the extent of its fairness to other races." Complimenting
blacks "on their spirit of forgiveness in view of the wrongs and injustice
practised against them," she agreed that they had "more than obeyed the
admonition of Christ to forgive seventy times seven." Given the expression of such sentiments, little wonder that the editor of Richmond's
black newspaper called her departure from Richmond "a distinct loss,"
and agreed that she carried "with her . . . the affectionate regards and
the sincerest best wishes of the humble people whose cause she has stead-
fastly championed, undeterred by biassed criticisms."[26]

White interracialists, too, paid tribute to Lucy Mason. L. R. Reynolds,
director of the Virginia Commission on Interracial Cooperation, said it
would be hard to keep the commission going without her. "Let me thank
you again for your untiring loyalty and helpful leadership in the cause," he
wrote. "I shall expect to find you fighting to the last minute for justice and
fairness, and while some of your friends may think you are too militant, no
one can accuse you of being a coward or a hypocrite." She certainly was

not, and throughout her life she remained a persistent fighter on behalf of civil rights for blacks.[27]

Though her various activities and attitudes did at times disturb her white friends and colleagues, her status and background nevertheless assured her a certain standing in the Richmond community and in the state of Virginia. In 1926 the Virginia state administration marked the occasion of the one hundred and fiftieth anniversary of the adoption of the Virginia Bill of Rights by the Virginia General Assembly with a commemorative ceremony. Naturally, George Mason's great-great-granddaughter was invited to participate, and there were many newspaper pictures of her reading the "famous document of her forefather" aloud to the invited guests, with Virginia's governor standing alongside her.[28]

Her respectability and her connections in part enabled Lucy Mason to leave her YWCA job for a while in 1931. She was certainly ready to do so. The periods of anomie and depression from which she had suffered since Katherine's death still came. The three months in Europe in 1929 had helped. She spent much of her time in England, visiting cathedrals and churches, and their very age gave her a sense of the timelessness of the Christian message of hope and redemption. Moreover, a chance encounter with an elderly woman on a train from Florence to Milan reinforced her growing conviction that death was simply part of a larger life. The woman, an Englishwoman who had been married to a Spaniard, said that her son Pietro had caught pneumonia during the war. The boy had apparently died. The young Italian doctor treating him, according to Miss Mason's notes,

> cast himself upon his body weeping—Pietro was withdrawn from body, hung above it looking at it and the doctor, thought to himself, "if he would use gymnastics on my body as they do drowning men, I could come back." Doctor seemed to hear a faint whisper in his ear, "gymnastics." He jumped up and said to his assistant, "We will try artificial respiration." Pietro saw them begin to work his arms; gradually breath came in his body; he suffered terribly in the attempt to reunite soul and body and thought, "If they would just let me alone and let me stay over here." But he came back.

This tale profoundly affected Lucy. It was one of the reasons she returned from Europe rested and ready to work again.[29]

Nevertheless, she longed for a break from the routine aspects of the

YWCA job and especially from "finances, cafeterias and residences." The chance to do so came rather unexpectedly at the end of 1930. A group of southern church and club women calling themselves the Southern Council on Women and Children in Industry, some of them with linkages to the National Consumers League, knowing of her long-term interest in protective legislation and aware that her lineage gave her a certain entree into society, invited her to work for two months in the southern states as their representative. Her task was to work to create a better climate of opinion for child labor laws and shorter working hours for women. Her salary was to be paid by the National Consumers League.[30]

As she remarked in her autobiography, "I accepted and had an illuminating time." For the months of January and February 1931, she traveled throughout the South, talking to governors, editors, ministers, college professors, labor leaders, industrialists, anyone who would listen, advocating the cause. The key industry was, of course, the textile industry, and upon this she concentrated. By 1931 it was in a perilous condition. The market was glutted, and prices were at their lowest levels. In an endeavor to meet competition by lowering costs, manufacturers had lengthened working hours, had increased night work, and had cut the already low wage levels. The voluntary agreement made by manufacturers in 1928, through the Cotton Textile Institute, to reduce night work and to prohibit it for minors and women, had been jettisoned in the depression. Working conditions were appalling. A twelve-hour shift was the norm, and effective wage rates of seven dollars a week were becoming common. Yet the industry remained profoundly depressed. Miss Lucy therefore found many a southern ear receptive to her message that the restriction of production by limiting of hours of work for certain groups might be one way out of the slide. There was even considerable agreement among mill owners that the only way of achieving this end was through state or federal legislation.[31]

Deftly, Miss Lucy attempted to capitalize on such inclinations. She wrote long letters of support to manufacturers who had expressed views favoring the proposed legislation. To W. M. McLauren, of the American Cotton Manufacturers Association, she explained that she "came down for just two months to help southern women organize the above named organization among women's clubs, churches etc. etc. This is going on swimmingly—but I suddenly found my best immediate ally is to be found in the liberal textile men who have their fingers on the legislative pulse in each state. So I go on organizing the women and talking to the wisest men." McLauren, she clearly inferred, was one such man. Stating that she sympathized with the manufacturers and recognized that "abuses in the industry are not the personal result of any one man, but the result of a system which no-one alone could change," she stressed constantly that she approached "the subject of legislation with sanity and perspective." "We have," she said, "reached one of those curious juxtapositions of forces when economic expediency, social wisdom and public conscience combine to point to legislation as the way out in the South." To Donald Comer, of the Avondale Mills in Birmingham, Alabama, one of the region's largest producers, she explained that she well understood the predicament of individual mill owners caught "in a vicious circle from which it is almost impossible for anyone to escape until there is a basic change in the whole industry" and admitted that she "little dreamed when I came here I would be looking upon leading textile manufacturers as the most hopeful support of legislation."[32]

It is difficult to judge how effective her two months' sojourn was. At the very least, she may have left local organizations able to maintain pressure on mill owners. She had helped convince some of them that protective legislation, and the consequent limitation of production which would ensue, might have some beneficial economic effects. After all, the idea of raising prices by restricting production was very much in the air at the time. Within two years it was to underpin the New Deal's recovery program. Miss Lucy thoroughly enjoyed her work in the South and was fulfilled by it. Her activities illustrated both the style and the nature of the task she was to undertake for the CIO just six years later. She gained some national attention, at least in reformist circles, as a result of her efforts. Florence Kelley of the Consumers League wrote to congratulate her.[33]

In March Lucy returned, reluctantly, to the YWCA. The work in the South had convinced her that it was indeed time for a change, both for her and for the institution. Within two weeks she had submitted her resignation. "There is a danger," she wrote the Richmond president, Miss Emily Thomason,

> that I may become conservative if too long engaged in the same type of work and not quick to sense the need of change. There is also grave danger that because I know this city well and assume leadership which in many cities belongs to volunteers, I may be permanently weakening the Association's

place in the city as an organization largely sponsored by volunteers. This is
probably one of the most serious reasons for my resignation.

The Richmond YWCA's Board of Directors, however, was in no mood to
let her go. Members wrote to her, requesting that she withdraw her resignation. "We do not feel that dispensing with your services at such a critical time would do more than add to the seriousness of the present crisis,"
said one. Another averred that no greater handicap could be placed in the
path of the Richmond YWCA's progress than for her to leave it.[34]
    In the end, she gave in to such pressure and agreed to stay. But she did
so most reluctantly. A long, intimate letter that she wrote to a close friend
revealed the strain she was under at the time and her ambivalence about
making a change. She was restless, she said, but did not know if "there is
an inner urge in me to change, or only because I so fear dominating a
situation and growing into it so that no one can pry me out." She "adored"
Richmond and did not want to leave, yet she did not know whether the
community really needed her or whether people were simply in the habit
of saying so without meaning it. She had her problems with Brownie Lee
Jones, she said, and believed that, deep down, Brownie Lee considered
her to be "an ancient fossil with antideluvian [sic] religious and psychic
ideas. There is no doubt," she continued, that Brownie Lee had done
much "to discount my faith in myself and on the other hand has stimu-
lated me to new enterprises and new ideas." She would stay, she had
decided, till "something presents itself that asks me to go and which is
compelling enough to make me feel I must." Katherine had always believed that she, Lucy, had a "curious conscience," which led her to think
that "if you want to do a thing it must be wrong for you to do it. Maybe I
have," she concluded, "and it warps my judgement."[35]
    Her ambivalence, her confusion, her restlessness—all were obvious.
She did decide to stay with the YWCA, however, for the time being. For
the first half of 1931, she was partly occupied with writing a pamphlet
about her experiences in the South earlier in the year. The booklet was
published by the National Consumers League and was entitled *Standards
for Workers in Southern Industry.* In it Miss Lucy gave a state-by-state
account of the working conditions she had encountered during her tour,
with particular emphasis on those for women, children, and blacks. In all
states she found long hours of work. The little existing protective legislation for women and children was inadequately enforced. In Alabama, for

example, there was no law limiting hours of work for women. A bill for a ten-hour day and a fifty-five-hour week had been supported by liberal manufacturers but had been killed in committee in 1931. Many mills operated on a twelve-hour shift seven days a week, with frequent closures between orders which left the employees wageless. Arkansas had a nine-hour day and a fifty-four-hour week on the books, but women textile workers fell outside the law's scope. Moreover the state provided only a tiny appropriation for its enforcement, and the measure was generally ignored outside Little Rock. In Georgia, sixty-hour-week schedules for mill girls were common. After describing existing conditions, Miss Lucy went on to argue the case for regulation and reduction of hours of work, stressing the social values that would accrue. "If the real wealth of a nation or state consists in the intelligence, health, vigor, initiative, happiness and public spirit of the citizens," she claimed, "then that wealth is seriously impaired by a work day for any considerable number of people of such length as to sap vitality and deny opportunity for the normal enjoyment of the world which lies outside the plan of work." This, she concluded, was the general situation in the South. The pamphlet was widely circulated. Indeed Frances Perkins used it as a discussion paper at her first National Labor Legislation Conference after her appointment as secretary of labor.[36]

Early in 1932, the citizens of Richmond decided to let Lucy Mason know how much they valued her and her work. At the YWCA's annual meeting in January, a book of letters of appreciation was presented to her. There were thirty-nine contributors, including the governor of the state, the mayor, and many of the town's leading figures. All spoke of her courage and generosity. Douglas Southall Freeman, editor of the *Richmond News Leader* and the distinguished biographer of George Washington and Robert E. Lee, described her as an "indispensable servant of the city." He admired her, he said, "for her many splendid qualities, but most of all because she is not afraid of tomorrow." Gordon Hancock spoke of the "diadem of service of this wonderful woman," again stressing Miss Lucy's concern for the city's black community, as did many others, white and black. Mrs. J. Scott Parrish perhaps best caught the spirit of all the contributors. "All hail Lucy Mason," she wrote, "the worthy daughter of two crusaders of the nineteenth century. A pioneer in your own generation, working for those vital issues which are striving for the greatest good to humanity. Your city, State and Southland will ever hold you in warm regard and appreciation."[37]

Lucy Mason, for her part, was overwhelmed by the gesture. It must have allayed those doubts she had expressed the previous year about whether the community in which she worked really needed her. Yet the tribute did not still her restlessness, her determination to answer the call to leave when something sufficiently compelling presented itself.[38]

Such a call came sooner than she expected. Florence Kelley, the first and only secretary of the National Consumers League, died early in 1932. Before her death, she had discussed her possible successor with her friend Molly Dewson, soon to be a woman of national importance with the advent of the New Deal. "Of course there is Lucy," she reportedly said. "She is known all over the South very favorably and carries great weight there. She has not written books, but she is a fine speaker. And she is consecrated to the work. I think she would take it." Years later, Molly Dewson confirmed that Lucy had been Mrs. Kelley's personal choice. "Sure, F. K. did suggest you to succeed her," she wrote, "and who should know better than I for she told me herself."[39]

Mrs. Kelley's favored candidate Miss Lucy may have been, but she was certainly not the only applicant for the position. Nearly forty people were interviewed before the league's board had settled on a short list of three, Elizabeth Magee of the Ohio League, A. Estelle Lauder of Pennsylvania, and Lucy Mason herself. Eventually Magee and Lauder both withdrew, leaving Mason as the only appointable candidate. Thus in spring of 1932, she was asked whether she would consider a call to fill the office of general secretary of the National Consumers League.[40]

This was the challenge she had been waiting for, and quickly she accepted it. Leaving Richmond was "painful," she told the YWCA board in her letter of resignation, but "the call to the National Consumers League both fulfills a life-long dream of working for the improvement of industrial conditions, and makes it possible for me to complete the effort made two years ago to resign my present position." This time the board did not attempt to persuade her otherwise. It accepted her resignation "with a depressing sense of the loss you will be to Richmond as well as to the Association." So amidst the tributes of her friends and fellow workers, her heart filled with excitement at the prospect of change and of fulfilling service and with some moments of apprehension, Lucy Mason left the South for the first and only time in her life—for the vastly different milieu of New York City.[41]

4

Turning on the Light

The National Consumers League

T he great days of the National Consumers League had long since
passed when Lucy Mason became the general secretary in 1932. Described by William O'Neill as "not only a model social feminist organization but a prototypical specimen of the Progressive mentality" and as
"dollar for dollar and woman for woman . . . the best buy in the history of
social feminism," it had exerted its greatest influence in the first decade of
the century and had been steadily dwindling since World War I.[1]

The first Consumers League resulted from a meeting organized in
New York in 1890 to protest the low pay, long hours, and appalling working conditions of the city's shop assistants. A committee of prominent
citizens, most of them upper-class women, was formed to investigate their
complaints. They called themselves the Consumers League. Their first
president was Josephine Shaw Lowell, a Civil War widow and a wealthy
philanthropist with strong interests in the labor movement. She brought
other wealthy upper-class women into the league, one of whom, Maud
Nathan, replaced her as president in 1896. By this time, other leagues
had been established in several cities. The National Consumers League
was formed in 1899 to coordinate their activities, with Florence Kelley as
its executive secretary. "This fabulously energetic woman," the daughter
of a wealthy Congressman, and herself a socialist, of whom it was once
said, that "everybody was brave from the moment she came into the

room," was to direct the NCL's activities from then until her death in 1932.[2]

Under Kelley's aggressive leadership, the league quickly grew. In a relatively few years there were ninety local leagues and twenty state leagues, all working actively for social reform, imbued with Florence Kelley's dictum, which was to become the unofficial motto of the NCL, "investigate, agitate and/or legislate." The league, she often observed, should be an instrument for "turning on the light," thus exposing all manner of social evils. In this approach, according to O'Neill, the league "embraced without reservation the cooperative ethic which distinguished Progressive social thought. It had complete faith in the power of reason to change society," he writes. "It investigated each problem as fully as possible, then it educated the public on the basis of its discoveries. Finally, it relied on the moral indignation thus aroused to influence public policy . . . it relied mainly on the Progressive formula of investigation, agitation and moral suasion." "No other social feminist organization," he concludes, "was as much a product of its age." In this approach it very closely reflected the views of Florence Kelley.[3]

The NCL was at first highly successful and used various approaches to achieve its aims. It sponsored a White Label campaign, by which clothing manufacturers with good labor policies were authorized to use a special NCL label. It lobbied Congress and state legislatures for protective legislation, especially for women and children. It prepared model bills for sympathetic legislators to introduce. Increasingly, however, largely as a result of its success in helping prevent an adverse court judgment on the Oregon ten-hour law, its main task became to provide logistical support for those defending reform legislation against court challenges. When the Illinois maximum-hour law was challenged, for example, the NCL produced a 600-page brief supporting it. The law was sustained, which prompted a remark from Mrs. Kelley that this feat alone justified the NCL's existence. In the course of this achievement and its other activities, the league always cooperated closely with the Women's Trade Union League, the National Child Labor Committee, and other organizations controlled by women reformers. The NCL was, in short, one of the most successful pressure groups for Progressive reform.[4]

It was also a training ground for socially active women reformers. Much of the NCL's work was performed by its salaried staff, all of whom were socially committed young women and many of whom in later years continued their commitment in government service. They included women such as Pauline and Josephine Goldmark, Molly Dewson, and, most famous of all, Frances Perkins, who during the New Deal was to be the first woman member of the federal cabinet. For such women, the NCL experience remained of prime importance throughout their lives. Indeed Frances Perkins once admitted that she did not take her appointment as secretary of labor as reflecting on her personally. "It was the Consumers' League who was appointed," she said, and "I was merely the symbol who happened to be at hand, able and willing to serve at the moment." The NCL, then, was an important component in what Susan B. Ware has termed "the women's network."[5]

From about 1915, the NCL's influence began to decline. There were several reasons. In the first place, the reform impulse had slowed. The league increasingly had to fight to maintain ground recently gained, let alone plow fresh fields. Further support was lost during World War I, in part because of Mrs. Kelley's uncompromising opposition to American entry in the war. Though the league emerged in 1918 relatively unscathed, confident, and with a bold ten-year plan of reform, including such measures as the eight-hour day, the elimination of night work for women, child labor legislation, and health insurance for workers, the 1920s was to be a decade barren of achievement. The social climate militated against further reform. The women's movement was riven by the struggle between the social feminists (the membership of the NCL was archetypical), those who supported protective legislation, and those, exemplified by the membership of the National Woman's party, who wanted all distinctions between the sexes removed by a constitutional amendment. Much of the league's and Mrs. Kelley's emotional and financial resources went into this struggle, a conflict which was beside the point, as the amendment had no chance of passage. Yet as Clark Chambers notes, the episode illustrated "the kind of irrelevant wrangle which so often engaged the social reformers during the twenties" as they dissipated their energies in "fruitless and rancorous debate."[6]

Most important of all, the United States Supreme Court began to strike down many of the measures for which the NCL had fought so vigorously in the heady years of Progressive reform. One after another, state minimum-wage laws, laws against child labor, and laws permitting the regulation of hours of work for women all failed the test of constitutionality. In

an endeavor to recover some of the gains of the previous decade, the
league spent much of its time and resources during the 1920s in support
of the Child Labor Amendment. It was a losing battle. The amendment
passed both Houses of Congress in 1922, but by 1930 only six states had
ratified it. The cause was dead, and its failure, again according to O'Neill,
"cut the heart out of both her [Mrs. Kelley] and the league," which was
demoralized. In Mrs. Kelley's last years at the helm, it drifted aimlessly,
lacking leadership, money, and influence. Clearly, Lucy Mason had a
daunting task before her as she took over the wheel.[7]

Lucy Mason moved to New York in September 1932, when the ravages
of depression were at their worst. She had decided to accept the Consumers League position, as she told Anne O'Hare McCormick, because it
had been agreed that she could direct its activities more toward the problems of the industrializing South, an area so far neglected by the NCL.
"Of course, the usual work of the League in the East and North will go on
and will constitute an active part of my duties," she wrote. "But I have
been chosen as executive as a recognition of the identity of interests of
manufacturers in New England and the South and the hope that we may
be able to enlist support in both groups." She hoped, she said, to spend
much of her time traveling in the South.[8]

Lucy's aspirations to redirect the NCL's activities fairly rapidly, however, had to be postponed because of the immediate problems of the third
year of the depression. Wage rates, which, as William E. Leuchtenburg
has noted, had held up remarkably well until 1932, in that year began to
plummet as industrialists, exploiting the drastic labor surfeit, began to cut
costs by slashing wages. Soon, sweatshop conditions prevailed in many
industries, and the hard-won gains of the Progressive reformers were effectively nullified. In New York, when a garment manufacturer advertised
for skilled workers at ten dollars weekly, the police had to break up a riot
as more than a thousand women fought each other for the few jobs available. In Cleveland, Ohio, a merchant who advertised for ten experienced
sales ladies at eight dollars a week had the window of his store smashed,
not through angry reaction at his exploitation of depression conditions,
but through the pressure of the crowd of women who answered his
advertisement.[9]

The Consumers League decided to throw all its meager resources into
the fight against such exploitative wage rates. Mason was soon in the thick
of the fray. Her first task for the NCL was the organization of a Conference

on the Breakdown of Industrial Standards, held in New York in December 1932. Molly Dewson chaired the meeting, and her opening address gave some indication of the depth of her concern. "The National Consumers' League had a sharp awakening this fall," she said.

> We had realized that wage levels were sinking, but we had not realized how rapidly wages were being cut—slashed in industry after industry beyond the subsistence level in many cases. We had realised that enforcement of the hours laws was not as good as it had been because it was impossible to keep up with the number of violations in certain places, but we had not realized that the industrial standards built up little by little after years of struggle are collapsing like card houses under the grim determination of the unemployed to get work at any price. The women are undercutting the men as they never have before. The better manufacturers are demoralized by cut in throat and fly-by-night competition.

The breakdown in standards was a challenge the NCL could not afford to ignore. Accordingly, it made plans for widespread publicity and for concerted pressure on state legislatures, all but five of which were meeting in 1933, to enact adequate wages-and-hours legislation. To that end a committee of league members, all experts on minimum-wage legislation, was appointed to draft a model minimum-wage bill that would be applicable in all states and would meet the test of constitutionality. The members of the committee, all soon to become familiar names, were Molly Dewson, Josephine Goldmark, Felix Frankfurter, and Benjamin V. Cohen. They finished their work by February 1933, and the bill quickly became a standard one. There was, however, no suggestion that action could or should be taken at the federal level.[10]

Yet these problems and others would soon be tackled at the federal level as Franklin D. Roosevelt and his New Deal came to Washington and changed the focus of American political action. As the legislative program of FDR's first hundred days unfolded, Lucy Mason, like many other reformers, began to comprehend that the political climate had changed dramatically—that a whole agenda of reform heretofore regarded as wildly impractical might now be possible. "Notwithstanding the anxiety and uncertainty of these days," she wrote her friend Emma Zanzinger in April 1933,

> I feel a curious sense of lift and thrill, as if some great adventure were just around the corner. Half of my friends, including Hermine, have lost so heav-

ily that it is a mystery how they are to live hereafter and I ought to be
depressed about that and the mass misery in our world, and yet here I am
eagerly anticipating changes to come that will mean a more decent sort of
society. We have to go through a hell of suffering from doing the wrong and
stupid things before we learn to do differently: the main thing is to learn the
lesson and avoid past blunders.

Her sense of eager anticipation was doubtless heightened by the fact that
the Consumers League, after years in the political wilderness, now
clearly had a strong voice in Washington, not only through Frances Perkins and Molly Dewson, as head of the Women's Division of the Democratic party, now a power in the New Deal constellation, but also through
Eleanor Roosevelt herself. The First Lady, a long-time member of the
New York Consumers League and a friend to many of the league's leaders,
could be relied upon to push its program whenever possible. Perhaps,
indeed, the NCL's long period of declining influence was over.[11]

Certainly such seemed to be the case in 1933 as Lucy Mason and the
NCL were caught up in the breathless pace of the "hundred days." Lucy
spent much of her time in Washington, testifying at hearings on the various National Recovery Act (NRA) regulatory codes, insisting that adequate wages-and-hours provisions be written into them. It was scarcely
surprising, given her southern background and her previous experience
with the industry, that she should have devoted most of her attention
initially to the Cotton-Textile Code. At the hearing in May 1933 she urged
that wages and hours be controlled, that child labor be prohibited, and
that safety provisions be rigidly monitored. She also fielded questions and
stated parenthetically that, if the textile workers' wages were raised, they
would spend the extra money on "better food, shoes for the children so
they could go to school in cold weather; the women in the family—and
men and boys too—would get some better clothes to wear to church and
on the street. They might go to a movie once in a while." In fact, she said,
the workers would do exactly what the president wanted, would spend
their money, and would thus promote recovery—an assertion, she said,
that was "greeted by roars of laughter and much hand-clapping."[12]

Lucy was to attend many such code hearings in the next few months.
She argued for a set of principles developed by the league which, it believed, should be embodied in all code labor provisions. These included
such standards as no employment of children under sixteen, no night
work for young people or women, the forty-hour week, specified overtime

rates, a defined lunch break, a minimum wage of thirty-five cents an hour, or fourteen dollars for a forty-hour week, and no wage differentials. In short, Mason argued for the inclusion in all NRA codes of the NCL's agenda of labor legislation, as it had built up over years of activity. The league, through Lucy Mason, bitterly criticized provisions in many codes which sought to discriminate against black employees. It filed detailed briefs with authorities, arguing that "it is economically bad for both white and colored wage earners that wage discrimination against Negroes should be perpetuated by NRA codes." It was in the interest of better race relations, ran one such brief, not "to perpetuate economic discrimination against Negroes. Though he himself is unaware of the cause of his antagonism, deep rooted in the southern white unskilled wage earner is fear of Negro competition. Whether consciously or unconsciously, employers have too often contributed to this fear by employment of Negro workers at sub-standard living wages." This emphasis on the problems of black workers was something relatively new for the NCL. As such, it may reflect Lucy Mason's concern to use her new position to address the economic problems of her native region whenever possible.[13]

Mason thoroughly enjoyed the heady atmosphere of New Deal Washington in the summer of 1933 and believed that her lobbying efforts were worthwhile. The Cotton-Textile Code hearing was a "thrillingly interesting and a history-making event," she wrote one friend. To another, in describing the frenetic activity of the recent weeks, she summed up the scope of her new job. "The program we have made for ourselves in connection with NRA," she said, "is to criticize the labor provisions of codes, whenever we think they are too weak or imperfect. Beginning with the Cotton-Textile Code, we have written criticisms on countless codes, and occasionally I have spoken at code hearings. Also we have worked behind the scenes with deputy administrators." This aspect of the league's activity, she added, was particularly effective.[14]

So expert did Lucy Mason become on the application of NRA codes that the agency's head, General Hugh Johnson, once asked that she be excused from the NCL temporarily in order to help explain the workings of the NRA to the nation's social, religious, and educational leaders. The NCL's board was willing to let her go, but Mason eventually decided not to leave from a conviction that "the publicity work in interpreting the NRA to social workers and allied groups would not give me sufficient opportunity to be critical of the weak places in the NRA." She therefore remained where she was, one of the very few people to turn down an opportunity to join the New Deal administration in those heady first few months. [15]

At NRA code hearings Lucy Mason had her first sustained contact with representatives of national labor unions, including some who would later profoundly influence her life. At this time she met Sidney Hillman of the Amalgamated Clothing Workers, his deputy Jacob S. Potofsky, and David Dubinsky of the International Ladies Garment Workers Union, all of whom would become friends and counselors. Moreover, although she had not yet met Mrs. Roosevelt, that lady's influence on Lucy Mason was already profound. Lucy had begun a correspondence which was to last the rest of her life. From 1933 onward she wrote to Mrs. Roosevelt frequently, asking her advice, reposing confidences in her, and, above all, telling her how much she was admired and loved. In December 1933, Lucy thanked God that "you [Mrs. Roosevelt] put your influence behind so many good causes and find time to be in so many places where your presence helps so much." It was but the first of literally hundreds of notes expressing such sentiments. Eleanor Roosevelt had quickly become one of the central reference points in Lucy Mason's life. [16]

On December 12, 1933, the National Consumers League held a second conference on labor standards exactly one year after the first. This time the atmosphere was sustainedly upbeat. Molly Dewson again presided and set the tone by referring to the NRA labor agreements as "a great pipe dream come true." Lucy Mason then reported on the effect of the NRA labor provision, which, she agreed, had been beneficial to the workers. They had come a long way in a year, she said, but there was still a long way to go. The job now was to ensure compliance with NRA codes as well as to seek still higher standards. In particular, there was need for continued pressure for minimum-wage legislation at the state level. Six states had already passed the NCL standard bill, which was most encouraging, but hard work was required to ensure that more did and to ensure that the gains made during the "momentous year just closed" became permanent. [17]

Nevertheless Lucy Mason had every reason to feel satisfied with her performance in her new position. Certainly she had reveled in the excitement of it all and had relished the Washington trips, the new faces, and

the sense, though she was outside government, that she was part of a
great new enterprise. Moreover, though not all that the NCL had advocated had been included in the NRA codes, the labor provisions were
sufficiently strong to enable her to think that the effort had been well
worthwhile. Her next tasks, now that the tumult of the New Deal's first
year was subsiding, were, first, to consolidate the gains made in the field
of labor legislation and, second, to implement the postponed policy of
redirecting the NCL's activities somewhat by giving more attention to
specifically southern problems.

The two aims could readily be combined, of course, given that working
conditions in the South were still the most barbaric in the nation despite
the NRA codes. The need for state wages-and-hours legislation was still
acute. Much of Lucy Mason's time over the next three years was devoted
to work for the passage of such legislation in the southern states. At first,
she concentrated specifically on promoting protective legislation for
women and children, continuing the oldest of Consumers League traditions and one to which she personally had long been deeply committed.
The aim of the league was to secure the passage of a model bill, the
"Frankfurter Bill," as it was generally called, after its distinguished drafts-
man. Later, however, the league worked for broader aims, including the
extension of such legislation to male workers as well.

In so doing, the NCL was much influenced by the close working relationship that Miss Lucy developed with Clara Beyer, the activist assistant
director of the Labor Department's Division of Labor Standards. Clara
Beyer, herself a member of the Consumers League and clearly part of the
women's network, became one of Lucy's firmest friends. Deeply committed to the same social concerns, they kept in constant touch with each
other. Lucy Mason supplied Clara Beyer with reports of her frequent field
trips, and Clara kept Lucy informed on the direction and developments of
federal labor policy. The Division of Labor Standards, too, provided the
league with draft legislation. By 1935 it was legislation supplied by the
federal government, rather than the league's own model bill, that Mason
urged state legislators to pass. In this regard she reflected an important
aspect of New Deal Washington, namely the fruitful intersection between
public and private agencies, the close cooperation between the federal
government and its supporters in private reform bodies. Lucy Mason,
after all, was not employed by the government, yet she worked so closely

and so well with government officials that it would scarcely have occurred to her not to feel directly a part of the New Deal enterprise. In a broad sense, of course, she was a part, and so was the NCL. The league always maintained the closest connections with its members in the administration and especially with the women's network.[18]

Lucy Mason approached the task of humanizing the South's industrial laws in several ways. In 1934, again in line with its traditions of "investigate, agitate, legislate," the NCL produced, in conjunction with Miss Gladys Boone, an economist at Sweet Briar College, South Carolina, and her students, a series of charts detailing the existing labor laws in twelve southern state departments of labor, including summaries and analyses of their child labor laws, their laws on hours and night work for women, and their workmens' compensation provisions. These charts received wide publicity and, indeed, were used by the Division of Labor Standards at several conferences and hearings on minimum-wage legislation.[19]

Next Miss Lucy took several extensive trips to the South in 1934. She made all manner of contacts and spoke wherever she could on behalf of labor legislation. Her report of one such trip, made between January 22 and March 25, 1934, gives a good indication of the extent and the nature of her activities. Because of the sparse NCL budget, she had had to secure the bulk of the trip's expenses through fees from local audiences. She had written, therefore, to 100 southerners the previous fall, saying, "I wanted to visit the South in the interest of state labor legislation, and . . . I was prepared to speak on that subject and on NRA codes. The result was that $200 in fees was guaranteed before I left New York." The trip cost the league only $75.55. Miss Lucy paid her own food bills and traveled by day coach. During the two months she visited twenty-seven cities and towns in eleven states. She gave sixty-nine talks to a wide variety of audiences at "Universities, Colleges, Leagues of Women Voters, YWCA's Rotary Clubs, . . . women's clubs, civic organizations, labor unions, unorganized industrial workers, adult Bible classes (both men and women), business women's clubs, social workers, community forums, and of course Consumers' League groups." On all such occasions, she spoke about the current industrial situation in each state, and advocated the cause of labor legislation. The audiences were eager to learn about the industrial situation, she reported, and discussion usually followed the talks. In addition to the contacts made through such formal occasions, she had many informal talks with newspaper editors and placed several special news stories about NCL work. She also saw "legislators, social workers, strategic community people, club-women—in fact all types of people who can help with the League program." Moreover, Molly Dewson had written to some of the leading Democratic women in her various ports of call, and they too made contact with her, offered help, and attended meetings. [20]

Although Miss Lucy saw "encouraging evidences of new interest in labor measures in the southern states," she nevertheless knew full well that the battle ahead would be a hard one. It would "take a long, steady pull of constant educational work to make the public and legislators aware that as the section evolved from an agricultural into an industrial area, industry must have legal traffic regulators or it will do great harm to itself, its employees and society." Still, the trip had been worthwhile, if only because it had enabled her to make contact with a nucleus of liberal and intelligent people who, she hoped, would become the stimulus for progressive labor measures in the future. Certainly, too, with respect to both the nature of her activities and the range of contacts made, the trip involved the same work that she would be doing in later years for the CIO. [21]

By 1935, the NCL believed that the time was right for Lucy Mason to concentrate her activities in two southern states where there seemed to be a chance of passing some labor legislation. She therefore spent much of that year in South Carolina and Virginia, lobbying intensively for the passage of certain bills, including draft wages-and-hours legislation supplied by the Division of Labor Standards. It was hard work. Moreover, what seemed so clear from the perspective of the nation's capital often looked very different, much more complex and murky, at the grass-roots level, where the influence of local and special interests had to be accommodated. "About your draft of the S.C. hours bill," Mason once wrote Beyer after a particularly difficult session with local labor officials.

> It is fine except for its coverage—we just can't get by with general coverage in such a state. The bills would invite the hotels, canneries, banks and many others to fight it. No one I talked with is willing to see a bill go in with so broad a coverage.
>
> Can you have this first page redrafted to include these occupations: manufacturing, factories, workshops, mercantile establishments, laundries, restaurants, telegraph exchanges, and hair dressing and manufacturing establishments. Also right after laundries, dry cleaning and pressing. [22]

It was exhausting work, difficult and sometimes frustrating, but she enjoyed it. Eventually she was able to get labor's representatives and their various friends in both states to agree to the NCL–Division of Labor Standards legislative program or to variants of it rather than bills of their own and to have the measures sponsored in the state legislatures. Now, the task was to secure their passage. Again Lucy Mason worked tirelessly, particularly after it was decided to postpone further action in South Carolina for a year, so that she was free to concentrate her activities on Virginia. She spent two full months in the state, working with the contacts she had made both during the long period in Richmond and through her various trips there, seeing state legislators, newspaper editors, and labor officials. She aimed particularly for the passage of a maximum-hours law and to "put minimum wage before the public to break the ground for actual passage of the bill in 1938."[23] She had hoped that labor representatives would agree to a nine-hour-day, forty-eight-hour-week bill, which seemed to her to have a good chance of passage, but labor held out for the eight-hour day. Finally she arranged a compromise whereby all groups agreed to support an eight-hour bill initially but with the possibility of later modification. She at first thought it would pass, and in fact it did sneak through the House of Burgesses but only to languish and die in the state senate's Committee on General Laws.

Mason was bitterly disappointed. "Virginia killed every social and labor bill except a mutilated amendment to the child labor law," she wrote a friend. "We got further with the hours bill than ever before and it would have been passed if it had gotten out of the Committee, where we lost by one vote." Some good, however, would doubtless come out of the defeat. "I believe," she said, "as a result of this dreadful showing that we are really going to have a Consumer's League of Virginia to carry on essential educational work on the State's need for labor and social legislation." Not all was lost—certainly not the war but simply a battle. This was clearly the view of the National Consumers League's Board, which in February 1936 expressed "its satisfaction and pleasure at the progress made by Miss Mason in Virginia believing that great headway had been made."[24]

For a time, though, in 1936, the Consumers League could have been excused for thinking that the war was certainly going against it. The Supreme Court's invalidation of the NRA, with its hard-won labor provisions, was bad enough, but when in June 1936 the court ruled that New York State's minimum-wage law was also unconstitutional, the whole

thrust of the NCL's program seemed to be in danger. The league was in
confusion, and Mason, for her part, curtailed her activities in the field in
order to devote herself to persuading the NCL's board of directors that
they should endorse an amendment to the federal constitution that would
give the states and the federal government power to regulate working
conditions. There seemed to her to be no other way of beating adverse
court judgments. The league's directors took some time to make up their
minds on the matter, but partly as a result of Miss Lucy's pressure, they
eventually decided to endorse the proposition. Lucy was delighted and
immediately set about drafting the amendment.[25]

She had scarcely begun, however, when the president revealed his own
solution to the problem of a recalcitrant Supreme Court in the famous
"court-packing" plan of 1937. Once again, the league was in confusion. It
decided in the end to go ahead with work for an amendment, hoping that,
after the battle for Supreme Court reform was over, FDR might then
support it. There was little interest in it, however, and before long the
league abandoned the idea in favor of the simple revision of its model bill,
the more so since the Supreme Court had obviously changed its perspective and was now upholding the sort of legislation that it had until recently
disallowed. Miss Lucy returned to the South to continue the campaign for
state action that she had been forced to abandon in 1936.[26]

She went first to South Carolina, to resume the battle that had been
postponed during the previous year. Again the Division of Labor Standards bill was killed in committee; its blanket provisions were simply un-
suitable for the variety of local interests and sectional concerns in the
state. Instead there passed an amended and far from satisfactory measure
that provided a nine-hour day and a forty-eight-hour week for women and
a ten-hour day and fifty-five-hour week for men but omitted several occupations. Lucy Mason was disappointed, though she recognized that
failure in part reflected the fact that the model bill did not accommodate
the realities of southern industrial life. "I wish that people who draft
laws," she wrote Louise Stitt of the Department of Labor's Women's Bureau rather testily, "and people who have spent years lobbying for them in
Legislatures could make a more practical combination of their experience. If an hours law is to contain reasonably high standards for some
occupations, it must make provisions for other occupations on a different
basis. I do not know of a single hours law in a state this side of the Mississippi which does not have these variations." Miss Stitt replied sooth-

ingly. She recognized the problems, she said, but the Labor Department's experience had been that laws "that enumerated the industries covered are the source of endless grief. No matter how inclusive your list of industries is, sooner or later, it develops that some industries or occupations which very much need coverage have been excluded due to inevitable omissions in drafting the law and to changed industrial conditions." Better, she argued, to take the high ground and aim for complete industrial coverage, even though the chances that state legislatures would agree to such measures were obviously much less. "I know how deflated you must feel after weeks of apparently fruitless lobbying and educating," she replied to Lucy Mason,

> but after you are dead and gone, those Southerns [sic] while taking their ease after working a 30-hour week, will say, "Our decent working conditions are all due to a woman named Lucy Mason, who, way back in the early part of the twentieth century, came down here and worked night and day that we might get a 9-hour day and a 50-hour week. She talked so hard and so long that we finally got shorter hours. Now we work 6 hours a day, are paid $30 a week and send all our kids to high school and Miss Mason's birthday is a legal holiday in our State." But in the meantime, I know one has to be content to shove on an inch at a time.

Lucy, however was, increasingly, not content to do so. The relative lack of gains as a result of her efforts made her doubt that, in the South at least, much could ever be expected in this area from state legislation. She had begun, therefore, to ponder other means of achieving a basic level of industrial justice in her region, and the growing industrial labor movement was becoming a most attractive alternative.[27]

It would be a mistake, however, to suggest that Lucy Mason's activities in her time with the NCL were confined to the southern states. Though the main thrust of her work was unquestionably directed there, she nevertheless pursued the fight for labor legislation in other parts of the country as well, usually in cooperation with state consumers' leagues. Thus Miss Lucy campaigned actively for the passage of minimum-wage legislation in the states of New Hampshire, Illinois, Michigan, New Jersey, New York, Ohio, and Rhode Island during her first three years in office and often visited these and other states in order to gain support for the cause. Moreover, she kept all state leagues alerted to her doings by producing regular newsletters and memoranda which detailed her activities. A

newsletter of May 24, 1934, for example, indicated that in the previous
month, in addition to visiting New Orleans and Texas, she had been in
Wilmington, Delaware, where she had talked on labor legislation to "six
groups in two days"; to Louisville, Kentucky; to Ohio, to campaign for a
higher minimum-wage law for laundry workers; to Rhode Island to work
for the passage of a minimum-wage bill and a child labor amendment; and
to New Jersey, to lobby for various pieces of labor legislation, including an
unemployment insurance bill, which were currently before the state legislature. She was shortly to leave for a speaking tour of Michigan. In all
cases, she had worked in cooperation with state and local consumers'
leagues. Thus although the South remained her prime focus, it was by no
means her sole concern.[28]

One reason why she was able to spend as much time in the South as she
did was that she could do much of her business with strong local and state
leagues in other parts of the country by correspondence and telephone.
Though personal visits were undoubtedly important, they were not crucial. Such was certainly not the case with the South, where the absence of
any state league structures meant that she had no one to work through.
One of her main aims, therefore, was to organize such state leagues in the
region. Indeed, she had scarcely taken office in 1932 before she was writing to scores of prominent southerners asking for their support in her
work. One of the first to be contacted was Frank P. Graham, the young,
feisty, and liberal president of the University of North Carolina, with
whom she was soon to form a long-term association and with whom she
would later work closely in the Southern Conference for Human Welfare.
Telling him that she planned to focus the NCL's work directly on southern
problems and that the league was making "an immediate drive for limitations of hours and night work for women in industry through state action,"
she asked him to serve on the NCL's southern committee if he could do so
without embarrassment. Graham readily agreed and noted in doing so
that "the man who is head of an institution that is charged by some 300 of
the leading citizens of the state as being the center of atheism, communism and what not, could hardly be embarrassed by being a member of
the National Consumers League." He suggested the names of other prominent citizens who might also be willing to join.[29]

Mason was able to set up a few regional and state leagues in the South,
using the good offices of such people as Graham. The NCL files contain

hundreds of letters to individuals asking for their support, some of whom responded positively. Yet there is little evidence that these committees functioned effectively or that the league ever established much of a popular base in the region, even among the middle-class women with whom Lucy corresponded so frequently. Indeed, in 1936 she described the membership situation in the South as "pitifully few," though "those few are of high quality." The following year, writing to Frank Graham, she expressed grave doubts as to the value of the league's southern work. "Sometimes I wonder if I am fooling myself as to the significance of the work we have done in the South these five years," she confessed. "So much of my time and energy are spent that I may have lost a sense of proportion as to the relation between the effort and the accomplishment." Indeed, she wondered whether the work was sufficiently important to be continued. Certainly, for all her efforts to achieve some sort of local or regional infrastructure for Consumers League activity there, the responsibility for work in the South continued to fall very much on her shoulders alone.[30]

Fortunately for Miss Lucy, her duties in the league's New York office were few. Throughout Lucy Mason's period as general secretary, the mundane duties of office management, together with the bulk of the fund raising, were handled by the efficient associate general secretary Mrs. Emily Simes Marconnier, assisted by a research officer, Rosilla Breed, and, after 1935, a National Youth Administration (NYA) trainee as a typist. It was a skeleton staff on which to run a national organization, especially with fund raising a constant battle. The relationship between Mason and Marconnier was not always an easy one. At times Marconnier became frustrated at Lucy's lack of interest in the administrative side of the operation, her increasingly frequent absences from the office, and her seeming unconcern with the NCL's always precarious financial state. "I have just told Miss Mason that she must have been absolutely out of her mind to give you the impression that my appeals for funds have been effective this year," an exasperated Mrs. Marconnier wrote to the president of the Cincinnati Consumers League on one occasion, pointing out that in fact the NCL was so hard up that it had to appeal to paid-up members for second contributions. Despite Lucy Mason's lack of interest in it, money was a constant worry for the NCL throughout her tenure of office. In part the reason was something the league could not possibly control, indeed, in a sense it was hurt by success. Molly Dewson explained what was happening in a letter to Eleanor Roosevelt. "I know that you and Franklin and Frances Perkins will be sorry to know that the New Deal program is, I think, the cause of the Consumer's League losing ground financially," she wrote. "The public that is interested in the Consumers' League seems to think that now we have the New Deal, it is not necessary to have a spearhead fighting for better hours, wages and conditions of workers." While this statement was undoubtedly true, much of the blame for the NCL's financial woes must also be attached to Lucy Mason. She simply did not concern herself sufficiently with this side of the league's work. Finances did not interest her, and she ignored them.[31]

Both Molly Dewson's letter and the fact that NYA girls were working in the league's New York office reflect one aspect of the NCL's activities during Miss Mason's secretaryship that deserves extended comment. In crucial ways, the organization during the 1930s became an adjunct of the New Deal. That it did so should scarcely be surprising, given that many of the league's goals now became legislative proposals and, of course, given that so many members of FDR's team, and particularly the women, had passed through it. The close working relationship between Lucy Mason and Clara Beyer at the Division of Labor Standards has already been noted. The two women were in constant contact, exchanging information, as in the case of the league's charts on southern labor conditions, while it was the division which provided the league with the draft bills it subsequently urged on state legislators.

Still Mrs. Beyer was only one of a number of officials at the Department of Labor with whom Mason worked closely. Most important was the secretary of labor herself. Frances Perkins did not forget the organization to which she had devoted so much time and energy. She had scarcely settled into her new office before she was in contact with Mason on league business. "Governor Green of Rhode Island," she wrote her confidentially as early as May 1933, "will be very glad to have the Consumers League cooperate with him in an effort to organize public opinion in Rhode Island for minimum wage and shorter hours legislation next year. I have just seen him and he is o.k. on it. Please do your part." Soon the two women had established a regular working relationship. In 1934 Mason wrote several articles at the secretary's request, urging people to respect NRA code labels. She was a regular participant in conferences and seminars organized by the Department of Labor on industrial matters, always at Perkins's request. For her part, the secretary found Mason's knowledge of southern customs and people invaluable when organizing regional conferences on labor matters. Indeed, as Molly Dewson once told Eleanor Roosevelt:

> For the last few years Lucy Mason has been drawing together and invigorating the liberal industrial opinion on the South. Frances Perkins has turned to her for the names of these interested persons for her conferences on Tennessee, Georgia and Virginia. This winter Miss Mason, in extensive speaking trips has included strong support for the Social Security bill and has also spent ten days in Washington lobbying for it.[32]

Whenever such a conference was scheduled, Mason would supply the secretary's office with a list of names of key people to be invited. Sometimes she would help with the organization of the program, and usually, as she did with the Second Southern Regional Conference on Labor Standards, held in Columbia, South Carolina in 1936, she would use the occasion to recruit for the Consumers League. Then, after the conference was over, the Consumers League would follow up on its recommendations, in particular those advocating the passage of wages-and-hours legislation by the various state legislatures. In this way, the NCL acted as a pressure group for the United States Department of Labor. [33]

Another member of the New Deal's women's network with whom Lucy Mason had regular dealings was Mary Anderson, head of the Labor Department's Women's Bureau since 1920 and an uncompromising supporter of labor legislation. As with Clara Beyer and Frances Perkins, the two women corresponded frequently, supplying each other with information, reinforcing each other's commitment. When the Consumers League, for example, decided in 1935 to survey wages-and-hours legislation in certain interstate service industries, including beauty parlors, hotels, and dry cleaning plants, Miss Lucy turned to Mary Anderson for her basic data. "We do not intend to do any original research," she wrote her, "but to use all we can get from your Bureau." Asking for suggestions as to how to acquire certain code hearings and other material free of charge, she requested that Anderson "put on your thinking cap and tell me all the answers to my questions." Throughout 1935 and 1936 they kept each other informed on the details of the various minimum-wage cases currently before state courts. In 1936, after the Supreme Court decision on state minimum-wage laws, Anderson personally nominated Lucy Mason to serve on an important Labor Department committee to study the decision's implications. The committee chairman was Benjamin Cohen. The two women sometimes took vacations together, their relationship thus becoming more than a professional one.[34]

Through Mary Anderson Lucy became involved in the drive to secure ratification of the "Women's Charter." Like Lucy Mason, Mary Anderson was an uncompromising opponent of the National Woman's party and any who supported the Equal Rights Amendment. The Women's Charter was supposed to provide an alternative to ERA, one social feminists could support and one which would safeguard the gains women had made in recent times through protective legislation.

The origins of the Women's Charter are somewhat obscure. It most likely arose from a decision taken by the League of Nations General Assembly in 1935 to investigate the political and economic situation of women with a view to recommending a treaty which gave all women rights equal to those of men. It was left to the International Labor Office to seek the information from the various countries on their reaction to the proposal. As a member of the international Women's Correspondence Committee, Mary Anderson was approached. She was highly suspicious of the idea because the wording of the treaty was suspiciously close to that of the Equal Rights Amendment which the National Woman's party had sponsored for years and which she, like most social feminists, bitterly opposed. Immediately she consulted with various women, all heads of national women's organizations, all opponents of the Equal Rights Amendment, and all hostile to the National Woman's party, to determine how the United States should respond. It was decided that a subcommittee chaired by Mary Van Kleek of the Russell Sage Foundation, but with Mary Anderson as its motive force, should "formulate a clear and brief statement of women's objectives and . . . outline the requested study on an international scale in such a way that it would throw light on those objectives." The idea was to produce an alternative to the equal rights treaty. The subcommittee met on September 9, 1936, drew up a draft statement on a women's charter, and then invited a number of prominent women to join a general committee to refine it and decide on a procedure for ratification. One of those invited was Lucy Mason, who accepted enthusiastically.[35]

The draft charter was a lengthy document. Its preamble stated that it was "a general statement of the social and economic objectives of women for women and for society as a whole insofar as these can be embodied in legislation and governmental administration." Its purpose was to codify the various causes to which a large number of women's organizations had already become committed. It recognized that many of the needs to which it was directed should "disappear as society develops the assurance of a more complete life for every person." In promoting certain objectives at this time specifically for women, it did not preclude the application of these in time to both genders. Rather it welcomed such a prospect.[36]

The charter itself stated in summary:

> Women shall have full political and civil rights; opportunity for education; full opportunity for work according to their individual abilities, with safeguards against physically harmful conditions of employment and economic exploitation; they shall receive compensation, without discrimination because of sex. They shall be assured security of livelihood, including the safeguarding of motherhood. The provisions necessary for the establishment of these standards shall be guaranteed by government, which shall ensure also the right of united action towards the attainment of these aims.
>
> Where special exploitation of women workers exists, such as low wages which provide less than the living standards attainable, unhealthful working conditions, and long hours of work which result in physical exhaustion and denial of the right to leisure, such conditions shall be corrected through social and labor legislation, which the world's experience shows to be necessary.[37]

The political purposes of the charter, at least as far as the split in the women's movement is concerned, can be discerned in the explanatory notes which accompanied the document. These stated unequivocally the view that legislation specifically directed toward guaranteeing certain rights for women only was not regarded as inadmissible. "The Charter does not necessarily call for legislation applying to women only," the notes read, "but it permits it if the experience of the women themselves . . . and the general legislative situation in the nation require it." Historically, after all, women had suffered "special handicaps imposed by custom or tradition." If protective legislation were needed to remove these, so be it.[38]

Mary Anderson's committee met on October 7 and immediately decided to form two additional committees, one to continue refining the draft charter and one to promote it among women and the community at large. Lucy Mason was appointed convenor of the second committee. The full committee, too, decided to remain in existence and named itself the Joint Conference Group of Women in the United States. Much of Lucy Mason's time, therefore, in the last three months of 1936 was devoted to this work, ensuring that the draft charter was circulated widely among women's groups for comment, publicizing it, and drafting the accompanying document explaining its origins and its aims.[39]

By December a draft of the charter on which everyone agreed was ready to be presented to the public, and this was done on December 28. It was immediately met with a storm of criticism, mainly from the national and state leaders of the National Woman's party, who had not been at all involved in its drafting and saw in its advocacy of special legislation for women an attempt to revive the horse-and-buggy concept of women's position in society. Mrs. Steven Pell, the NWP's national chairman, deplored the charter as dangerous because it denied the very principles of equality it purported to uphold. "Only by presenting a united front against the menace of restrictive labor laws applying to women and not to men can women preserve the opportunities they have gained and prevent new discriminations against women from being written into the labor laws," she claimed in denouncing the document. Elsie Hill, a veteran campaigner for equal rights, argued that the charter "echoes and re-echoes the anti-suffrage psychology familiar to the campaigners for the Susan B. Anthony amendment." It advocated one law for men and another law for women in a world that required men and women to live and work side by side.[40]

Stung by the intensity of such criticism, the members of the Joint Conference Group decided to suspend their activities in promoting the charter while they considered the feasibility of accommodating some of the NWP's demands. This action was bitterly opposed by Lucy, and she moved to sever her connection with the charter's advocates. "I want to put myself on record as saying," she wrote Mary Anderson, "I think it is impossible for those of us interested in the Charter ever to meet the Woman's Party point of view. The more we concede to them the more danger there is that they will misinterpret what we have said." She wrote to the secretary of the National Woman's party, telling her in no uncertain terms what she thought of certain changes to the charter which the party

had proposed. "It seems hardly necessary to say that I completely disagree with the changes made by you and your associates," she said. She
would under no circumstances support a revision of the charter on NWP
terms. Lucy Mason refused to attend any more Joint Conference Group
meetings or to devote time to promoting the charter movement, which, in
the event, languished, bereft of substantial support, for a few further
months before being decently and quietly buried.[41]

The charter episode is significant for two reasons. It shows graphically
the extent of the divisions still existing within the women's movement in
the United States, and it clearly indicates the nature and limits of Lucy
Mason's feminism. She remained, as she had been all her life, very much
in the social feminist mainstream, committed to the cause of protective
legislation for women and implacably opposed to those who would deny
that, for social and historical reasons, women needed any special treatment. Only in this way, she averred, could real equality be achieved while
at the same time maintaining the differences between the sexes that were
determined by their differing roles.

Lucy Mason's intensely active public life in New York left little time for
private pursuits. In fact, little can be reconstructed of her private life at
this time. She did, however, visit the Gerwicks, Katherine's family in
Zanesville, Ohio, whenever she could. "You doubtless know," she once
wrote a friend, "that Katherine Gerwick was my closest friend and in a
sense I adopted her family—in more ways than one." "Auntie Gerwick,"
Katherine's mother, wrote Lucy every week, and she was always welcomed in Zanesville like a returning daughter. "It is so hard to talk about
all the things we want to in a hurried visit," she once mused regretfully,
"and then there are always two or three old friends of Katherine's in Z.
who always want little private talks." Katherine's death had indeed left a
wound, but a wound possibly assuaged to a degree by her acceptance into
the family—indeed she became almost a substitute for the beloved dead
daughter. [42]

Lucy vacationed with two or three other women friends from time to
time. One was Mary Anderson. They liked to go to Three Hills, a large
house near Warm Springs, a spa in the Virginia mountains, where Mason's cousin Eloise Johnson took paying guests. The writer Mary John-
ston, Lucy's friend from the far-off days of the Richmond Equal Suffrage
League, also lived there, and she and Mary Anderson spent some pleas-

ant times together driving around the hills or bathing in the sulphur pools. "Nice hot, soft water, full of bubbles," Lucy once wrote. "I love it and go in daily." Sometimes, too, she spent the weekend in Washington with Molly Dewson, a visit which she always enjoyed. Busy as she was, she found some time to relax.[43]

Work, however, was always paramount. Her little free time she often spent working for the same liberal causes through other agencies. She was a member of the Social Policy Committee, a group of prominent New York liberals who met together from time to time to support New Deal programs. Others in the groups were Bruce Bliven of the *New Republic*, Paul Kellogg, Helen Harris of the NYA, and Oswald Garrison Villard. It was as a representative of this group that she first met President Roosevelt. She was a member of a delegation which in 1934 presented FDR with a petition calling for a stronger NRA. Mrs. Roosevelt she saw more frequently, usually at meetings, where they sometimes spoke on the same platform. Life for Miss Lucy was full and rewarding.[44]

After severing her ties with the Women's Charter movement, Mason went back to Consumers League work ready to fight for the cause of a constitutional amendment giving federal and state governments the right to regulate hours and conditions of work. The Consumers League board decided in December 1936 to support such an amendment and, delighted, Lucy began to draft one and to plan an extensive tour to drum up support. Notwithstanding the president's "court-packing" plan, the league decided to go ahead with the project, but the tour never came to pass. A crisis in the New York office caused Lucy Mason to abandon these and other plans and was soon to prompt her to resign from the Consumers League.[45]

There had been, as previously noted, some tension between Lucy Mason and Emily Marconnier regarding Lucy's lack of interest in the fund-raising side of the league's activities. By 1937, the league was desperate for money, and Marconnier, fed up with minding the store while the general secretary traveled around the country, had decided to resign unless Lucy, too, shouldered some of the fund-raising duties. Lucy Mason had no choice, therefore, but to postpone all thoughts of trips in support of the constitutional amendment or labor legislation and devote her time to the business of alleviating the league's desperate financial plight. "The raising of our budget has become so difficult," she wrote one friend, "and Emily

Marconnier is so worn down by it that I have decided I must either raise several thousand dollars each year myself, or leave the League." Accordingly, she busied herself seeking contributions from such people as Bernard Baruch and Eleanor Roosevelt. To Mrs. Roosevelt she observed that there was still need for private agencies such as the league, even though "the popular impression in these days is that government will do it." Without a substantial increase in the league's budget, she said, its work would be "so crippled as to be largely ineffectual." She asked for some assistance from the money the First Lady presumably made from radio talks. Mrs. Roosevelt replied that, as she had no radio contract at this time, she had "no money to give away. However, if I do get a contract, I will surely keep you in mind."[46]

Responses such as this one depressed Lucy profoundly. She disliked office work, and the fund-raising task in particular she found distasteful. In this mood, she began to doubt the efficiency of the league's activities, especially in the South, as she told Frank Graham. When it became clear that her shouldering of some of the fund-raising burden would not prevent Emily Marconnier from resigning, she, too, decided to leave the league. Both of them submitted their resignations on the same day, May 28, in an atmosphere not without bitterness and tension.[47]

By the time the board met to act on these resignations, Mason already had another job, one which had come completely out of the blue. In her autobiography she spoke of the circumstances. John L. Lewis, the towering, passionate leader of the fledgling and feisty CIO, had recently purchased a home in Alexandria, Virginia. The transaction had led him to have some business dealings with Lucy Mason's brother-in-law, Taylor Burke, husband of her sister, Ida, and a respected Alexandria banker. According to Lucy, the two men had become firm friends. She happened to be visiting the Burkes in June 1937 and during dinner expressed the view that, with the Consumers League job now over, she would like to go back to the South to work with organized labor and interracial groups if a suitable position could be found. "Why not try John Lewis," her sister reportedly said. A meeting was quickly arranged. Lewis was impressed with the prospect of having this prim, respectable middle-aged woman of impeccable pedigree working on the side of the CIO in the South, where organizing activities were just beginning, and the deal was practically settled then and there. She would work in the South as a publicist and public relations representative for the CIO and, in particular, on behalf of the Textile Workers Organizing Committee (TWOC).[48]

 There are other versions of how she came to be offered the job. According to Virginia Durr, Mrs. Lewis's influence was considerable. She was desperate to be accepted by Alexandria society, of which Ida Burke was the prime social arbiter. In particular, she wished to become a member of the Alexandria Gardening Club, of which Ida was president. Partly in response to his wife's social aspirations, then, Lewis offered Lucy Mason the job, Mrs. Durr said, hoping thereby to ease Mrs. Lewis's path to social acceptance. Whatever the reason, the offer came. The details were soon settled with Sidney Hillman of the Amalgamated Clothing Workers, director of the TWOC organizing drive. What she termed her "rather amazing adventure" was to begin on July 7. She was to operate out of Atlanta.[49]

5

The CIO

The First Years

H istorians have finally begun to ask new questions about the structure
of the post–Civil War industrial South, less with a view to overturn-
ing the conventional wisdom than to remove certain misconceptions as
to detail and tone. The development of the structure itself has been
brilliantly outlined by Jacqueline Hall, Robert Korstad, and James
Leloudis in a recent article. The impoverishment of southern farmers
after the war was "industrialization's driving force," they claim, and the
textile mill its most potent symbol. Merchants who had accumulated capital through control of the agricultural system used it to finance the
growth of the region's textile industry, which by the 1930s was the largest
in the world.[1]

Textiles provided the model for southern industry generally. Two of its
most "cherished" traditions were low wages and paternalistic control. As
George Tindall has noted, by the beginning of the New Deal era these
provided "the great magnet for outside capital, the foundation of industrial
growth." Furthermore, according to the New South myth, the paternalistic
attitude of the region's employers, their concern for their people, and their
determination to serve the impoverished mass of southern rural whites by
providing them with sanctuary in their textile factories and mill villages
rendered union activity unnecessary. In addition it was "unsouthern."[2]

The grim result of the twin traditions could be measured statistically by

1930. The regional wage differential stood at about 35 percent, that is, the average wage for southern workers was about 65 percent of that for the rest of the country. Legislation regulating the conditions of labor lagged well behind that in other parts of the United States to the extent that the differences were more in kind than in degree, while the southern labor movement was weak. Largely based on a few craft organizations centered in the towns, the southern labor movement had little relevance for the vast number of the region's industrial workers, especially those in the textile and the tobacco mills, who remained virtually unorganized, working long hours for low wages, often in unregulated conditions, living in the social isolation and systematically rigid control which was the mill village's reason for being.[3]

This familiar picture retains considerable force and truth, but needs some modification. Recent studies have shown, for example, that mill village culture was more than a thin and static creation of the mill owner, breeding an essentially passive "social type." Rather it had both richness and depth, and it continued to evolve. Similarly, the proper emphasis on labor's weakness should not obscure the fact that there was a tradition of labor protest in the region, one the mill owners could certainly repress but not entirely destroy.[4]

The New South's industrial system may have ensured a large measure of control, but it did not bring social harmony. Indeed it often produced a sullen class consciousness in the workers and a simmering class resentment, which at times could be channeled into militant labor activity. The year 1929, in particular, saw violent though localized labor revolt in Tennessee and the Carolinas. One incident, the strike in the Loray Mill in Gastonia, North Carolina, quickly entered the mythology of both the Right and the Left. In Gastonia a Communist-led local of the National Textile Workers Union precipitated a strike which was eventually to lead to violence and death and, inevitably, to the shattering of the union.[5] The same year saw other such manifestations of class resentment, economic desperation, and paternalist reaction. They jolted a few southern editors into a realization that all was not well with labor relations in the region, prompted a few enlightened industrialists to think about labor matters, occasioned expressions of concern among some members of the southern middle class—as indicated by Lucy Mason's two-month stint on behalf of the Southern Council on Women and Children in Industry—and even forced the American Federation of Labor (AFL) to decide on a southern organizing drive in 1930, a drive which collapsed with the onset of the depression. Yet although all generalizations have their exceptions, it is still true enough to say that southern labor remained in 1932, as it had been throughout the century, impoverished, unregulated, and largely unorganized.[6]

The New Deal brought the most sustained unionization drive in the region's history. Sparked initially by the labor provisions of the National Industrial Recovery Act and their attendant publicity—"The president wants you to join the union" was the most compelling battle cry—labor organizers moved into the South, determined to reshape the region's traditional industrial structures. Among the first was John L. Lewis, who mounted an intensive campaign in the region's coal fields. The United Textile Workers, too, entered the fray. As Tindall says, "energized by the New Deal spirit," it increased its dues-paying membership from 15,000 in January 1933 to 270,000 in August 1934. Emboldened by the spirit of the times, the UTW precipitated a general strike in southern mills that September, a strike which, as Irving Bernstein notes, arose as much from the mill workers' anger at the gulf between promise and actuality in the working of the NRA textile code as from Tindall's more positive assertion. The wage increases supposedly provided by the code had been negated by shorter hours, higher commodity prices, and an increase in the stretch-out. After a year of the New Deal, there had been no material improvement, and the strike seemed to be the only sanction left. Whatever the reason, the decision to strike was a disaster. State militia men were used against the workers. In Georgia, Governor Herman Talmadge imprisoned many in hastily constructed compounds which quickly became known as "concentration camps." As at Gastonia, there was violence and death. By the end of the month, the strike had collapsed, the union had been discredited, and the NRA soon became a victim of the Supreme Court. The first New Deal unionization drive was clearly a failure.[7]

From failure, however, came renewed growth. The death of the NRA was a prime cause for the enactment of the National Labor Relations Act, the most important single piece of labor legislation in the history of the United States. The provisions of the Wagner Act would eventually alter the relationship between capital and labor throughout the nation dramatically, and the South would not remain untouched. Second, the failure of the AFL to sustain the organizing drives of the early New Deal and the inability of its craft union orientation to deal adequately with the vast mass of the unorganized industrial workers, together with personal rivalries at the top, caused the momentous split in the labor movement which led to the founding of the CIO, its base firmly rooted in the ideal of large-scale industrial unionism. Soon labor's cohorts would be in the South again, this time under John L. Lewis's banner, attempting once more to organize the region's industrial workers, its miners, its tobacco workers, its rubber and steel workers, its lumbermen, and the laborers in its thousands of textile mills. Marching with them was Lucy Randolph Mason.[8]

In a letter to Frank Graham written just after Lewis first offered Lucy the job but before she had formally accepted it, she described the work she was being asked to do.

> Briefly, the plan of work would be for me to live and travel in the South, reaching all possible groups—college, church, club, conference, whenever people gather to listen to a speaker, interpreting the union movement. I would make contact with editors and teachers and ministers. On the other hand, I would go into mill towns, among unorganized workers, to preach the gospel of organization—though I would distinctly not be an organizer, merely an interpreter. As far as possible I would make contacts for the liberals and labor greatly intensifying what I have done in this direction for the last five years. Also and perhaps increasingly I would urge workers to use their political power in electing men—and *women*—who would represent their best interests. Needless to say I would avoid giving aid to the demagogue.

There were some shifts of emphasis over the years and a few additions and widenings as the times changed, but essentially Lucy Mason had just outlined the work that she would do for the rest of her career. She had described the parameters of her career as "Miss Lucy of the CIO," labor in which so many of the concerns which had motivated her activism heretofore would coalesce.[9]

First, however, she needed a place to live. Soon she was installed in a small, comfortable apartment in Myrtle Street in northeast Atlanta, an apartment which would serve as office, archive, and home for many years to come. Having settled in, she attacked her new job with a will, initially with rather more enthusiasm than realism. Indeed, if she had ever thought that winning southerners over to the side of the CIO would be a relatively simple task, she was soon thoroughly disabused. "Even with my intimate knowledge of the South," she wrote Lewis after only two months on the job, "I did not know of the misunderstanding and hostility to the CIO and TWOC in this section" and the "campaign of lying and misrepresentation" on which it was based. "The work is infinitely slow," she wrote gloomily. Indeed, she was far from sure that her contribution would make any difference. For this reason she insisted that Lewis reduce her annual salary from $5,000—the amount that the Consumers League had been paying her—to $3,600. Even then, she was not sure that she was worth it.[10]

Her first report to Hillman was similarly pessimistic. "You people in New York don't know what it means to have the politicians, the local and state administrators, the press and the public lined up with the employers and against the workers," she told him, in the tones of the field worker reporting to a distant home base. "So far I have not found a single editor in Georgia to whom I can go without the danger of having all that I say used against our work." The whole matter of her appointment was a gamble, she said, which might not pay off. True, there was some light in the "dark picture," notably the willingness of workers to join the TWOC, but the struggle was going to be much harder and more protracted than she had ever imagined.[11]

Indeed, the evidence suggests that in those first few weeks the magnitude of her new job and the hostility confronting her all but overwhelmed her. She wrote long letters to friends and people of influence back in Washington describing the conditions she found and appealing for aid. Indeed, she even approached President Roosevelt. "When I came South I had no idea of the frequency of attacks on people peacefully pursuing legitimate purposes," she told him. "I am appalled at the disregard of the most common civil rights and the dangers of bodily harm to which organizers often are exposed," she stated, urging him to use the Department of Justice to prevent such illegalities.[12]

Lucy Mason's reaction to this new world of violence and illegality so different from the genteel, upper-middle-class environment of the Consumers League and the ordered procedures of New Deal Washington, and her sense of alienation and powerlessness, were nowhere more evident than in a long appeal for help that she addressed to Molly Dewson early in September 1937. "I thought labor was at least getting strong enough to defy the politicians," she wrote. "I was wrong. The dice are loaded against organization so far as state and local governments are concerned—but I think labor is going to organize anyway, only more painfully and perhaps more violently because of the politicians." Still, the task was going to be terribly difficult. Civil liberties were flouted "every few days" and organizers worked in constant physical danger. The press, due to "a conspiracy of silence," failed in its duty to defend basic civil rights. Indeed, she said, in words which illustrate dramatically her sense of shock and confusion, the South was "Fascist . . . the domination of the Negro had made it easier to repeat the pattern for organised labor"—bitter words from someone who was as proud of her southern heritage as she and as much a product of her region. Change could not come unless the few brave folk working in such danger were given the support of the federal government. "Molly, my darling, if you would persuade the President to educate the southern governors and would be senators or representatives on this labor question it might relieve the tension some. The workers are his friends." The need for White House support of a federal antilynching bill was even more urgent, not simply to prevent the killing of blacks, but also to protect organizers and union members. "Do what you can, Molly dear," she concluded desperately.[13]

Gradually, however, as Lucy Mason began to adjust to the new situation, the sense of panic that had marked her initial exposure to the realities of southern labor relations gave way to a dogged determination to bring change no matter how long it took. The reason was partly that she began to make sympathetic contacts in the wider community and also to develop a real sense of solidarity with others working for the TWOC in the region. The first of these included Steve Nance, former president of the Georgia AFL but in 1937 director of the TWOC's southern drive. More than anyone else, the tall, principled, imperturbable Nance helped Lucy Mason adjust to the realities of working for the labor movement in the South, encouraged her in those first difficult months, and taught her that "the only possible way to work" in the South was "with infinite patience and diplomacy." Nance quickly became her trusted guide and mentor. His death in April 1938 at the age of forty-one, largely from overwork, was for her a cruel personal blow.[14]

In these first few weeks, too, Lucy met two other young organizers who were to become sources of inspiration and firm friends as well. One was

Paul R. Christopher, in 1937 South Carolina's director of the Textile Workers Union but soon to become CIO state director for Tennessee. The other was Bernard "Buck" Borah, a young graduate in psychology and philosophy from the University of Tennessee, who from 1937 to 1942 was southern director of the Amalgamated Clothing Workers of America. Borah had by this time volunteered for the armed forces, and he and Lucy Mason kept up a correspondence during his training period. The friendship and support of young men such as these helped her find her feet in those first few months.[15]

By the end of the year, too, Miss Lucy had begun to systematize some aspects of her new job. True, newspaper editors were generally unsympathetic to her work—even her "beloved V. Dabney"—and were reluctant to talk with her. As Jonathan Daniels, one of the few exceptions, said, the number of his editorial colleagues "that would trust even George Mason's descendant in connection with labor unions in the modern South is strictly limited."[16] Nevertheless Miss Lucy could still communicate with them through press releases and information sheets, and this she did. She produced regular accounts of her activities on the CIO's behalf which she sent to more than 250 editors in the region. One of the earliest, sent on October 5, 1937, was fairly typical. In it she described various events on a tour of the Carolinas that she had recently made. She spoke of the denial of civil liberties that union organizers there were facing and refuted charges that they were all "outside agitators." She also reproduced various statements from mill owners in the region which reflected favorably upon unions. On December 18, 1937, she provided editors with statistics purporting to show the success of the TWOC drive. She was prompt in responding, through the correspondence columns, to any editorial criticisms of labor actions and distortion of labor's aims.[17] Gradually, some of the region's editors began to warm to her, including a few influential ones. Grover Hall, of the *Montgomery Advertiser*, was one of the first to do so. In an amusing letter inviting her to call he proposed to her in jest and asked her to "be a good girl and do not stab any textile executives. In the end you will need them to sign the contracts." In reply, she promised not to murder any. "I am a pacifist," she said. In press circles the ice was gradually broken, and her views, and through her those of the CIO, began to be heard.[18]

Contact with the region's clergymen, most of whom were hostile to labor's aims and many of whom had their salaries paid by mill owners, also initially took place through mimeographed statements. The first of these went out just before Labor Day, 1937. In it she urged ministers, on the Sunday closest to Labor Day, "to speak clearly and courageously on behalf of the right of workers to organise and bargain collectively through Representatives of their own choosing." The southern labor movement was stirring, she said. Textile workers would organize; the weight of recent history was on their side. Deploring the violence practiced against unionists, "often incited by employers or by company deputies," she talked of the great opportunity the church had to contribute to "public understanding of labor's legitimate aspirations" and implored ministers not to be deceived by the "smokescreen of charges of Communism and atheism" raised by labor's enemies. She was no Communist or atheist, she concluded, but a lifelong Christian lady who had chosen to work in the South as an interpreter of the organized labor movement "in the hope of contributing a little to its peaceful development."[19]

Miss Lucy's initial approach had the desired effect. A number of clergymen responded, and though most were decidedly not persuaded by her argument, still believing, like the Reverend Arthur J. Barton, that "the CIO is doing much harm in many ways," they at least agreed to see her, though, again to quote Reverend Barton, "with no thought of approving the CIO or co-operating in its efforts." She had wanted only a foot in the door, but a few of those who responded supported her position. By the end of the year she was much more confident about the possibilities of success and the value of her own contribution. "The thing that impresses me more than anything else," she told Hillman, "even in the discouragement of this time of bitter suffering from unemployment among the textile workers, is that at last a southern labor movement is in the making. Always before the southern textile workers have been deserted and have had to struggle along. At last they have leadership that stays by them and they are responding to that leadership." She had been traveling constantly the last few weeks and had met "courage and persistence" everywhere. The experience had clearly fired her own determination. Lucy Mason was in the fight to stay.[20]

In 1938 she first became involved in an aspect of her work that was to become increasingly important, namely her intervention when acts of lawlessness against organizers occurred. On April 15, Charles (Jimmie)

Cox, a young textile union leader from Tupelo, Mississippi, was kidnapped by two carloads of workers opposed to unions and was driven
twenty miles out of town and there savagely beaten. Lucy Mason had
earlier taken an interest in Cox, had arranged a short-term scholarship to
the Highlander Folk School for him, and had helped support his family
while he was away. When she heard of his abduction she went immediately into action, wiring the Tupelo County attorney, the governor of Mississippi, various congressmen, and, as she was to do so often in such situations, President and Mrs. Roosevelt, insisting on "immediate action on
behalf of Cox." She also wrote Mrs. Roosevelt, expressing both her own
sense of impotence in the face of such situations and also her sense that
action by the president could have some effect. "I am sorry to have bothered you," ran the letter, "but I felt desperate last night and have dis-
covered that if I send the President a telegram about a situation and then
wire some person back in town where the trouble is that I have appealed
to him and the Governor of the State for protection for the worker involved it seems to have a good effect." There were to be plenty of such
letters and telegrams in the years ahead.[21]

A few days earlier, she had written to the president, ostensibly to congratulate him on a recent speech but really expressing her continued
shock as the South she had never known, or had preferred not to think
about in her busy world of middle-class women reformers, continued to
become her new reality. "Since I have lived in the deep South," she told
him, "I have seen the feudal system leaning on the fascist system as I
never saw it before. Perhaps the Bill of Rights is so engrossed in my faith
because the Virginia Bill was written by the direct ancestor of both my
father and mother, who were third cousins. At any rate it is because I take
it seriously that I left the Consumers League last June and came to the
labor movement." The president almost certainly never read this letter or
most of the many others she wrote to him, though Mrs. Roosevelt may
have done so. The act of writing them was cathartic, however; moreover
they did provide her with a sense of connection both to the federal government and to something much more personal, as did her brief visits
with Mrs. Roosevelt, which began at this time. They enabled her to feel
that the president was on her side, not an unimportant consideration
when one realizes how lonely and vulnerable these few advocates of labor's right to organize must have felt in the South in the 1930s. For Lucy

Mason, lacking at this time a sustaining personal life, these feelings must
have been the more acute. Writing to the Roosevelts was one way of as-
suaging them.[22]

Lucy Mason called upon the White House for aid in another dispute at
the same time as the Cox kidnapping. The case involved the Dallas Textile
Mill in Huntsville, Alabama. The mill had closed the previous fall after
having declined to renew a contract with the Textile Workers Union. Recently, however, the management, backed by a "citizen's committee," had
asked the state employment service for sufficient workers to enable it to
reopen on a nonunion basis, completely ignoring the previous employees.
The situation held potential for large-scale violence. The TWOC wanted
Alabama governor Bibb Graves to arbitrate. The mill management, on the
other hand, insisted that he call out the state militia to protect the non-
union workers. Lucy Mason, claiming that "Huntsville is being made a
test case by Southern textile manufacturers," appealed for White House
intervention. "A phone call from the White House to Governor Graves
urging him to refuse troops and to insist on arbitration will tremendously
strengthen him," she claimed. "He is between two fires—while the citizens are visiting him, the union strength of the United Mine Workers,
the SWOC in steel and the TWOC in textiles is pouring in to him letters
and telegrams. Help if you can—and quickly." She concluded in her best
conspiratorial style. "No one shall ever know I have written this letter,"
ran a handwritten postscript.[23]

If the White House placed a phone call, it went unrecorded, and probably there was none. The militia was not sent to Huntsville, and indeed,
the management at the Dallas mill did finally capitulate and agreed to
reopen with union labor, partly because of a lack of support in the state
generally for its position. Miss Lucy was partly responsible for this turn of
events. If her letters to the White House had had little effect, those to
Alabama's editors had much more. She was constantly in touch with the
newspapers, presenting the CIO's side of the dispute and urging report-
ers to use their columns to support arbitration. When Carroll Kilpatrick of
the influential *Montgomery Advertiser* told her that his publishers were
pressing him to oppose the CIO's actions in Huntsville, she replied with a
long, lucid rundown of the situation. The citizen's committee, she said,
"was playing the game for the mill—doing things that the Wagner Act
does not permit the mill management to do." She appealed to Kilpatrick

to plead for investigation and arbitration. "The blind stupidity of it is incredible," she concluded. "The hate that will be sown where no hate need be. . . . these things might be avoided by any justice and common sense and fair play." She was tireless in expressing this position to the state's editors. The fact that the Dallas management received little support outside the local area might well have been due to her efforts. If so, it would indicate that her work was finally receiving a level of acceptance, even of legitimacy, in the region.[24]

The White House, too, accorded her some recognition. When the National Emergency Council was asked to prepare a report on the economic condition of the South—the report which led to the president's famous designation of the region as "the Nation's No. 1 economic problem"—Mason was one of a number of distinguished southerners invited to advise the council.[25] Then, too, there was evidence that at least a few of her frequent requests to the White House for action on labor-related problems were being taken seriously. In November she wrote to Mrs. Roosevelt on behalf of the Erwin Manufacturing Company, a small cotton mill in Huntsville, Alabama, which she described as "unique" in the town "because it has a history of friendly co-operation with its organized employees." The TWOC had a union contract with the company which was working well. The company's president, L. O. Erwin, had sought to borrow from the Reconstruction Finance Corporation on several occasions but without success. He believed that the reason was partly the influence of other manufacturers, who resented his relations with the TWOC. Lucy Mason asked if there was anything Mrs. Roosevelt could do. She immediately passed on the request to her husband, who in a personal note to Jesse Jones of the RFC asked him to consider the latest loan application favorably. "I am told they [Erwin Manufacturing] have a good record," the president said. "Can we fill their application?" In the event, nothing could be done because of the company's level of indebtedness, but the incident does show that Lucy Mason had become a person of sufficient value to have her requests treated with some seriousness. Even the president himself acted on them occasionally. She was becoming established as a genuine spokesperson for labor.[26]

Then, too, the routine side of her job, the trips to small community after small community, seeking to present labor's position particularly in communities where the CIO had begun to work, was beginning to take

shape. Her report of a visit to Milan, Tennessee, in March 1938, a small
textile town where National Labor Relations Board hearings had recently
been held following defiance of an NLRB decision, gives some idea of the
type of people she sought to talk to, and the reactions she often provoked.
First there were the ministers, including an old Presbyterian minister,
whom it was "hopeless to try to educate . . . too old to learn," and the
Methodist pastor, who, she said, "looked scared and ineffectual" and
would not let her come into the house, so they talked at the door. He
realized that the "Methodist Church social creed involved collective bargaining" but said it did not apply to this situation. Another Presbyterian
minister was so reactionary that he opposed joining any organizations except the church—even the American Legion. "So ended the chapter on
religion in Milan," she commented after talking to him.[27]

The town's leading businessmen were similarly intransigent. The mayor
was described as "stupid, ignorant." He insisted that all had been peaceful
in the community until the CIO had come to town and escaped from her
as quickly as he could. An insurance man who "looked like Mickey
Mouse" and was "scared to death" of her listened for a few minutes but
refused to talk further, saying that they could not get anywhere. The phar-
macist was polite until she told him who she was, then "turned stiff and
hard" and refused to talk further. The dentist, also courteous initially,
"turned into an 'intense point' of anger" when she presented her card,
"got very white, drew himself up and bowed stiffly, saying 'I do not think
it is necessary for you to come back again." One insurance company president did talk to her, mainly about Virginia and even asked a few questions
about her work, but, she said, he would not help her in any way. Her
parting shot to them all was a warning that when they fought the union
they took on the federal government and the Supreme Court as well, but
this had little effect. She made hundreds of such visits during her years
with the CIO, often receiving similarly negative responses, though attitudes in time did begin to change. The first years, however, were years
of hard work and precious little reward.[28]

There were some signs of success in other areas, however. She began to
receive invitations to speak, to state the CIO's point of view, mainly from
church groups and from colleges. She accepted as many of these as she
could, speaking extemporaneously most of the time, engaging in discussion with the audience, as she loved to do. Moreover, the TWOC *was*
winning some NLRB elections, *was* securing new contracts and renewing

old ones, and this at a time of severe depression in the textile industry. The CIO's approach to organization seemed to be having some success. "The old method of organizing by the United Textile Workers, an AF of L affiliation," she told Jonathan Daniels,

> was to rely on strikes in time of stress, or to send in an organizer who collected initiation fees, received half for his reward, signed up and collected dollars, moved on to a new place, leaving nothing solid behind him. Now unions are built first and dues come when something has been accomplished. Do not ever quote me aloud on this, as we are not flaunting any red rags in the faces of what is left of the UTW leadership.

She could feel herself to be part of these successes, and this helped her in the rough patches.[29]

Then at times her influence was directly effective, even in cases when labor people had run foul of the law. In July 1938, three CIO members had been jailed in Covington, Virginia, allegedly for illegal picketing. Mason went directly to the governor, James Price, and the state comptroller, LeRoy Hodge, both of whom she knew personally, and quickly secured a pardon. This was an enormous boost for her—direct evidence that she could be effective—and she left for a break in Maine, to look after the children of her ailing sister, Ida. She was in the most positive frame of mind she had felt since joining the TWOC.[30]

Finally, there were the encouraging tributes of her friends. "I am so thankful that you are having a chance to do such swell work," wrote Molly Dewson. "I know how happy you must be. The NCL carried the candle during all those dark and bleak years, but the situation is different today. With all the workers trained and seasoned you can really make a fight." Small successes, her slight connections with the Roosevelts, and the support of friends in higher places than she—all these helped her as a pattern developed to her activities in the South. The year 1938 thus closed on a note of cautious optimism.[31]

Apart from her union work, Lucy Mason was not slow to become involved in other aspects of southern political and social life after her move to Atlanta. I will discuss her continuing and important connection with the Southern Conference for Human Welfare (SCHW) shortly. More generally, she became active in Democratic local and state politics, always, of course, on the New Deal side. Initially her involvement took the form of work for particular candidates behind the scenes. She supported Eurith

D. Rivers in the 1938 Georgia gubernatorial primary, for example, as "the lesser of other possible evils" and also worked for the election of Olin Johnson in South Carolina.[32] As might be expected, she always let the White House know what was happening and what she was doing. From 1938 on she wrote frequent lengthy letters to both the president and Mrs. Roosevelt, explaining Georgia politics and suggesting courses of action they might take. Early in 1939, for example, her lukewarm support of Rivers had already cooled. In a long letter to Mrs. Roosevelt she explained the reasons for her break with the new governor: "His New Deal attitude is purely for political purposes. He would jettison the New Deal at any moment that it would seem to promote his own career to do so." She then discussed the fragmented and feud-ridden state of Democratic politics in Georgia, analyzed the close connection between anti-CIO activity and certain Baptist revivalists, and provided a list of local politicians who favored the New Deal and whom she thought the administration should be supporting. In line with her own commitment she strongly advocated the appointment of a woman to lead voter registration drives among the women of the state. "She should be a native Georgian," she said, and someone who was popular among women. Noting that the retroactive poll tax did not apply to women until after they had registered to vote, and that therefore it did not cost them anything, she argued that there was an untapped course of liberal support among them. Lucy Mason also had comments to make, not all of them complimentary, about the various federal officeholders in Georgia and about the textile industry. It contained, she said, "some of the most reactionary manufacturers in the country and an unusually smart and vicious secretary for its state organization." About the state's press she observed, "I do not know of a state in the South so devoid of a progressive paper as Georgia." Weak as the region's liberal press was, there were in the other states at least a few papers that could be counted on.[33]

Such letters did show that Lucy Mason had quickly become involved in the details of state politics. Mrs. Roosevelt certainly considered Lucy's information of sufficient value to warrant sharing it with the president. She did so and told Miss Lucy that she had. Thus encouraged, Miss Lucy continued to report frequently to the White House on all manner of issues until FDR's death. Doing so undoubtedly helped her feel important, even part of the administration, but also she undoubtedly did provide some useful information, an informed perspective on regional politics of which from time to time the president may have taken notice. Sometimes she had specific requests to make. She suggested, for example, that a woman be made head of the Federal Security Agency and nominated Josephine P. Roche. Mrs. Roosevelt did not support the idea, but most often her White House correspondence was more in the nature of keeping in touch. As a single woman living on her own, she did have, despite her busy life, time to write.[34]

Lucy Mason had other reports of a more routine type to submit, of course. She kept the national CIO officials in Washington well informed of her activities. Initially her point of contact was Walter Smethhurst, Lewis's executive assistant, but from early 1940 when her responsibilities were broadened to encompass public relations work for the whole CIO and not solely the TWOC, her regular contact was the CIO's director of organization, Allan S. Haywood. From her reports to Haywood there emerges a picture of the varied nature of her activities as she defined her job. Her account of October 15, 1940, on her activities in August and September, is representative.

First, Miss Lucy had spoken at the Highlander Folk School, and to students at Sewanee University. She had attended a banquet in honor of Philip Murray, the CIO's vice president, and had spoken at the SWOC convention in Birmingham, Alabama. There she had also called on the editors of the city's main newspapers. From September 29 to October 12 she had visited Nashville, Memphis, New Orleans, Baton Rouge, Mobile, and Montgomery, where she had talked with local CIO officials, community leaders, newspaper editors and publishers, public officals, and politicians.

In New Orleans, where she stayed the longest, she had spent a considerable amount of time with the Catholic archbishop, who, she said, had changed his mind about the CIO and was now willing to cooperate with it. When she was in Baton Rouge, she had a long and "good" interview with the governor of Louisiana. In addition, she had provided information on the CIO in the South for "the usual number of college professors, students and otherwise." She had supplied special material for a large number of union representatives and had sent out a bibliography of labor books "to nearly a thousand people." She had spoken to teachers for the Works Progress Administration (WPA) on labor's attitude toward national defense, had led discussions with several groups of social workers, and had involved herself in state and local politics. Without directly supporting Eugene Talmadge in the Georgia gubernatorial primary, the CIO had secured a great many promises from him, and as a result the organization was in a better political position in the state than it had ever been. Moreover a majority of CIO-supported candidates were successful in local primaries in Atlanta and elsewhere.

Finally, she had made contacts with black ministers and other black leaders in Georgia. She had supplied information for the Commission on Interracial Cooperation on CIO activities among blacks and had accepted an invitation to join the commission, as "this seems a further opportunity not only to help in race relations but the CIO program." It had been, in short, a busy, if routine, two months.[35]

During her first three years with the CIO, Lucy Mason also kept in fairly close touch with John L. Lewis, whom she clearly regarded as a combination of patron and mentor. She wrote often to him, letters which he only briefly acknowledged, usually to ask his advice. When she had to make a choice, for example, between moving to Charlotte with the Textile Workers or remaining in Atlanta and working more generally with the CIO, she turned first to Lewis for counsel. "I have no lien on this job," she told him. "I have loved doing it and would like to go on with it, believing that it has validity and is of service to the greatest Labor movement in the world." She would do whatever he thought best, however, even if that meant resignation.[36]

Her admiration for and dependence on Lewis was such that his decision during the 1940 presidential election campaign to abandon Roosevelt, the Democrats, and most of his CIO colleagues for the parvenu Republican Wendell Willkie caused her the deepest personal tension. Forced to choose between the two men she most admired, she issued a press statement to the effect that she intended to vote for Roosevelt and then wrote Lewis offering her resignation. "It is deeply distressing to me that I have no alternative but to differ with you on this matter," she told him, stating that, if he found her continued employment with the CIO embarrassing, she would immediately leave. Lewis assured her that she was free to occupy any position her conscience dictated and that he looked forward to her continued service with the CIO. In her distress, she decided to make a last attempt to change his mind. In a long letter she urged him to support FDR because "the CIO needs you as its president—only you can hold it together." The letter was never sent, however. Instead she told him that, if Willkie was to be elected, the only benefit, in her view, would be that "the greatest labor leader in America would be in a position of great influence with him." Roosevelt's triumphant reelection was marred for her by the knowledge that it would inevitably mean Lewis's departure from the CIO. Few events in recent years had distressed her as much as the seeming defection from the cause of a man she had admired and trusted and to whom she considered herself beholden.[37]

Again she offered her resignation, this time to Philip Murray, now president of the CIO inasmuch as Lewis had made good his promise to resign in the event of Roosevelt's reelection. As Lewis had appointed her, she said, "it seems proper that I should now leave the slate clean for you to decide whether you wish this work to go on, and if so whether you wish to select someone of your own choosing." Murray was quick to assure her that he wanted her to stay, and before long she felt for him the admiration and affection that she had formerly attached to the CIO's founder. Nevertheless, she continued to keep in touch with Lewis and to profess her admiration for his achievements. "To you more than anyone else, the Congress of Industrial Organizations owes its inception and accomplishments, and I am sure history will so record," she once wrote. His resignation would long remain a painful matter for her.[38]

An aspect of her work on which she began to spend more time concerned the CIO's attitude toward organizing blacks. The CIO's drive to organize America's industrial labor force was bound to have its effect on the nation's black work force. CIO policy recognized no racial boundaries, and its organizers moved aggressively to cut through lines of prejudice and fear on both sides in order to bring black workers into its swelling ranks. The results were immediate and impressive. In all regions of the country, there was a steady increase in black union membership, and in some industries, such as steel, which mounted an aggressive organizing drive under the aegis of the Steel Workers Organizing Committee, blacks became unionized in even greater proportions than did whites.[39]

The thrust to organize the black worker had its effect in the South, as it did in the other regions of the nation. Given the region's unique social structure, the problems confronting southern organizers were extraordinarily difficult, but they battled onward. After the mid-1930s, whites and blacks began to come together in CIO-formed unions, usually in trades where blacks had always been a considerable presence, such as the mining, iron, and steel industries. Of the 22,000 coal miners in the Alabama mineral area in 1935, for example, 12,000 were black. Half of Alabama's 12,000 iron and steel workers were Negroes, as were more than 70 percent of the state's iron ore miners. Procedures had been developed in such unions for integrated meetings. Blacks usually sat on one side of a central aisle and whites on the other, with officeholders from both races having clearly defined tasks. Such meetings were always risky affairs, however, given the region's racist history, and provided the prospect of conflict as well as conciliation. One of Miss Lucy's jobs came to be helping to minimize tensions.[40] After all, the CIO's professed policy was one of complete racial equality, yet the South was still a Jim Crow region. Unemployment rates ran high, violence against blacks was commonplace, and blacks had heretofore been almost entirely excluded from many industries in which they might conceivably compete with white labor. For the first two years of Miss Lucy's employment in the South, when she devoted the bulk of her efforts to the textile workers, an industry with no black employees save at the janitorial level, the issue hardly came up, but after 1940, partly because her responsibilities had broadened to include the whole CIO and partly because of the economic revival which was soon to become the wartime boom, the situation increasingly commanded her attention.

She first confronted the issue in the larger cities with a history of some black union activity. Early in 1941 she was asked to investigate the disappearance in Memphis, Tennessee, of one Robert Cotton, an employee of the Warner-Tamble Transportation Company, a barge line, and a member of the Inland Boatmen's Union. Cotton had been suing the company for back wages, and the evidence suggested that company officials had simply done away with him rather than fight the case. When Mason arrived in Memphis she found, to her horror, that Cotton was but the last in a line of Warner-Tamble employees, most of them black, who had disappeared under similar circumstances. Once more, when faced with the ugly underside of southern life, Miss Lucy appealed for aid, and again it was to Mrs. Roosevelt. Claiming that the local authorities were so much under the control of "Boss" Ed Crump that they would do nothing to protect CIO members, she implored the First Lady to pressure the FBI to enter the case. Mrs. Roosevelt tried to help, passing the letter on to the attorney general, Robert H. Jackson, with the comment "Cannot something be done about this?" The answer was probably "not very much."[41]

In addition to appealing desperately to federal authorities for the protection of black workers, Lucy Mason adopted the more positive approach of working for the recruitment of blacks in CIO unions. In industries where blacks represented the bulk of the workers, as in the lumber industry in Memphis, for example, recruitment was not particularly difficult once the confidence of black community leaders had been gained. Lucy Mason, with her obvious warmth and complete lack of racial arrogance, was usually successful at winning trust. Indeed, in May 1941, she again wrote Mrs. Roosevelt about the Memphis situation but this time in much more positive tones. "The unions are still growing fast," she reported,

> and Negroes constitute the greater part of the membership. I spoke to a number of union meetings and was keenly interested in what many negroes had to say in the meetings—they have a wit and aptness of expression which is intriguing.
>
> All meetings opened with a prayer and a hymn or spiritual. Usually the prayer leader "lined out" the prayer—even the Lord's prayer—and the group repeated it after he read out the words—or rather said them from memory. The variations on the Lord's prayer were new to me, and apparently were optional with the prayer—that is the pray-er.[42]

The most difficult tasks for her in the area of race relations within a union context still lay ahead. In the shipyards and factories of the booming wartime southern cities the employment of blacks for the first time in a number of skilled and semiskilled jobs gave the matter of race relations real urgency. The issue nevertheless occupied more of Miss Lucy's time in 1941, a development which she embraced gladly, given her long-standing concern to improve race relations in the South.

In 1941, too, Miss Lucy ventured on the first in a long line of extensive speaking tours. Her audiences were mainly on college campuses, and she was sponsored by a body other than the CIO, which, however, continued to pay her salary, given that the organization and its advancement were always the focus of anything she had to say. The first tour she made from late February to early April 1941, under the auspices of the YWCA's national student council. Her report to that body's president suggests the tour's extent and its strenuous nature.

Starting in Washington she moved first to New York, visiting several

Miss Lucy speaking at an early morning union meeting, held outdoors.

northeastern campuses, including Vassar; the Yale Divinity School, where she spoke to several of Liston Pope's classes; the New York School of Social Work; Union Theological Seminary; and the New School for Social Research. Moving south in mid-March, she went to her hometown of Richmond, where she spoke at Virginia Union University, at Westhampton College, and to YWCA groups and a group of Richmond social workers. Next, she swung west to Pennsylvania, speaking first at Crozier Theological Seminary in Chester, where she addressed members of a religion and labor seminar, and then to Philadelphia, again to speak to YWCA groups. Back south, she spent a week in North Carolina, speaking at Guilford College; the Women's College of the University of North Carolina, where she found "the differences in information concerning organized labor between northern and southern students very evident"; and North Carolina State College for Negroes in Durham.[43]

Going home to Atlanta at the end of March, she sat on a panel at the Georgia Student Christian Conference which discussed the relation of religion to economics and labor questions. As she was so often to comment about southern meetings, she said "the group started out with almost no information concerning organized labor and with a great deal of misunderstanding." She completed her tour at Talladega College in Alabama on April 1. There she conducted a faculty seminar, observing that the women faculty "seemed better informed and more in sympathy with labor unions" than the men.[44]

Such tours became a regular part of her activities, and she enjoyed them thoroughly. She especially liked being with young people because she felt that they were at least open minded about what she had to say and that she was able to remove a few prejudices or, at the very least, to provide unbiased information on which judgments could be made. She spoke to the students usually without a prepared script and engaged them in debate and discussion. She became a familiar figure on southern college campuses during the 1940s. There, she believed, she met a positive response.[45]

It was hard to say the same about others to whom she spoke or with whom she corresponded during these first years with the CIO. Indeed, some long-term relationships were strained or perhaps even broken as a result of her new job. One such was with her old friend Virginius Dabney, the editor of the *Richmond Times-Dispatch*. Regarded then, by some

scholars even now, as something of a liberal in the southern context—
Morton Sosna, for example, calls him a "publicist for a liberal South"—
Dabney found Lucy Mason's views on labor and especially her support of
strike action, impossible to take. Their correspondence, formerly between "Dear V," and "Dear Miss Lucy," deteriorated to the extent that by
1941 he was referring to her as "Miss Mason" and was observing that they
were "so far apart on some of the fundamental facts in this matter of industrial disputes at a time of national crisis, that there isn't much point in our
trying to get together." The "average American" was "awfully sick" of labor's demands and, contrary to Miss Mason's views, found many of them
unreasonable. "I honestly fear that *anything* demanded by the union
would be regarded by you as reasonable," he claimed. He hoped that they
could "continue to disagree amicably." Their friendship, which had
existed for more than twenty years, was nevertheless under serious
strain.[46]

It nevertheless survived. Dabney came to Miss Lucy's defense later
that year when a columnist in a Charlottesville paper accused her of
slighting her distinguished Confederate ancestor Senator James Murray
Mason and also hinted that her relationship with John L. Lewis was more
than a business one. Scandalized, she wrote to Dabney, imploring that he
tackle the offending journalist. She noted that there was "no particle of
truth," in what had been written about her and that the last thing she
would do would be to jibe at her famous relative in print. Dabney did as
she asked, and their relationship became warmer from then on, especially
after the break with John L. Lewis. Soon it was "Dear V" again. "Lewis
seems a tragic failure where his egotism is concerned," she wrote him in
1942, ". . . and I shall not see him anymore." These were sentiments of
which Dabney wholeheartedly approved. Her job with the CIO did not
cost her this particular relationship, though it threatened to do so for a
while.[47]

Her own attitudes were becoming sharper because she was being called
upon increasingly to troubleshoot, was managing better, and was seeing
at first hand just how labor was exploited and how the rights of organizers
under the Wagner Act could be subverted, given the southern climate of
opposition. In January 1941, for example, Paul Christopher asked her to
come to Nashville and to work with Myles Horton to combat antilabor
legislation currently before the Tennessee state legislature, legislation os-

tensibly directed at saboteurs but with the real purpose of harassing union members. There she became involved in the case of a young unionist named Blair, an employee of the Washington Manufacturing Company, a manufacturer of cotton garments, which she described as a "notorious defier of the Labor Relations Act." He had clung to his job despite repeated harassment but had recently been fired, allegedly for sabotage. The company had been awarded a government contract, and Blair had accidently nicked some cloth too deeply, according to him because of a defective cutting knife about which he had repeatedly complained. For that act of sabotage he had been dismissed.[48]

Blair told Miss Mason that the management urged workers to work at a pace which made mistakes inevitable. The government inspector, he said, then rejected work as defective, giving management the chance to fire those held responsible, all of whom would inevitably be union activists. Such practices, with which she was becoming all too familiar, aimed at subverting the New Deal labor legislation. Often, too, they involved an unwitting federal government. For these reasons she rejected more and more summarily the antilabor views of men such as Dabney. Her commitment to labor, always strong, was deepening as the result of what she saw and heard in the course of her daily work.[49]

Indeed, at times her commitment led to disagreements even with president and Mrs. Roosevelt. When John L. Lewis and his mine workers threatened and finally implemented stoppages in 1941 over the issue of universal contracts, and in defiance of federal orders, he did so in the face of almost universal criticism, criticism not only from the traditional enemies of labor but also from many friends. Any legitimacy the issue may have had was lost in the emotional response of those who claimed that even to contemplate strike action in a time of such national emergency was tantamount to treason. The president, no friend to Mr. Lewis, took the opportunity to denounce him roundly. Lucy Mason was upset and said so to Mrs. Roosevelt. "Perhaps you can imagine my perturbed state of mind at the present moment," she wrote. "But the situation is different with me from what it was last fall—when I publicly stated I thought Mr. Lewis was wrong in supporting Mr. Willkie. Today I think the United Mine Workers are right in asking the same contracts for all miners, regardless who the owners of the mines may be." The administration had not incorporated labor into the defense program, she insisted. In the

United Kingdom, labor was "on the inside"; in America, however, it was "still on the fringes." The president had talked about using troops, if he had to, to keep the mines open, but sending soldiers was hardly an answer. "There must be some other solution. John Lewis is not tactful, but he has brains to an unusual degree. I think he has his eyes on the war's aftermath—he remembers the last after-war period when we returned to 'normalcy' to the 'American tradition of the open shop,' and practically destroyed the labor movement for twelve years." In England employers tried not to smash unions but to work with them. Why could not the same thing happen in America, where, she said, labor was still "Democracy's strongest bulwark"? Mrs. Roosevelt did not agree with her perspective but passed the letter on to her husband nonetheless. He read it but made no comment. Lucy Mason had become such a dedicated advocate of labor's position that she was willing to oppose even the revered Roosevelts if they seemed to be wavering in the cause.[50]

One other aspect of Miss Lucy's work during these first years with the CIO should briefly be mentioned. Newspaper editors began to call on her to review books on aspects of labor policy, and in these reviews she was able to advocate particular stands on issues. Moreover, she made her first radio addresses during this time as well and became adept at doing so. She was extremely nervous about her first broadcast, however, over Radio WIS in Columbia, South Carolina in April 1940, shortly before the NLRB election at Columbia's Duck Mill. On the air she urged the workers to choose the Textile Workers Union of America (TWUA) and not an independent union, refuting charges that the CIO was tainted with communism and stressing the fact that local union meetings began and ended with a prayer. Producing an argument that she was to use often in such circumstances, she noted that Mrs. Roosevelt was a CIO member through her association with the American Newspaper Guild and asked, "Aren't you proud to be part of an organization to which our first and greatest lady belongs?" Lucy Mason became an effective user of the mass media to publicize labor's position. She was often asked to write radio scripts for others to give, as well as making broadcasts herself.[51]

As her work became better known, Miss Lucy began to be asked to write or speak on broader themes than simply labor matters. One of the first people to make such a request was Lillian Smith, who in 1939 solicited a piece for the *North Georgia Review* in a symposium entitled

"Southerners Look at the South." Lucy was delighted. In her contribution she discussed the economic problems of the region and spoke of the spirit of hope engendered by the first meeting of the Southern Conference for Human Welfare that these problems could finally be met in a humane and liberal way. Lillian Smith, who was to become a good friend, was pleased with the article and wrote that the *Review* planned to feature her in a future issue on southerners who were making a "distinctive contribution to the enrichment of southern and national life. We think of you because of your personality, your magnificent work and the influence which you are exerting . . . , because of your consistent emphasis on human values." Lucy Mason was becoming known in the region as one of the leading liberals, and this recognition was a source of pride to her.[52]

Of her personal life in these first Atlanta years, little is recoverable. Given the hours which she worked, her traveling, and the diversity of her involvements, she had virtually no time for herself. Any vacations she took were normally spent in Virginia, first with her sister and her family and later, after Ida's death in 1939, either with Ida's children or with her friends Carrie and Hermine Moore, whom she still assisted financially. She continued, however, to "communicate" with Ida, talking about it so matter-of-factly with friends that some of them asked her to give her dead sister messages from them as well. "Lucy dear," wrote one such, "ask that Ida might if possible bring me some word of or from my child." Spiritualism, then, remained very much an aspect of her belief system, a part of her world view. "It seems to me that the only basis for invincible happiness," she wrote at this time to the minister of the church she had joined in Atlanta, "rests in a conviction of—immortality—the wholesome and unbroken continuity of life—the safeness of our universe and our at-homeness in it. . . . it is just as true to me that we have communion with all we have ever loved and who have gone ahead of us as we do with God." She and Ida still met at this level, she said, "sharing the deepest, sweetest realities of life." She concluded that a person had no "right to invincible happiness until *identity* with others" had been realized.[53]

This feeling of identity had brought her into the labor movement, she told him, where she could work "with the dispossessed and submerged." Once this "identity" was realized, "it burns away social indifferences to injustice and human suffering." Such had been her experience. Certainly it must be said that her Christian faith, her conviction of the continuity of life unbroken by death, and her firm belief that she was doing God's work had all helped sustain her during these difficult years as she established herself in her new position and in a new town. Moreover, she had made some new friends, including Margaret Fisher, who was to become particularly close and would indeed eventually fill the gap left since Katherine's death. By the end of 1941, then, she was confident in her job and content within herself as, after December 7, the labor movement began its period of adjustment to the realities and needs of a nation at war.[54]

6

The CIO at War

L ucy Randolph Mason's commitment to pacifism was both deep rooted and long standing. Forged, as was that of so many others, in the horror of the First World War and the loss of her brother Randolph, it developed during her years with the YWCA and through her relationship with Katherine Gerwick. Miss Lucy was a committed pacifist throughout the 1920s, attending conferences, often with Katherine, on the causes and prevention of war and being very much a part of the international peace movement. The cause of peace was very dear to her. It took a fearful realization of the prospect of a world dominated by Hitler for her to relinquish it. Even then, something had to be put in its place. As she told Mrs. Roosevelt in 1941, "Many of us who have slowly and painfully abandoned the pacifist position we took largely as a result of disillusionment following 'the war to save democracy' want to believe that a better and more just national and inter-national economic system will be built when this war is over. We know that the President holds this hope and will work for its realization." On December 7, 1941, Lucy Mason, having reluctantly come to support war as the only way to resist totalitarianism, was ready, within the labor movement, to help FDR build a better world.[1]

Lucy Mason's retreat from pacifism and her eventual acceptance of an interventionist American foreign policy tended to reflect the shifts in attitude of the CIO itself. Initially the organization's leaders were far from united about the increasingly internationalist course of Roosevelt's foreign policy, with its corollary of putting the American economy on a war footing. John L. Lewis, in particular, argued that such a policy would strengthen labor's enemies at home and would lessen the prospects for further social advance. Even after the Nazi blitzkrieg across western Europe, Lewis continued to oppose American aid to the Allies, advocating an isolationism which put him on the same side as the American Firsters. One of the reasons for his split with Roosevelt in 1940 was his fundamental disagreement with the president over the course of American foreign policy.[2]

The rank and file, however, repudiated Lewis, and with his defeat went any suggestion of an independent stance for the CIO on the matter of intervention. The new leadership, the pragmatic, cautious Philip Murray, and the New Dealish Sidney Hillman, with his close White House connections, were much more inclined to support the president's foreign policy directions. Perceiving, as did Lewis, that the labor reforms of the New Deal, and the attendant incorporation of the labor movement into the bureaucratic structure, had, in Nelson Lichtenstein's words, created a situation where "the fate of the labor movement largely rested on its relationship to government power," they, unlike Lewis, welcomed rather than deplored the relative loss of labor's independence. Lucy Mason and most of the CIO's leaders, together with the rank and file, had by the beginning of 1941 come to believe that an interventionist foreign policy to preserve global democracy was labor's most important priority. As Lichtenstein wrote, "Given this liberal interpretation of American war aims, most CIO leaders easily rejected the sullen counsel of John L. Lewis and vowed cooperation with Roosevelt and the military in the rapidly expanding mobilization effort."[3]

Such broad cooperation did not of course mean an immediate end to labor disputes. In fact, rather the contrary occurred. As employers and reactionary state legislatures began to use the state of national emergency in order to roll back some of labor's painfully won gains of the past few years, a series of CIO-led strikes resulted, the most violent being the North American Aviation strike in California in June 1941, which was eventually broken by the use of federal troops. This strike and the manner of its breaking marked, as Lichtenstein has observed "a turning point in defense era labor relations." By failing to oppose the use of troops, the CIO leadership virtually acquiesced in the government's demands that strikes be suspended for the duration of the emergency, and that industrial disputes, including the maintenance of real wage rates, be settled through federal mediation, first through the National Defense Mediation Board and then, after Pearl Harbor, through its successor, the National War Labor Board (NWLB). Its relationship with this aspect of the federal bureaucracy, then, became an increasingly important aspect of the CIO's work during the war years.[4]

The CIO became increasingly involved with other wartime bureaucratic structures, too, with which field workers such as Miss Lucy had to come to terms. One was the War Manpower Commission (WMC), set up in April 1942 under the directorship of Paul V. McNutt, a former governor of Indiana. Its task was to determine where workers were needed and to apportion them between industry and the armed forces. At first its function was coordination, reflecting FDR's belief that federal control over a person's job should be kept as light as possible for morale purposes, but gradually it was given more power, including that of preventing rapid job changes in the new atmosphere of full employment. The development and maintenance of relationships between such arms of the wartime bureaucracy as the NWLB and the WMC, then, marked a shift in emphasis of CIO activity which characterized the war years.[5]

The South, like the rest of the country, was affected by the development of the wartime bureaucracy. The war boom resulted in considerable industrial growth in the region but not as much as elsewhere in the nation. The South's major contribution during World War II was probably in the provision of space for training camps but was significant nonetheless. In some industries, such as shipbuilding, chemicals, and nonferrous metals, growth was spectacular. Unionization developed in consequence. Though the AFL reaped most of the benefits, the CIO also grew, though more slowly because of employer and community hostility. Moreover, the determinations of such bodies as the War Labor Board had important implications for labor relations in the South. In particular, certain of its rulings on equal pay for equal work had a profound effect on the region's traditional racial pay differentials. These were often bitterly opposed by southern employers. Labor organizers constantly found themselves in the position of defending the bureaucracy and its conclusions.[6]

No wartime bureaucratic creation caused more antagonism in the South, of course, than the Fair Employment Practices Commission (FEPC). Created by executive order in 1941 in response to intensifying black discontent over the issue of discrimination in defense employment,

its purpose was supposedly to ensure that plants holding defense contracts accorded blacks equal treatment as employees. It achieved a lot
less. It had limited power to enforce its directives, and its moral censure
bothered few employers. It did have some positive effects, however, although its very presence was an affront to most white southerners. "Oh!
This is the beginning of a communistic dictatorship," Mississippi congressman John Rankin once remarked of the FEPC. The CIO supported
the FEPC and maintained a close relationship with the members of its
regional offices, including those in the South. The South's CIO officials,
including Lucy Mason, found it a new and difficult task to justify such a
position to union members still solidly steeped in the support of segregation.[7]

The creation of the FEPC, its limited successes in the South, and the
reaction to it there drew attention to a broader problem for the CIO in the
South, one which the war had made urgent. Southern blacks were moving
into the region's work force in significant numbers and were entering industries such as shipbuilding and rubber which the CIO was attempting
to dominate. The union would have to develop policies to meet the
changed situation, to make union membership attractive to black workers, to mollify white ones, to prevent racial tension—in short, to hasten
the development of biracial union structures. Miss Lucy, with her commitment to a better deal for southern blacks, would have an increasing
role to play in this area. In late 1942, for example, she spent some time in
Savannah, Georgia. There the CIO and the AFL had been competing for
the loyalties of recently hired workers in the city's booming shipyards.
The AFL, which had a history of acquiescence in discrimination against
blacks in the industry, was signing up most of the white workers, and the
CIO was getting the blacks. The situation in the community was tense,
according to Miss Lucy, and there were fears of a race riot. "The CIO is
blamed for this," she told Philip Murray, "rather than the unfair practices
which the Negroes have endured." She had gone to Savannah with hopes
of relieving some of the tensions, to talk to community leaders of both
races, to representatives of the industry and to federal officials. She was
making some headway, she thought, in communicating the CIO's perspective, though the community remained overwhelmingly sympathetic
to the AFL.[8]

She was often to find herself in such situations during the war years. In
May 1943, for example, she was involved in a strike at the Alabama Dry

Dock and Shipbuilding Company's works in Mobile, Alabama, one which had involved the use of federal troops. Again, the issue was race, and its details indicate the problems caused by the war boom. The company had had an excellent history in the employment of blacks but not as skilled laborers. Many of these blacks were in the CIO. The union had attempted to secure the employment of some skilled blacks by enlisting the War Manpower Commission and the company in a plan to set up two shipways to be manned entirely by Negro labor, including every skill used in ship-building. Black unionists agreed with the plan, but just before it was due to be implemented, the company, in Miss Lucy's view in order to discredit the FEPC, "suddenly placed a number of Negro welders with white workers in various parts of the yard," often with newly recruited whites who were not union members. The result was abuse, violence, and eventually a wildcat strike, for which the company's management blamed "the President's race discrimination order." Miss Lucy and Frank Constangy, the regional War Manpower Commission official, hastily drafted a scheme to dampen the tension, whereby blacks of all skills would build the hulls and white labor would complete the rest of the work. This arrangement would provide blacks with better work opportunities than they had ever had while at the same time preventing the integrated work situation which in the South was always a potential source of disruption. The plan, which was accepted, as she told Mrs. Roosevelt in describing the incident, illustrated "what we said at lunch, that this race issue cannot be solved by too much publicity, but rather by quiet, effective work."[9]

This incident and its solution indicate the role that Miss Lucy played in attempting to mitigate some of the racial tensions engendered by the wartime employment situation while at the same time helping to improve employment opportunities for blacks. Recognizing the realities of southern life, she never attempted to force the integration of plants and yards. To do so would have been counterproductive. Instead she sought to make advances within the framework of a segregated society, chipping away at the edges, perhaps, but rarely attacking the foundations. When she spoke at Tuskegee Institute in December 1942 on "the Negro and Organized Labor," she had come to know her subject well. She understood its complexity, how far one could go, and what could realistically be expected in the contemporary South. The issue occupied much of her time during the war years.[10]

Lucy Mason's association with Frank Constangy during the Mobile strike illustrates one aspect of her approach during World War II, namely the way she worked, wherever possible, in concert with the wartime federal bureaucracy. She had little contact with the NWLB inasmuch as her work was seldom associated with such matters as wage differentials, cost-of-living increases, and so forth. She did, however, have sustained contact with the War Manpower Commission and, as she had in Mobile, sometimes worked very closely with its representatives. There were times, indeed, when she tried to influence particular appointments to the commission. Writing to Mrs. Roosevelt in 1942, for example, she urged the appointment of Clark Foreman to a senior position on the newly created body, having first secured Philip Murray's support. More important, she intervened actively in 1944 on behalf of Constangy, deputy administrator of the WMC in the southeastern region, seeking his promotion within the agency. She wrote to Mrs. Roosevelt on his behalf, calling him "one of the key men in the South, and one who is going to count even more in the future." She even contacted Malvina Thompson, asking her to use her influence to secure Constangy an interview with the First Lady. Miss Lucy liked Constangy. He had been on the TWUA payroll for a time and was thus sympathetic to labor, she thought. She had forged a fine working relationship with him. In her concern to have good relations with those in the federal bureaucracy whose interests impinged on hers, and to have persons sympathetic to labor in such positions, she both recognized the tightness of the link which had recently been forged between the Roosevelt administration and the CIO and tried to influence that link from labor's end. [11]

The Roosevelt-CIO link was most starkly demonstrated during the election year 1944, through the activities and influence of the CIO's Political Action Committee, the CIO-PAC. The PAC was formed quietly in July 1943, partly as a result of the blows that labor and the Democrats had suffered in the 1942 congressional elections, when millions of working-class voters had stayed away from the polls either from apathy or from disaffection with the course of domestic politics. The result was a Republican triumph, and labor now faced a Congress anxious to roll back some of its recent gains. Part of the purpose in forming the PAC, therefore, was to prevent a similar disaster in 1944 and, indeed, to ensure Roosevelt's reelection on a liberal platform so that the postwar political world would continue to reflect the New Deal's liberal values.

A second reason for the PAC's establishment, however, had to do with the internal politics of the CIO. There was growing disaffection among certain left-wing unions, both with the accommodationist policy of Philip Murray and other national leaders where the federal government was concerned and with the administration itself. As a result there was a growing demand that the CIO should take a more independent political stand in 1944 or at least maintain a more active political presence so that the gap between labor and government would widen, not narrow. The PAC was formed in part as an attempt to blunt some of this disaffection.[12]

The PAC was always safely in the New Deal camp. It was chaired, until his death in 1946, by Sidney Hillman, who kept it firmly under his personal control. There were some Communists and popular-fronters in its employ, for by 1944 they were, of course, loyal supporters of the president. Missing were the supporters of John L. Lewis and the advocates of an independent position for labor. Under the PAC's direction the CIO became a crucial component of the Democratic party's campaign machine in 1944, with a chain of organization reaching to the ward level, aimed at reversing the loss of the working-class vote which had occurred in 1942. There were some successes—not nearly enough to ensure claims that it had determined the outcome of the election but sufficient to ensure its continued existence. The new Congress was a little more liberal than the last one. A few of its most reactionary members, such as Martin Dies of Texas, had gone; some new progressive ones, like William Fulbright, the young senator from Arkansas, had appeared. Nothing spectacular, but the drift of 1942 had at least been checked.[13]

During the 1944 campaign, a number of CIO local officials were directed to spend all or part of their time working with the PAC. One of these was Lucy Randolph Mason, and this political involvement represented a further extension of her work. From early 1944 she cooperated closely with the southern PAC director George Mitchell, son of her old Richmond mentor Samuel Chiles Mitchell and himself a valued friend, on a wide variety of PAC matters. As the year progressed she spent more and more time on political activity, attending most regional strategy sessions, tirelessly canvassing local union members on the PAC's behalf. She enjoyed the task and particularly working with her friend Mitchell. They concentrated their activities on the primary elections, of course, and were encouraged by some successes. The results of several primaries in Alabama and Florida had been good for the CIO, she wrote Allan Haywood in early May. "The CIO helped in both," she claimed, "but especially in Alabama."

In recognition of her efforts for the PAC in the South, Sidney Hillman appointed her in late July to the executive committee of the National Citizens Committee of the PAC. The NCPAC, as James Foster explains, was a device to provide "a means for the PAC to carry on a campaign outside the immediate labor community without being burdened by the restrictions that the Smith-Connally Act placed upon the CIO." Principally a fund-raising body, its executive committee as well as comprising top CIO officials, also included distinguished liberals such as Freda Kirchwey, publisher of the *Nation*, Gifford Pinchot, and politicians such as George Norris and Elmer Benson. Lucy Mason was honored and delighted to join their company and especially loved the trips to committee meetings, which were normally held in New York.[14] From then till the election she worked almost full time for the PAC. She certainly had no doubts as to the value of its activities. Calling its accomplishments "magnificent" and claiming that it was "responsible for the changes made in Congressmen for the South," she urged Philip Murray that its work be extended. In a long letter stating her case, she outlined a view of her region and its potential for change. In its optimism—its faith in a liberal future—this view typified the outlook of many of the region's liberals as the war drew to a close and the possibilities of a Roosevelt-led peace began to be glimpsed. At the time Lucy identified two outstanding developments in the South.

> One tends to Fascism, reaction, labor baiting, Negro hating, and to the support of the reactionary element in Congress which aligns the worst of the Republicans and Democrats against all progressive measures. The other southern force is for good, for progress in liberal political, economic and social action; for support of men and policies of benefit to the South and to the nation. The South can become the worst seedbed of Fascism in the country, or it can move in the direction of a liberalism based on the mass strength of labor, such small farmers as can be drawn in, and the best of Southern liberals, plus many obscure people who can be appealed to by what is sound and right and good.

The CIO, she said, had "the greatest power to influence the South in the right direction." The need to develop a "South-wide movement, founded on labor," drawing to it other liberal bodies such as the SCHW—"best instrument for promoting such a movement"—was urgent. The PAC could be of the greatest help there, she added in urging its retention. Obviously, she had found the new experience of working for labor in the political arena to be an exciting one, and she wished for more.[15]

Much of her work during the war, however, differed little from that which she had undertaken during the years prior to Pearl Harbor, as she was defining her job. There was still a lot of troubleshooting to be done. She needed to visit communities where the civil liberties of organizers were being violated, where their rights under the National Labor Relations Act were being ignored. Indeed, such incidents seemed to increase rather than diminish during the war, as management, secure in its government contracts, confident in the burgeoning wartime prosperity, and wrapping the cloak of patriotism around itself, openly defied labor's rights. Management often did so, believing that the growing climate of hostility to labor would make it possible to evade retribution. Miss Lucy always had her hands full, investigating such situations, reporting them to the CIO leadership, the United States Department of Justice, and, often enough, to Mrs. Roosevelt.

From late July 1944 until late September, Lucy Mason spent what time she could in Milledgeville, Georgia, where the R. J. Reynolds Corporation operated a naval ordnance factory on behalf of the Navy Department, which owned it. R. E. Starnes of the Steelworkers had gone to Milledgeville to organize the plant's employees and had faced a constant barrage of harassment, obstruction, and, eventually, physical attack. Earlier the city had passed a local ordinance requiring union organizers to pay a license fee of $5,000 for a permit from local authorities and to have resided in the city for at least twelve months. Starnes refused to comply and was twice arrested and once savagely beaten.[16]

The incident represented a clear violation of the Wagner Act, not to mention the Constitution, and Miss Lucy went to investigate. She found the situation disastrous; officers of the United States Navy who shared in the management of the plant were as hostile to union activity as were the local officials. The executive officer at the plant, Lieutenant Commander Neal K. Banks, had publicly equated CIO unionism with lack of patriotism, had formed a company union, and had dismissed CIO members. Miss Lucy collected all the facts she could and called on the Department of Justice for an investigation. "It is a blot on the spirit of democracy for which we fight, and a disgrace to the Navy Department which is committed to upholding the laws of this country, including the National Labor Relations Act, that this situation exists in Milledgeville," she stated. She also appealed to Mrs. Roosevelt, though with "only a very faint hope that you can do anything."[17]

Indeed, little enough was done in Milledgeville. Miss Lucy herself said that she returned because of the hope that her presence might be conducive to law and order— "and this because the people there know that I constantly report anti-union activity to federal authorities"—rather than from any expectation that these authorities would act upon her complaints. Mrs. Roosevelt did ask the Navy Department to investigate. The investigating officer's report exonerated the department of all charges of conspiring with local officials in the harassment of union members while conceding that "Lieutenant Commander Banks was over-zealous in his efforts to get out production and unquestionably was indiscreet." His actions, it was thought, were "largely attributable to the fact that he had recently returned from the Pacific War Theater and takes quite seriously any interference with production. . . . His extreme devotion to the task of getting out production, combined with his inexperience in labor relations has resulted in some imprudence which has caused union criticism that is not without some justification." Banks had been warned to keep out of labor matters, according to the report, and the problem was not likely to recur. Meanwhile, a local judge had struck down the offending ordinances. Thus, though there was no Justice Department investigation, and no one was punished for beating Starnes, Miss Lucy's efforts had had some minimal effect in relieving the tension in the community and in protecting the rights guaranteed labor by federal legislation.[18]

One of the problems with preventing such harassment, or in securing the punishment of the harassers, was that the local federal law officers charged with doing the job themselves often held profoundly antilabor sympathies. Such was certainly the case in the Mississippi communities of Jackson and Vicksburg. Miss Lucy visited both towns in March 1944 in connection with the violation of the civil rights of three representatives of the International Woodworkers Union who had been organizing there. In Jackson the three men had been arrested, held without charge, and denied access to counsel. They were eventually released without explanation. The men then proceeded to Vicksburg with a Jackson police car trailing them all the way there. In Vicksburg they were arrested a second time, again without charge, fingerprinted, and given a lecture on the CIO by Chief of Police Hogaboom, whom the usually circumspect Lucy Mason later described as "the most utterly stupid chief of police I have ever met. He is very old, having served in all wars since the Spanish-American." Afterward the men were once more released.[19]

Lucy Mason went first to Jackson and called immediately on the chief of police, J. D. Holden. There she met with courtesy and charm until the police officer realized that this seemingly respectable elderly lady was actually a CIO representative, when he expressed "antagonism and dislike." After Miss Lucy informed him that he had violated the organizers' civil rights in having them arrested, he became quite agitated. "Everybody was talking to him about civil rights," she reported him as saying, "but what were civil rights for two or three people when our country is at war." He refused to accept her view that the wartime situation did not make such violations legal and angrily claimed that the men "had sneaked into town like snakes . . . , and for all he knew they were planning to bomb the war industries of Jackson." He asserted that he did not care whether the right to bargain collectively, and "the right to have civil liberties," were guaranteed by both the Wagner Act and the Constitution, nor was he concerned with what happened elsewhere in the United States. He did not propose to have the CIO or any other people endangering the war plants in Jackson.

Miss Lucy received a more courteous but equally hostile response from Jackson's mayor; in Vicksburg General Hogaboom had seemed completely unable to grasp the points she was making. "My conversation with him [Hogaboom] was very funny," she reported to Victor Rotnem, chief of the Department of Justice's Civil Rights Section. "All I got out of him was such comments as 'you did'—'they did' or 'you are' hurled at me in booming tones." She was certainly not amused, however, at what had happened to three men who had clearly broken no law and had been forcibly prevented from exercising rights guaranteed organizers under the provisions of the Wagner Act. She asked Rotnem to make a thorough investigation of the whole matter as "a reminder to local authorities that the Constitution of the United States and the Acts of Congress are law as much in Mississippi as elsewhere."[20]

An investigation was carried out by Toxey Hall, United States attorney for the southern district of Mississippi. A Mississippian himself and an old acquaintance of Mr. Holden's, he was less inclined than Lucy Mason to invest the situation with much concern. Her complaint against Mr. Holden had been an isolated one, he said, and as he had subsequently informed Holden that federal law guaranteed labor unions the right to organize, he expected no more trouble. As for Hogaboom, far from being "utterly stupid," Hall had found him to be a sincere and decent man with a history of honorable service to his country in the Spanish-American War and on the battlefields of France, a man with two sons currently serving their country. One of the sons, in fact, was a prisoner of the Japanese. Hogaboom, for these reasons, had "his whole heart set on winning the war." Hall realized, of course, "that none of these things would justify the violation of the Civil Rights statutes," but nevertheless they "might give some insight to his point of view." True, Hogaboom did believe the CIO to be "unpatriotic and communistic, and for the sake of a few dollars, has tied up War Industries [sic], cut down production and deprived the armies of vital war materials, which will cause delay in winning the war and probably result in the death of many of our boys." As he assured Hall that he was not about to take vengeance on any CIO people, nor "arrest them or cause their detention because of his personal feeling," however, there seemed little point in pursuing the inquiry, and Hall had advised the Justice Department accordingly.[21]

Miss Lucy was far from pleased with Hall's report and the Justice Department's subsequent acceptance of it, but she was scarcely surprised, for she had learned through bitter experience that federal intervention on behalf of labor organizers rarely resulted in anything more substantial than a slap on the offender's wrist. Besides, the Woodworkers Union had reported to her that, though no action had been taken against either Holden or Hogaboom, nor would it be, there was much less harassment of local officials in the two cities. "It is my opinion," wrote the union's director of organization, "that your intervention in the case has gone a long way toward making organization less difficult in Mississippi." She therefore contented herself, as she had so often, with a sense of a small success—plus another letter to Hall, in which she asserted that far from being communistic, as Hogaboom thought, he would, if he were familiar with the real situation, "know that the CIO has been responsible for an enormous increase in production, that it is highly respected in many sections of the country, and that no group in America has done more to promote the war in every phase than have the CIO and its nearly six million members." The statement was probably as much for his edification as for that of the aged chief of police. Sending a copy of Hall's letter to her on to Eleanor Bontecou of the Civil Rights Section, she commented wryly that "more enlightened district attorneys has [sic] gotten me spoiled in believing that district attorneys really do mean to uphold labor's rights and do not think the CIO is a subversive organization." Hall was clearly not such a district attorney.[22]

Still, some Department of Justice officials did take the protection of the organizers' civil rights seriously. One such was Neil Andrews, of Atlanta, Georgia. When Mason complained to Rotnem that organizers in the mill village of Ellijay, Georgia had been savagely beaten by a mob led by the local sheriff, Andrews was asked to investigate. He went immediately to Ellijay, saw the mayor and the chief of police, and warned them that if there was further interference with the rights of labor to organize, they would certainly risk prosecution. T. Hoyt Davis, of Macon, Georgia, was another federal district attorney who usually acted swiftly and firmly on her complaints. When she told him in March 1944 that the police in Albany, Georgia, were preventing union meetings, he promptly investigated and assured her within a week that there would be no more trouble from that quarter. Davis did what he could, too, to ease the situation at the Milledgeville ordnance plant during that particular crisis. As a result of his efforts three of the men who had attacked the organizer, Starnes, were placed under peace bonds. Such officials did make it worthwhile always to appeal to the Justice Department, as stronger action than that taken by Toxey Hall sometimes resulted. Her faith in the federal government's commitment to guaranteeing the legal and civil rights of CIO workers, though often shaken, was never completely destroyed.[23]

Lucy Mason's activities as a public speaker explaining CIO policies and programs were unaffected by the war. Indeed, she was more in demand than ever as the CIO was increasingly charged with lack of patriotism and "hindering the war effort." Again, it was on college campuses that she spoke most frequently. Her regular reports to Haywood usually mentioned at least one speaking engagement on a campus, often before a church-affiliated society or group. One such visit, to Vanderbilt University, in January 1943, actually involved her in a lively though brief controversy. She had been invited to address several classes there on the churches and labor unions during Vanderbilt's "Religious Emphasis Week." During discussion following one class, several antiunion students attacked her, focusing particularly on the race issue and accusing the CIO of having "stirred up the Negroes, and gotten them out of their place" so that they "would not cook and do housework any more." She opposed them cautiously but firmly and thought no more about it till a letter in the university's newspaper appeared denouncing her as a "labor monger" and claiming that radicals like her "had no part in what should have been the most revered week of the Vanderbilt curriculum." Indeed, 300 students eventually signed a petition attacking Religious Emphasis Week on the grounds that its organizers permitted the expression of "injurious" racial, social, and political views under its guise. The *Nashville Tennessean* reported on January 30 that the university's chancellor, O. C. Carmichael, had decided to investigate certain aspects of the week following the petition but that most faculty and students seemed to think it had been a great success.[24]

Mason was concerned at the controversy she had caused, though buoyed by the public and private support she received from members of Vanderbilt's faculty. George N. Mayhew of the university's School of Religion, for example, stated that the furor reflected "both the intellectual immaturity of many of our students, and the failure of our university to acquaint them with the actual world they are living in." He believed that the week was one of the best things that had happened to Vanderbilt in recent years. In a public telegram to the *Nashville Tennessean*, Lucy Mason regretted the lack of awareness, on the part of some Vanderbilt students, that most churches, including the Methodists, Episcopalians, and Baptists, had endorsed labor's right to organize. "I believe," she continued,

> that the greatest wealth of the South lies in developing its resources and increasing the skills of its workers of both races. Also that the higher economic status won for labor through organizing adds to the South's wealth. I believe in democratic and representative government in which all citizens share through the ballot. I take my religion most seriously and always have struggled to live as nearly as I could in accordance with the teachings of Jesus Christ. I talked about these things at Vanderbilt.[25]

Privately she expressed shock at the students' attitudes, and worried that the controversy might hinder her effectiveness on other campuses. To one critic she pointed out that, as this was the "first college in where [sic] a reaction of this kind occurred, I confess I think the onus lies with the social, religious and economic attitudes of the students more than upon the speakers." At the time Vanderbilt was an extremely conservative campus. She had often spoken there during her years with the Consumers League, but since she had joined the CIO, "not a professor of the many formerly inviting me has dared ask me to speak to one of his classes." She need not have worried that the controversy would have any wider repercussions, as she continued to have more invitations to speak than she could possibly accept. Nevertheless, labor was a sensitive issue in the South when even Lucy Mason could be deemed a radical, a "labor monger," and an advocate of subversive and unpatriotic views.[26]

Other aspects of Miss Lucy's work which continued during the war included her regular newspaper bulletins on CIO activities and her radio broadcasts. Indeed, the broadcasts grew in importance. In most of her radio talks she emphasized the CIO's contribution to the war effort. In a broadcast she made in Greensboro, North Carolina, in 1943 on this theme, for example, she stressed the need for unions in modern industrial life, spoke of the example of "our splendid ally" Great Britain, with its enlightened attitude to unions, emphasized the support of most churches for labor, and praised the "miracles in getting out war production" that were being performed by the CIO. The main theme in Lucy Mason's wartime radio broadcasts rarely altered. Continually she stressed the patriotism of the CIO, its commitment both to the war effort and to shared American values, an emphasis easy to understand in a region where so many of its inhabitants harbored the deepest suspicions about the labor movement's ultimate loyalties and intentions.[27]

She continued to write for journals and magazines whenever she could. For the most part she produced shortish pieces for regional church or college papers, but occasionally she did some more substantial work. One such, "The CIO and the South," which she published in April 1944 in the highly respectable journal the *South and World Affairs,* was widely reprinted. In it, after surveying the growth of industrial unionism in the region, and pointing to the shift in public attitudes which now meant the CIO representatives could appear on "a college campus, [or] before a civic association or ministerial union," she went on to argue that the growth of labor unions led to greater community involvement generally. "Industrial unions," she said, "have made better citizens and better co-operators for war and peace," and black southerners had particularly benefited from the "experiments in education and democracy" which labor unions clearly engendered. "The mere business of running meetings and conducting union affairs contributes to this education," she stated confidently. In summary, she argued that the benefits of the CIO to the South and to all southerners had been entirely positive. "It often seems to me," she concluded, "that these national unions are doing more to unite the South with other sections than almost any other factor. Common national interests, common ideals for lifting the living standards of the submerged masses . . . , these draw together working people. . . . Beyond that, unions are coming to share the dream of Vice-President Henry A. Wallace for a world in which all people, everywhere, shall have more of the things that make life worth living."[28]

In such articles, and she wrote many, Lucy Mason gave the clearest expression to her ideal that the CIO was one aspect of a broad democratic movement stemming from the New Deal which would help create a more egalitarian, juster society, without revolution or violent social change. The South, she was sure, would become part of this democratic consensus, and the CIO would lead the way to a more thoroughgoing American welfare state. There was hardly a hint of Marxist influence in her social thought; rather it was derived from the most traditionally American of sources. Many of her CIO colleagues, if not Marxists, at least acknowledged their debt to Marxist analysis in helping shape their social views. Not so Miss Lucy; whatever egalitarian notions she held came straight from her progressive, Christian background and her total commitment to the attitudes and tendencies which were articulated in the New Deal of Franklin Roosevelt.

Again, the importance of the social gospel notions she had carried with her throughout her life cannot be stressed enough in explaining the wellspring of her social and economic thought. To say that she was not influenced by Marx is not to say that Lucy Mason and women like her were comfortable with unregulated and unrestrained capitalism. Obviously they were not. As McDowell has noted, they believed that excessive acquisitiveness "violated the principles of the kingdom of God they were

trying to extend," and they were "distinctly uncomfortable with an economic system that seemed to reward raw greed." If, like Marx, they considered unregulated capitalism to be unjust, however, unlike him, they
did not believe that change would come only through conflict. Quite the
contrary; the system could be changed, injustice could be rooted out, the
Kingdom could be extended in the social and economic spheres through
peaceful means and through established American practices and traditions. Surely Franklin Roosevelt's New Deal was proof of this point. In the
past, Mason's social gospel convictions had always enabled her to transfer
her sacred concerns readily to a secular setting. They did not fail her in
this instance.[29]

Moreover, in her optimism, in her faith in a New Deal future, and in
her conviction that the CIO had a vital part to play in that future, Miss
Lucy was at times prone to ignore the continuing realities of southern life
and to exaggerate the pace and the scope of change. True, the CIO had
made considerable advances, and there had been change, but as the postwar years were to show so graphically, much remained the same. The new
day, which in her articles she called close at hand, remained a long way
off. Hers were affirmations of faith, not statements of reality.

A large amount of straight publicity work remained to be done. In September 1942, for example, Philip Murray decided to make a southern
tour, culminating in a rally to be held in Atlanta on September 27. Miss
Lucy was given the job of organizing all the publicity and, indeed, of
making the arrangements for the Atlanta meeting. She immersed herself
in it, even refusing an invitation to lunch at the White House because of
it. She would "love to come," she replied to Mrs. Roosevelt, but could not
because of the Murray visit. "All of the publicity, invitations, liaison work
etc. has been my job," she wrote, "even the decorations and the music. It
looks as though we are to have the most significant labor meeting ever
held in the South." Certainly, she was tireless in her checking and re-
checking of the arrangements and was effective in persuading a number of
influential public figures, including Georgia's governor-elect Ellis Arnall
and Ralph McGill, the editor of the *Atlanta Constitution*, to participate at
the rally, which, according to Mason at least, was "a glorious success."
Murray, Miss Lucy said, captivated all who heard him and received widespread and favorable press coverage. "My highest hopes for the good that
a visit from you would accomplish have been fulfilled," she told him. The

CIO president, for his part, paid fulsome tribute to her organizing skills and indeed to the general value of her work. She was "one of the most able and sincere members of our staff," he told Margaret Fisher.[30]

One aspect of Lucy Mason's work which did not diminish as a result of the war was her function as a political lobbyist at the state level on labor matters. If anything it increased, as state governments, claiming to use the wartime emergency as their justification, pressed ahead with "right to work" and other antilabor legislation. In January 1945 a committee of the Georgia House of Representatives actually favorably reported a proposed right-to-work amendment to the state constitution by a vote of 19 to 16. Miss Lucy immediately went into action, swamping state politicians from Governor Arnall down with information to the effect that the amendment ran contrary to several federal laws and would inevitably be challenged successfully in the courts if it passed. The fact that the legislation went no further was doubtless due to a number of factors, one of which, according to the governor at least, was the vehemence of her fight against it. Arnall, who opposed the amendment, depended on her for material to use in the fight against its proponents. Similar amendments were defeated in Arkansas, Texas, and Tennessee at the same time, and she was active in each state. Defensive political lobbying was always an important part of her work.[31]

Miss Lucy also worked to secure the election of local and state candidates considered favorable to labor. She threw her support behind Ellis Arnall's Georgia gubernatorial campaign in 1942 and was thus bitterly disappointed when he allegedly made a statement which condoned violent action against blacks attempting to counter southern segregation. She took the Bill of Rights seriously, she admonished him, and said that it frightened her "for the future of democracy when public officials, or men aspiring to public office, threaten action in defiance of law and the Constitution." She hoped that in future he would rather speak of the maintenance of justice and civil rights as part of his concept of government; she warned him that her continued support would depend upon his response.[32]

His answer was quick in coming. He did not believe in violence, Arnall told Miss Lucy, but rather "in civil rights under the Constitution and the laws of this State." The statement attributed to him had been erroneous, he said. She felt sufficiently mollified. Given his support of labor's interests, she continued to work for his election and understood the speed of his response as indicating the importance he placed on having her with him.[33]

In the same primary season she was asked to go to Virginia and campaign against the powerful and reactionary congressman Howard W. Smith, who was currently under challenge from Emmet Davison. She refused, not out of any regard for Smith, whom she considered as "reactionary as any man in Congress and a bitter foe of labor," but because she did not think much of Davison either. Besides, she knew Smith's district well. She had friends and family there, including her brother-in-law, all of whom thought, she said, that "I had lost my mind when I came with the CIO." She believed she had more influence in Atlanta than in that part of her home state, and at sixty years of age, she was disinclined to put effort into a manifestly lost cause. Nevertheless, the fact that she was even asked is indicative of her value as a political campaigner on labor's behalf.[34]

During the 1944 campaign season, most of her political activity was bound up with that of the PAC. The PAC of course enabled her to synchronize her CIO work with the broader cause of creating a liberal South. In particular, she was able to fuse her job and her commitment to the Southern Conference for Human Welfare, without doubt her most important connection outside the CIO. Until her ultimate rupture with the SCHW in 1947, she believed that it represented "the best instrument for creating a democratic South," and she worked constantly to bring the two bodies closer together. She kept Haywood and Murray apprised of the SCHW's activities and always in the most positive of terms. "There was a quality of earnestness and conviction about it that was simply great," she reported to Haywood on the initial meeting of the Georgia SCHW. "It thrilled me deeply. We are touching tap roots of democracy in this state and are going to release new forces for good and right. And our unions are going to go along with us in confidence and enthusiasm." The fusion of aim between CIO and SCHW was a prime reason why she found the 1944 election campaign such a positive experience.[35]

An additional reason was that the SCHW included within its ranks the people closest to her in personal terms at this time. There was Josephine Wilkins of the Georgia League of Women Voters, who had become a close and valued friend. There was also Lillian Smith, at whose camp for girls she spent several weekends. Then, too, there was Margaret Fisher. Of all the relationships Lucy Mason was to make during her years with the CIO, that with Margaret Fisher was to become the most important. She had first met Margaret, who came from Andrews, North Carolina, in 1941 when Margaret was in her early twenties. She was the contralto soloist in the church Miss Lucy attended, and indeed, the older woman confessed that it was her beautiful voice "that first attracted me to her." Before long, despite the difference in ages, they had become firm friends, finding that they shared a common commitment to fighting for a liberal South. Soon Lucy Mason was referring to Margaret as her "adopted child." Margaret became quite simply the center of her personal life, in what was easily the most significant relationship she had formed since Katherine Gerwick's death. Lucy became involved with all aspects of Margaret's life and refused for example, to attend the CIO's regional convention in 1942 because Margaret was in a fragile emotional state after an "overwhelming personal loss." On another occasion Lucy arranged for Margaret to meet Mrs. Roosevelt so that she could fulfill "one of her dreams." It was the first of a number of such meetings. Lucy's attitude toward Margaret was exactly that of the proud mother she felt herself to be. She was "the sort of young person Mrs. Roosevelt likes," she told Malvina Thompson in seeking the initial interview for Margaret. "She has a keen, quick mind, wide social sympathies and such marked ability that I predict she will be one of the outstanding women of the South."[36]

Not everyone had such a high regard for Margaret. Virginia Durr, for example, remembered her as a "rather large and rather loud" young woman with a distinctly self-righteous streak about her, but Lucy Mason, like most mothers, could find no fault in her. Lucy followed her protégée's career with intense interest and promoted it where necessary. When Margaret became regional liaison officer between the War Manpower Commission and the FEPC, Lucy Mason was quick to inform Mrs. Roosevelt of the promotion, as she did when Margaret left the WMC to join George Mitchell's staff on the Southern Regional Council. "The very fact that Margaret immediately wanted you to know of her new and challenging work is testimony to what you mean to young women with vision, imagination, and courage," she told the First Lady, expressing the hope that Margaret would be able to see her "from time to time . . . as something in her work will be of interest to you." To Philip Murray she proudly described the organizational meeting of the Georgia state branch of the

SCHW, the Committee for Georgia, as a triumph for Margaret's administrative and social skills and predicted a successful future for the committee, given that Margaret had agreed to become its full-time secretary. Her
pride and obvious love for Margaret and involvement in her life filled the
emotional void that had been with Lucy Mason since Katherine's death so
many years before.[37]

During the war years her friendship with Margaret Fisher blossomed
into a sustaining and close relationship. She formed another warm personal association with Bernard "Buck" Borah, the young southern director of the Amalgamated Clothing Workers of America. During her first
five years with the CIO she had had frequent contact with him, and this
she maintained by mail after he volunteered for military service in 1942.
Indeed, throughout 1943 she battled on his behalf in an effort to get him a
commission, yet again enlisting Mrs. Roosevelt's aid in so doing. Borah,
then attending officer candidate school, she wrote her in January 1943,
was unjustly suspected of leftist leanings because his first wife had been a
member of the Communist party for a few months. The taint was likely to
interfere with his commission, even though he had not known of the affiliation until after the marriage had ended. Could Mrs. Roosevelt do anything to help? Later that year, after Borah had written that he was unable
to become an officer because of his membership in the CIO even though
he had received an FBI clearance, she wrote to a number of influential
people on his behalf, again including Mrs. Roosevelt, pleading for presidential intervention. Allan Haywood took up the case with the Department of War, and Mrs. Roosevelt, too, promised to take action.
Eventually, after almost a year, the pressure, initiated by Miss Lucy, had
its effect. In December 1943, Borah was summoned to Washington, was
interviewed by a special military tribunal, and shortly afterward was sent
to officer training school. He was commissioned in May 1944. Though
Mrs. Roosevelt's intervention in the case was doubtless of prime importance, it is nevertheless true that Buck Borah owed his commission
above all to his friend Lucy Mason and her determination to see justice
done.[38]

Buck Borah wrote frequently to Lucy Mason. His long, newsy letters
spoke of his training, discussed more general issues, and at times let her
know how much he valued her work and her friendship. "The year in the
South was made easier because of the work you did," he wrote on one

occasion. "Often in specific situations the job would have been impossible without your help." The letters she treasured, and their friendship grew even stronger. She felt no alarm when he wrote in August that he was in hospital for routine thyroid surgery, nor was she surprised that in the course of the letter he talked, not only about the CIO and its future, but also about God, religion, and death, affirming his love of life. "A man who loves men and loves life," he said, "and loves justice—then to this man life becomes more important than death, and he must strive to be good and build goodness on earth." They had often had such conversations, usually when driving together to some union meeting or trouble spot. It was natural that he should seek to continue them, even when separated physically from her, especially now that he had some leisure time to do so.[39]

Yet within a week Buck Borah had died of unexpected complications following surgery. Utterly bereft, Lucy wrote Eleanor Roosevelt for solace, sending her a copy of Borah's last letter. "You know the pure joy our young friends can give us," she mourned. "Watching them learn and grow and expand is a wonderful experience." Now he was gone. Though she could not think of him as dead, believing as she did "that life goes on in unbroken continuity beyond what we call death," nevertheless his earthly loss was a deeply painful experience for her. Mrs. Roosevelt wrote to comfort her. "It is indeed sad to lose a young life which had so much promise," she agreed, but she was glad Lucy had faith that there was unbroken continuity. Despite such sympathy the loss remained hard for Lucy Mason to bear.[40]

If Margaret and Buck were the two people most important to her at this time, other contacts which she maintained gave her pleasure. Her sister, Ida, had had two children, Landon and Charles (Sonny) Burke, who were now grown and wrote often and warmly. "You must be doing an awful lot of work for one human being," remarked Sonny on one occasion, "especially as you are getting on in years. Lucy, aren't you *ever* going to stop working and just sit down and relax?" Landon often called her "Loocy" and teased her gently. "Don't go marrying any Norwegian on us," Landon once admonished her, referring to an occasion when Lucy had reportedly squired a visiting Norwegian labor leader around Atlanta. Lucy kept in regular and warm contact with other relatives, too, including cousins such as Major L. M. Blackford, a doctor in a military hospital in Italy, who violently opposed the CIO, the New Deal, and just about everything she stood for. "I am resigned to four more years of your friend FDR," he once wrote, no doubt with tongue in cheek, "but I still wish his wife would meet with a fatal accident in the near future."[41] Loved friends, and continuing family relationships, then, helped make the war years in Atlanta as fulfilling for her personally as they clearly were professionally. As the war drew to a close, Lucy Mason, like most other liberals, looked to a continued and expanded New Deal and FDR's leadership as well as to a new world order based on his "four freedoms." Thus the sacrifices of the past years would be vindicated. The CIO would certainly be in the vanguard of this reaffirmation of democracy, which, she confidently expected, would finally bring social and economic justice to her beloved South.

7

Operation Dixie

The CIO emerged from World War II twice as large as it had been in 1939. Its dues-paying membership had increased from 1,838,000 to 3,937,000. It had helped reelect the president in 1944. Its officials had worked closely with the federal bureaucracy throughout the conflict while at the same time defeating dissidents within its ranks. It had, in effect, achieved during the war a degree of legitimacy, of acceptance, and could reasonably consider itself part of the national consensus.[1]

Yet, as Lichtenstein has observed, its leadership in 1945 felt far from secure. Roosevelt was gone, and after his death, many of his most experienced advisers and officials departed, leaving the whole issue of the CIO's relationship with the White House and the Democratic administration to be renegotiated with an inexperienced and little-known chief executive. Moreover, peace brought serious new problems and potential sources of conflict between labor and management as issues postponed during the wartime consensus could no longer be ignored. They were issues which the problems of reconversion from a wartime to a peacetime economy exacerbated. The CIO prepared itself for a new wave of conflict with an aggressive managerial class, confident in its wartime prosperity and in the attendant climate of government-business amity, hopeful of rolling back some of the gains labor had made during the previous decade. The CIO leadership anticipated a fight simply to maintain the position it had recently achieved within the industrial system.[2]

One of the means used to maintain this position was to increase membership. Given that the region where unionism was weakest was the South, it was natural that the CIO should seek to increase its strength there. Despite wartime gains, most southern workers in 1945 remained unorganized. Textiles, for example, the region's most important industry, remained only about 20 percent organized in 1946, and the position was even weaker in other crucial areas. The result was that both the AFL and the CIO decided to mount drives to organize the South.

The CIO named its drive "Operation Dixie." Van Bittner of the Steelworkers was appointed director, with six assistants and an advisory Southern Organizing Committee headed by Allan Haywood. Twelve state directors were appointed, with regional and area directors under them. In order to counter AFL charges that the CIO was filled with Communists and foreigners, more than 85 percent of the Operation Dixie staff were native southerners. It was, said Philip Murray, "the most important drive of its kind ever undertaken by any labor organization in the history of the country."[3]

Important it certainly was, yet from the beginning there was trouble. Money was always short, there was continued tension at the top, particularly between George Baldzani of the Textile Workers, one of the assistant directors, and Van Bittner. When in 1949 Baldzani defected to the AFL, he effectively destroyed Operation Dixie. Indeed, more effort from then on went into keeping what the TWUA had gained than in organizing new locals. Moreover, the growing Cold War mindset in the United States which in time was to split the CIO internally also worked against the organization in what was politically the most conservative region of the country. Constantly beset with charges of Communist domination, the organization found itself after 1949 always on the defensive. Operation Dixie was officially terminated in 1953, though it had actually puttered to a halt two years before. It was hardly the success its organizers had hoped for. Though total membership did increase during the years 1946–1951, and important gains were made in such industries as steel, rubber, and packinghouse workers—and even in textiles—in 1953 the bulk of the South's organized workers remained outside the CIO. Indeed, as Ray Marshall notes, while the AFL's share of the South's total union membership increased between 1939 and 1953 from 62 percent to 64 percent, the CIO's share had declined from 23 percent to 20 percent, and the bulk of this decline had occurred in the postwar period. In 1953, of course, as in 1946, most southern workers remained unorganized. Operation Dixie would seem to have been a failure. Certainly Marshall thought so.[4]

Barbara Griffith, too, in her excellent study of Operation Dixie, talks

Philip Murray, CIO president, pictured with Miss Lucy in 1946 during an Atlanta rally where he was the keynote speaker.

about its failure. "In the end, calm and quiet closed over Operation Dixie," she writes, "leaving the South, to all appearances, pretty much as it had been before." Business domination of the economy continued, textiles remained largely unorganized, and southern workers were still the nation's lowest paid and most exploited. If the aim of Operation Dixie had been to change the southern industrial system, then clearly it had not succeeded.[5]

Yet both Griffith and Marshall also note that many of those who participated in Operation Dixie are much less ready to accept this judgment of failure. Marshall quotes a former member of the Southern Organizing Committee as saying that the drive "had to take place," given labor's position in the South, and notes that a number of the region's labor leaders in the 1960s were initially brought into the union because of it. Griffith shows that even the modest gains of Operation Dixie were eroded in the years that followed, but she too quotes the views of the participants, many of whom she interviewed nearly forty years later. For them, despite the relative lack of measurable success, the effort had still been worthwhile. Each generation had its last frontier, said one, and "for the old CIO guys," theirs was Operation Dixie. As Frank Parker, an Alabama CIO organizer, said, "I lived through the whole thing. . . . And I'm happy they came. I'm happy they helped. But it could have been better."[6] The drive clearly did not achieve what it had set out to do; the strength of antiunion sentiment in the South and the sheer power of the opposition were too great. Yet perhaps the presence of the organizers exerted an effect on the lives of southern workers, albeit fleetingly—the sense that there were people who cared for them and who wished, against all the odds, to redress the balances between capital and labor in their favor—that might make the conclusion that it failed completely seem too simplistic. To quote one of Barbara Griffith's informants from Georgia, "Operation Dixie *did* do good!"[7]

Whether or not Operation Dixie was a failure, it certainly absorbed the time and the energy of a large number of people, one of whom was Lucy Randolph Mason. Her job under Operation Dixie was initially little different from what she had always done. She was to go into communities before the organizers arrived and prepare the way for them, seeking to allay fears, to prevent confrontation, and to warn of the consequences of illegal action. It was a task with which she was already quite familiar. Thus she continued to investigate charges of the violation of the civil rights of organizers and to report these to the Department of Justice for action when necessary. When the sheriff of Claiborne County, Mississippi, attempted to intimidate striking woodworkers in the small town of Port Gibson by threatening to "shoot their damn heads off" and assaulted several strikers in the process, Miss Lucy was quick to refer the matter to Theron L. Caudle, assistant attorney general, with a request for immediate action. In this event there was an uncharacteristically swift response. Department of Justice officials visited the town, and harassment ceased.[8]

In August 1946, recognizing her expertise and experience in the field of civil rights violations, Van Bittner asked her to concentrate her activities in this area. For the next two years she did little but travel about the South, usually at the request of the state Operation Dixie directors, attending to such matters. The testimony of these directors, together with the demands they made on her time, indicates the importance of her work. "Lucy Mason took care of our civil liberties matter in Canton, North Carolina," reported that state's director to Van Bittner in 1946. "She visited United States District Attorney Henderson's office and after long conferences worked out the matter with the United States District Attorney agreeing to write to the Mayor of the City of Canton demanding that our organization be given the right to distribute literature. I think this was a job well done and handled very efficiently by Miss Mason. Our troubles in this city are now cleared up."[9]

In January 1947, Paul Christopher, the Tennessee state director, wrote thanking her for the "fine work" she had done in three Tennessee towns. A few months later he was urging her to go to Tullahama, Tennessee, to "take on" the sheriff and chief of police there. Ernest Pugh, the Virginia director, in April of that same year sent her what amounted to an SOS. "You are needed in Pulaski, Virginia," he wrote, "and I mean needed desperately." He wanted her to come immediately to assist in a delicate lockout situation. She was unable to do so. She had been promising for weeks to go to four different towns, three in Georgia and one in Tennessee, she said, and these must remain her first priorities, given that the pressure of work on her was so great and that she had repeatedly been forced to postpone an earlier promised visit there. She was, in fact, never able to respond to all the requests from organizers for her time during these years. That she was able to satisfy as many as she did is a remarkable tribute to the stamina and commitment of a woman who, after all, turned sixty-five years of age in 1947. [10]

One of the toughest towns she had to work in at this time was the small southeastern Georgia town of Tifton. Her activities there indicate both her approach and the opposition she often confronted. She was asked to go to Tifton by G. H. Hathaway, southern director for the United Packinghouse Workers of America. The Packinghouse Workers, whose membership was predominantly black, had been on strike at the Armour plant just outside the city limits for seven weeks. There were allegations that the sheriff, his deputies, and the city police had been systematically violating the civil rights of the striking workers. Accordingly, Miss Lucy was asked to investigate.

She arrived in Tifton on May 2 and immediately began work. She talked to workers who claimed to have been assaulted by the sheriff or his deputies, including Andrew Rittey, a black man who had been so savagely beaten that both his eyes were completely closed and his "face badly swollen from jaw to forehead" when Lucy Mason saw him. Next she saw the deputy sheriff, John Duffy, "a man of most extreme stupidity and ignorance," who flew into a rage, advanced on her, and roared at her to stop meddling in what was none of her business. He was, she told Abbot Rosen of the Justice Department, of "all the unpleasant persons I have ever met, . . . probably the most so." The chief of police, whom she saw next, was intelligent and polite but "exceedingly anti-union." He categorically denied having intimidated any strikers. In any case, he said, the Armour plant lay outside his jurisdiction. [11]

Next she filed her report with the Department of Justice, requesting an immediate investigation, "lest there be bloodshed," with the black unionists as the victims. That night, she and others patrolled the Negro district of the town in CIO cars, as did the sheriff and his deputies. No incident occurred, however. There was an investigation by the FBI, the sheriff was warned, and the strike was eventually settled. The workers went back on the job. Miss Lucy's intervention may well have prevented further violence and even death. [12]

The scale of Miss Lucy's activities in towns such as Tifton at this time earned her, for the first time in her life, some national publicity. There was a long article in the *Week,* a Miami-based periodical. "Send for Miss

Lucy," which Van Bittner liked very much, emphasized her aristocratic lineage. "Ed." Townsend did a piece on her for *Business Week,* "Southern Blue Blood for the CIO," and Lawrence Lader wrote a lengthy article for the *New Republic* in January 1948 entitled "The Lady and the Sheriff." Lader's piece focused particularly on her struggles with local law enforcement officials regarding the civil rights of organizers. Calling her "the CIO's No. 1 trouble-shooter," Lader described her bravery in facing "tough-fisted sheriffs" in tense and violent situations. In so doing, he emphasized two of the keys to her success apart from her obvious courage. These were her lineage and, even more important, her sex. The potential for violence was so great in these southern towns, Lader argued, that "big, strike-hardened organizers" could not be sent there. Miss Lucy was different. "After all, who'd hurt a little, white-haired old woman?" Lader may have somewhat exaggerated the potential for violence in southern labor situations, though it was always real enough. He was, however, absolutely right when he suggested that Miss Lucy's sex and her appearance enabled her to go places and to say and do things no male organizer would have been permitted to say or do. It was her greatest single asset. The other was her lineage. As Milton McKaye remarked in an article on Operation Dixie for the *Saturday Evening Post,* "Any Southern editor, however hard-boiled, will think twice before he ejects from his office a representative, as Miss Mason is, of not one but two of the first families of Virginia."[13]

Miss Lucy had probably never been busier than she was in the first years of Operation Dixie and was probably never happier in her work. "God bless you Molly—especially for your all important part in opening the various doors that led me to the CIO," she wrote her friend Molly Dewson in May 1947, a letter that amply attested to the fulfillment she found in her job. Yet the pace and the scale of her activities were beginning to take their toll. She was, after all, an elderly woman. Toward the end of 1947 she began to complain of physical aches and pains. She could not go to Buena Vista in southern Georgia to investigate alleged police intimidation of striking black lumber workers, as Paul Christopher had requested. The reason was that she had hurt her right knee "and nearly put it out of commission on the picket line and tramping the little towns of Cordele, and before that Cuthbert"—in itself a comment on her energy and commitment. She reminded Christopher, however, that most routine violations of the law by police officers or members of the sheriff's department could be handled by telephone and confirmed by telegram or letter. She was now disposed to respond in this way more frequently in order to conserve her dwindling physical resources. She had worked out a formula for such eventualities, she told Christopher. "It must be an officer of the law," she wrote, "not just thugs or even a mob." A telegram should then be sent immediately to Turner Smith, the new chief of the Department of Justice's Civil Rights Division, with whom she had developed a fine working relationship, requesting an immediate investigation "of denial of civil rights by so-and-so," accompanied by a clear statement of just what had happened, signed by a person "who actually knows what has happened, or learned it first hand from a reliable party on the scene." If the particular United States district attorney was "good," then a similar telegram should go to him. This procedure did the trick in many cases, especially given Smith's sympathetic position on the rights of labor organizers. Certainly it saved her hours of increasingly tiring travel and confrontation.[14]

Nevertheless, she could not cut out all travel, and it was clearly becoming too much for her. In August 1948 Paul Christopher again asked for her help, this time to go to Morristown, Tennessee, to investigate alleged civil rights violations there. Again, she was forced to refuse. "Late in July," she told him, "I spent two intensely hot days walking the streets of Pell City, Alabama, and got a mild case of heat exhaustion." Her doctor immediately ordered her to take a break. She had done so and had come back "feeling fine." As soon as she had begun to walk around in the heat again, however, "my head got dizzy all over again." The experience had repeated itself the day before. Reluctantly, she concluded that she was no longer physically able to make long, tiring trips. In the future she would have to leave much of the investigation of civil rights violations to others. She did so, but Lucy Mason did not give her civil rights work away entirely. Indeed, at the age of seventy she walked a picket line in Thomasville, North Carolina, where she had gone to investigate alleged interference with the civil rights of striking furniture workers. After 1948, however, the bulk of her effort went into less strenuous activity.[15]

In 1946, John Gates Ramsay, director of church and community relations for the United Steelworkers, had been appointed to Operation Dixie as a liaison between churches and the Southern Workers Organizing Committee (SWOC). Ramsay had been born in Oklahoma but had spent most of his working life in the steel mills of Bethlehem, Pennsylvania. In 1936, he joined the SWOC and soon became its public relations representative. In an effort to combat opposition to labor from religious leaders, Philip Murray asked Ramsay, a devout Presbyterian, to concentrate exclusively on church and labor relations for the CIO. This was to be his task when he joined Operation Dixie. Though he was called director of community relations, his emphasis was to be on working with church people and particularly ministers, trying to ameliorate to some degree their often violent antipathy to the CIO.[16]

Among the first people he contacted when he came south was Lucy Randolph Mason. He wrote to her early in 1946, telling her of his new job and asking how to arrange a luncheon in Atlanta between "fifteen clergymen, interfaith, and fifteen labor leaders." The group should be interracial, he insisted; if a luncheon was not possible, an afternoon meeting would suit. Mason replied that she would be happy to work with him on such a meeting but had a few suggestions of her own to make. She thought twenty would be a more appropriate number of men to invite to the meeting, but she thought it would be "well to ask a few outstanding church women leaders" also. Did Ramsay not agree? He did, and the lunch went ahead with some women guests. In such ways Lucy Mason supported the cause of women's rights whenever she could—which, of course, in the masculine world of industrial unionism was not as often as she might have liked. This was the first time Ramsay and Miss Lucy had worked together. They liked each other, understood each other, and soon became firm friends. Indeed, Ramsay recalled, Lucy Mason was almost one of the family in those years. Increasingly, as the responsibility for checking civil rights violations proved too much for her physically, she put the bulk of her efforts into supporting Ramsay in his task of attempting to bring labor and organized religion together.[17]

A considerable amount of the work she did with Ramsay still involved field trips, but of a much more leisurely and far less confrontationist kind. She would visit communities on his behalf, contacting as many of the local ministers as she could, and in particular those of prominence in the local ministers' association. She spoke to them about labor matters in general and tried to persuade them to invite Ramsay to their community to speak to them or to hold a joint meeting with representatives of local labor organizations. Between 1948 and 1950 she visited scores of villages and towns for this purpose and, as usual, sent Ramsay detailed reports on each one, commenting on each clergyman she talked to and estimating the extent to which it would be valuable for Ramsay to visit the community. During a week in Staunton, Virginia, in October 1948, for example, she spoke with 13 Protestant ministers (all white, as the Negro ministers could not join the ministerial association), plus the local president of the Girl Scouts Association. She found most of them friendly, and some, such as the minister of First Presbyterian, Dunbar H. Ogden Jr., were extremely liberal. Dr. Ogden had recently left the Ministers Association because of its segregationist policies. He was definitely okay on labor, she told Ramsay. So was the president of the Ministers Association, Reverend John Sawyer of the United Brethren, who had a number of prominent local union people in his parish. Unfortunately, he was unwilling to ask his association to meet with Ramsay as a body, though he would be glad to see him personally. Mason said she was unable to budge him on this. As the other ministers would not move without him, she considered the visit to have been less than successful despite the general goodwill she had encountered.[18]

Other visits ended more positively. Twelve ministers in Greenville, South Carolina, agreed to attend a meeting with Ramsay after she had visited the town. Only the parson of a mill village Church of God refused to see her. In May 1949 Lucy and Ramsay organized a successful religion-labor fellowship meeting in Birmingham, Alabama. Here twelve "good union folk" sat down at lunch with twelve of the city's clergy and then heard an address from Ramsay on Christianity and labor, aimed at showing that there was no disjunction between the two. Not all the union representatives came from the CIO. Both Ramsay and Miss Mason aimed to attract as wide a cross section of the labor community to these affairs as possible, and on this occasion AFL people were present as well as representatives from the independent Mine Workers, all of whom "were really interested, even the miners." The lunch was a success in large part because of Miss Lucy's careful planning. To many in the labor movement this sort of activity must have seemed peripheral, yet in the South, with its deeply religious tradition and the authority accorded the minister in most Protestant denominations, labor could expect to make little headway without the support of the churches or at least their neutrality. In this context, their efforts had a considerable degree of relevance.[19]

In addition to visiting ministers and arranging fellowship meetings between churchmen and unionists, Ramsay and Lucy Mason produced a
number of pamphlets and leaflets emphasizing that it was the official policy of most Christian denominations to support labor's right to organize.
Perhaps the most important of these was *The Churches and Labor
Unions*, compiled initially by Lucy Mason in 1945 before Ramsay's arrival
but updated frequently by them both and very widely distributed
throughout the South. This six-page leaflet contained statements from a
number of church groups, usually culled from official proceedings such as
that of a recent meeting of the Presbyterian Church of the United States,
Synod of Tennessee, stating that "the Right of labor to organize and to
bargain collectively with employers is clearly an inalienable right in a
democracy and has so been recognized by our government. Surely the
church can do no less than to recognize these rights and uphold labor as it
seeks to exercise these rights." The pamphlet quoted the official policy of
the Congregational Christian Churches, which stood for "the replacement of the autocratic organization of industry by one of collective effort
of organized workers and organized employers."[20]

Also included were statements in support of labor's right to organize
from a number of the region's leading clergymen of various denominations. There was the view of the Reverend Lee C. Sheppard, a leading
Baptist pastor from Raleigh, North Carolina, that "we should regard as
suspiciously un-American any idea or movement which would hinder la-
boring men and women from organizing to secure decent wages and living conditions for themselves and those who follow them." Reverend
James A. Crain, of the Disciples of Christ, expressed his concern "over
attacks on organized labor by groups and publications that masquerade
under the name of 'Christian', but which in fact have no connection with
the churches and do not represent the convictions of the great body of
American church-men and women." No organization or publication, he
warned, could speak for the churches of America without authority to do
so, and most of the larger denominations had already endorsed collective
bargaining and had developed close and friendly relations with the labor
movement. "Leaders of reactionary anti-social and anti-labor crusades
should be challenged to show by what right they identified their movements with Christianity," he concluded.[21]

Ramsay and Miss Lucy both regarded the revision and widespread distribution of this pamphlet as being of the utmost importance. Miss Lucy was always trying to add new denominations, sects, and individuals to the list, and used all her charm and tact in the effort. She was particularly concerned to secure an endorsement from the Church of God, which was strong in the mill villages. "Gentlemen," she wrote to the Executive Council in June 1948, "Having met a number of your ministers in my travels through the South, I have a high regard for the quality of leadership and a respect for those I meet who are in charge of your local churches." They were invariably in sympathy with the aims of the CIO, she said. What she wanted was a general statement of support from the church's governing body, which she would then include in *The Churches and Labor Unions*. Eventually, such a statement did come. The church's general overseer responded that it was friendly to labor unions. Delighted, Miss Lucy included the statement in the revised edition of her pamphlet. [22]

The Reverend Crain in the pamphlet had decried antilabor groups and publications which claimed to be Christian but which in fact had no official church connection. One of Lucy Mason's tasks in her later years with the CIO was to expose these. She went about it with a will. In particular she was concerned to destroy the influence of two papers which circulated widely in the mill villages and were virulently anti-CIO. One, edited in Columbus, Georgia, by the self-styled "Parson Jack" Johnson, was called the *Trumpet*. The other, *Militant Truth*, was a Chattanooga, Tennessee, publication backed by a considerable amount of right-wing money. Both published a constant stream of anti-CIO invective.

Of the two, the *Trumpet* was probably the more extreme. Its issue of November 14, 1946, for example, was entirely devoted to attacking Operation Dixie and castigated the ministers in Columbus, Georgia, for allowing Ramsay to address them. The *Trumpet* was always an irritant to the CIO, partly because textile manufacturers often distributed it free to their workers until the National Labor Relations Board ruled in 1949 that it was an unfair labor practice to do so. After Miss Lucy had exposed "Parson Jack" as a liar for falsely claiming to be an affiliated Baptist minister, however, his credibility was somewhat reduced, even among the mill workers to whom the paper was directed. Later, he became an organizer for the Ku Klux Klan. [23]

Militant Truth was perhaps the more influential even though it, too, was eventually denounced by the NLRB as being antiunion and employers were enjoined against distributing it to their workers. The publisher, Sherman Patterson, however, had the financial support of enough southern textile manufacturers for him to mail the paper direct to any worker in a plant the CIO was planning to organize. Moreover, the paper was occasionally able to affect respectability. For this reason Lucy Mason and other CIO organizers were distressed when, in October 1950, a sermon by the young Reverend Billy Graham, already an evangelist with a considerable national reputation, appeared in its columns, surrounded by the usual anti-CIO propaganda. The potential damage of such an association was considerable. Miss Lucy desperately tried to see the Reverend Graham in order to secure a public denial of any antiunion sympathies.

She was eventually granted five minutes of the busy man's time. He told her that he had never heard of *Militant Truth* and that the sermon had been reprinted there without his knowledge, but despite her continued requests he refused to make a public statement. Rather Graham and his public relations man gave her what she described as "a complete run-around." Indeed, Mason and other CIO officers were forced to repair the damage as best they could by contacting liberal syndicated columnists such as Drew Pearson and Tom Stokes, providing them with information on *Militant Truth*, and asking them to use it in their columns. The information showed, among other things, that one of the paper's regular advertisers was Joe Kamp of the Constitutional Educational League, one of the nation's most outspoken anti-Semites, a supporter before the war of numerous quasi-fascist organizations, including the Silver Shirts and the German-American Bund, and an outspoken admirer of Adolf Hitler. Few of the journalists could use the material, however, and in any case, it was a poor substitute in the South for a statement from Graham himself. *Militant Truth* continued to attack CIO activity in the region throughout the decade.[24]

In 1950, both Ramsay and Miss Lucy devoted considerable time to procuring statements from as many sects and denominations as possible on the need for interracial cooperation. These they collated and published in 1951 in a form similar to that used for *The Churches and Labor Unions*. The new leaflet was entitled *The Churches and Brotherhood*. It included a wide variety of statements. There was a resolution of the Southern Baptist Convention that "the Convention recognize its responsibility for the promotion of inter-racial goodwill, and urge upon our Baptist people and all Christians the duty of ordering our racial attitudes and actions in accordance with Christian truth and Christian love." There was a statement from the Discipline of the Methodist Church, adopted in 1948, that all church meetings should henceforth be integrated and "that we individually and wherever possible, collectively stand for equality of political franchise and of economic and educational opportunities for all races." There was a commitment by the church of the Brethren, adopted at its annual conference in 1950, that the church "unhesitantly" supported equal rights, "regardless of race and ancestry." The statement further insisted that "people of all races should be freely welcomed into the membership of any and all congregations with no requirements or restrictions other than those ordinarily asked for anyway." All the statements in some way or another involved support for interracial cooperation. The pamphlet was widely distributed especially among unionists in an effort to lessen some of the prejudice against integrated locals in the South.[25]

The effort that Miss Lucy and Ramsay put into this pamphlet marked the end of their sustained work together. By March 1951 she was talking about imminent retirement, as even the relatively relaxed field trips she had to make in the course of her work with Ramsay were leaving her exhausted. She mentioned this possibility to Dick Conn, a publicity director for Operation Dixie, who immediately envisioned her writing an autobiography describing her fourteen years with the CIO. John V. Riffe, Operation Dixie's new director, was equally enthusiastic, and they made her an offer. She would remain on full salary, free from all other duties, and would be given all possible assistance, including stenographic services. In return, she would work full time, setting down her story. Initially, she was reluctant. She could not write, she said, but eventually she changed her mind. Soon she was telling friends that she was "more interested in this than I have been in anything for a long time" and was anxious to get to work. So developed the idea for what was to become *To Win These Rights*, which was to occupy her almost totally for the next eighteen months.[26]

Miss Lucy approached her new task, characteristically, with a will and initially enjoyed it immensely, especially the renewing of contacts with literally scores of people to whom she had once been close in the course of seeking information on which to base aspects of her tale. She even wrote

to Mrs. Roosevelt, telling her all about the project and asking permission
to use some of the stories in which she had been involved. She found the
business of arranging her material, however, completely beyond her. "I
am pretty well worn down trying to do this strange job," she wrote, much
discouraged, to Paul Christopher in September 1951, "for I never wrote
before and am dumb at it. I can only set down the facts. Well, if I can't get
a publisher it has at least been good discipline for my soul." Still, she was
making little headway, her health was suffering, and when, in January
1952 the book was still incomplete, she was ready to give it up, completely defeated by the task.[27]

Fortunately, a boost to her morale and practical assistance were both
close at hand. Harper and Row, having read some of her drafts, agreed
tentatively to publish the work if she could provide "a better organized
story." Her old Richmond friend George S. Mitchell, now with the Southern Regional Council and based in Atlanta, agreed to work with her regularly until the job was done. With his aid, she at last made progress.
Mitchell called in every day on his way home from the office and spent a
couple of hours with her, reading her drafts, commenting on them, and,
most important, bringing some sort of order to the mass of material she
had produced. His involvement was decisive. With him to guide her,
Miss Mason found the work "fun instead of labor," and the completed
manuscript went to the publishers in late February. The task, however,
had absolutely flattened her. "I am worn thin and shrink from any work,"
she told Aubrey Williams and indeed was ordered away by her doctor for
a period of complete rest as soon as the book was finished.[28]

To Win These Rights was eventually published in October 1952, complete with a brief but gracious foreword from Mrs. Roosevelt paying tribute to Miss Lucy's courage, acknowledging the importance of her work,
and saying how "proud" Mrs. Roosevelt was to have known her. The book
itself was partly autobiographical, partly a tribute to the men and women
with whom she had shared so much during her years in the CIO, and
partly an expression of faith in the continuing potential of liberal democracy to create a better future. It was well received and had gone into a
second printing by July 1953. Miss Lucy enjoyed all the attendant publicity and particularly the favorable reviews she received in many newspapers and journals. The *Atlanta Constitution* gave her several columns,
Ed. Townsend, in the *Christian Science Monitor* called her "a very real

Miss Lucy pictured in January 1952, shortly after signing a contract with Harper and Row to publish *To Win These Rights*. (*Winston-Salem Journal and Sentinel* photo.)

legend," and of course the Richmond papers made much of her. The CIO Organizing Committee gave a reception in her honor, at which she was photographed autographing copies of the book while an admiring John Riffe stood by. Most of all, she was gratified by Mrs. Roosevelt's foreword. "I am grateful to you beyond measure," she wrote, "very humbly thanking God that through our friend Molly Dewson we came to know each other. I cannot think of anything that would be better than what you have so generously and frankly written. It is just like you—so kind, so gracious, so untiring in the cause of democracy." Lucy Mason retired from the CIO as an employee as of February 1, 1953, at the age of seventy. She left on a note of triumph.[29]

Lucy Mason was less involved with Democratic party politics and campaigns in the years after the war than she had been in 1943 and 1944. Her work with Operation Dixie left little time for PAC activities. Indeed, the political activity in which she did engage was more on behalf of the SCHW and its state affiliate, the Committee for Georgia, than the CIO. She became extremely active in one campaign on the CIO's behalf, however. When Robert Ramspeck, the Georgia moderate and House majority whip, announced on New Year's Day 1946 that he had decided to vacate his seat midterm, Mason was very much involved in the choice of his successor. She and Ramspeck were good friends. Indeed, when he told her he was planning to leave Washington, she said the CIO would miss having him there. He was, she said, "the only member of the entire Georgia delegation with whom I could talk frankly and count on your understanding, even when we might disagree on a measure." She determined that labor would have some say in deciding who followed him.[30]

The context in which the election would be held was complex. First, the United States Supreme Court, after years of dispute, had unequivocally ruled that the southern Democratic "white primary," the only real contest in the one-party South, violated the Fifteenth Amendment. This decision paved the way for an increase in black voter registration, particularly in urban districts such as Ramspeck's, which included much of Atlanta. Second, Georgia state politics, and its attendant complexities, became crucial in determining who should succeed him. Ramspeck himself had presumed that his executive secretary for seventeen years, Thomas L. Camp, would take the seat. Camp was well known in Georgia, was widely respected, and was well liked by the state's most powerful political figure, former governor Eugene Talmadge.[31]

Talmadge's dominance had recently been challenged, however, by the current governor, the liberal Ellis Arnall. For Arnall simply to nominate Camp to fill the vacancy, as he was initially expected to do, would be to concede to the Talmadge camp an important political office without a fight. Accordingly, the governor quietly encouraged the candidacy of Helen Douglas Mankin, the New Dealish state representative for Fulton County, which included much of the Atlanta metropolitan area, as a challenger to Camp. Mankin had built a reputation in the Georgia state legislature as an opponent of Herman Talmadge, as a supporter of the liberal Arnall, and as a friend to labor. Moreover, she had welcomed the Supreme Court's ruling on the white primary. Lucy Mason had known her since she had moved to Atlanta and admired her politics while disapproving of her rather flamboyant lifestyle; Mankin was an agnostic who chain smoked and liked a drink. When Mankin announced for the vacancy, the CIO was quick to endorse her.[32]

The union's main contribution was to organize a voter registration drive, aimed at getting new voters of both races to the polls for the special election which had been called for February 12, 1946. Mason worked extremely hard on Mankin's behalf, and when she narrowly won the election, mainly as a result of the huge majority she gained at Ashby Street, an all-black precinct, Lucy Mason felt that the CIO could claim some credit for the victory. In speaking to James Carey, the CIO's secretary-treasurer, Miss Lucy described her as "the Georgia Congresswoman we helped elect."[33]

Mankin's triumph was short-lived. In July she lost the Democratic primary for the seat she had so recently won. Though running far ahead in the popular vote, she carried only Fulton County, one of the three counties in the congressional district, and thus became a victim of Georgia's notorious county unit system, whereby a victorious candidate had to carry the majority of the counties in the district or state, depending on the office he or she was seeking. In the November election, her write-in candidacy was turned back by a combination of legal maneuvers, intimidation and downright fraud remarkable even in Georgia. The CIO, in common with other liberal bodies like the Committee for Georgia, gave her what support it could, though it steered clear of overtly supporting the Committee for Georgia's vigorous campaign against the county unit system itself, knowing full well that many of its members supported it. The forces against Mrs. Mankin were too powerful, however, and she never held public office again. Lucy Mason would remain vitally interested in politics, but the Mankin campaign was the last one in which she would become actively involved.[34]

Writing about her personal life at this time, Lucy Mason said: "About my hobbies, I don't have any spare time to speak of. My friends are great joys, and I know they are there, real and sure, even when I don't have time to see much of them. I love reading—particularly good novels—but rarely have time to read anything but papers, articles and books on labor and economics." Lawrence Lader described her three rooms in the Myrtle Street apartment as quiet and lined with books. And it is indeed quite obvious that Lucy Mason continued to be so active that there was very little time for her to experience the loneliness of a solitary old age.[35]

Of those closest to her, clearly the most important remained Margaret Fisher, who since early 1945 had been executive secretary of the Committee for Georgia. Increasingly Miss Lucy spoke of the two of them as a team. "Margaret and I think very highly of Stetson [Kennedy]," she wrote Mrs. Roosevelt in 1946. Indeed, in many ways they were a team. She gloried in Margaret's activities on behalf of the committee, and proudly told her friends about them. "Our Margaret has done a job that makes her friends who know about it immensely proud of her," she wrote Mrs. Roosevelt as Margaret Fisher battled the county unit system. In the most obvious sense, Margaret had become central to her life.[36]

In May 1947, Margaret returned to her hometown of Andrews, in the North Carolina mountains. She was not in the best of health, and it was thought the mountain air would be beneficial to her. Moreover her family needed her desperately. Her father had become incapacitated, and there was no one to take over the family drapery business. She had to go. Miss Lucy was bereft. The two women nevertheless continued to see each other frequently. Lucy often drove to Andrews for the weekend, and they always took their holidays together. Moreover, each Sunday without fail Lucy Mason called Margaret to share the week's news. Margaret often came to Atlanta to shop for her store, and she naturally always stayed with Miss Lucy when she did so. Their relationship survived physical separation, and the two women remained extremely close for the rest of Miss Lucy's life. [37]

Other friends, such as John Ramsay and George Mitchell, helped fill the gap left by Margaret's departure. In addition there were visits to her family, much less frequent now but just as enjoyable when they occurred. Miss Lucy had seen all her nephews and nieces, she told Brownie Lee Jones after one such visit. "All of these young people met me with open arms and made my evenings and visits with them most happy." She grew old alone but was not necessarily desperately lonely. [38]

She stayed in contact by mail with friends from other days. Molly Dewson wrote frequently from her retirement cottage in Penobscot, Maine, and the two of them discussed all manner of issues. "Hello Lucy, you old now or never woman," began one such letter in 1951 before launching into a long disquisition on communism. "Every corpuscle in my body goes against the basic idea of being handed a party line and nailed to it. . . . The world is too closely knit and so large, socialism just could not work out. Democracy has many weak spots and bad performers here and there but it is in tune with the aspirations of man and his nature." The two of them continued to swap views and experiences for as long as Miss Lucy was able to write. [39]

Finally, there was still Mrs. Roosevelt. Though the two women rarely saw each other after Mrs. Roosevelt had left the White House, Miss Lucy continued to write to her regularly, sharing news, seeking her advice, occasionally asking her help. "It was a blessing under the providence of God that you were a President's wife," she told Eleanor Roosevelt in 1951, "and then became 'the first lady' of the world when he was gone." Miss Lucy continued to ask her help in all manner of labor matters, at times seemingly oblivious of the fact that the former First Lady now had a greatly diminished ability to shape events. Thus in November 1945, when Miss Lucy wrote, asking for assistance in a civil rights case in Columbus, Georgia, Mrs. Roosevelt replied, promising to do what she could but warning her, "I have no great hope that it will have any influence." Lucy did not seem to hear, or if she did, it did not matter to her. She continued to treat Mrs. Roosevelt, not only as a symbol of all that was good in the world, but as someone who could always be of real help. And perhaps she always was if only through inspiration. Eleanor was, after all, in Miss Lucy's view, "one of the two or three greatest people in the world." As a

One of the last pictures of Miss Lucy, taken in March 1952 after she received the annual social justice award from the National Religion and Labor Foundation. On her left is Allan S. Haywood, CIO director of public relations.

result it was probably more important to maintain the contact than to believe that Mrs. Roosevelt could continue to influence events as she had formerly done. Yet from time to time she was still able to help. "Our Eleanor Roosevelt has been the greatest help to me in my civil rights job," Miss Lucy told Molly Dewson as late as 1951, "and helped protect such rights for many a man being knocked around by the sheriff or police. I have grown to love her deeply and wish there was more time to see her."[40]

In March 1952, the National Religion and Labor Foundation, a small ecumenical body aimed at reconciling the interests of labor and the churches, honored Lucy Mason and her work by presenting her with its annual Social Justice Award. The accompanying citation spoke of her as embodying "at one and the same time the voice of the church speaking to the ranks of labor and the voice of labor speaking to the church." It praised the way she had translated her religious faith "into a life of service on behalf of unionism, social justice and human rights." In a very real sense," it concluded, "your life is your message to America and to the World." Allan Haywood made the presentation at the foundation's convention, and in his speech noted that Mrs. Roosevelt had won the award the previous year. To be following in the footsteps of the woman she admired most was probably the greatest satisfaction Miss Lucy gained from the occasion. As she looked toward retirement, the award must have seemed a fitting capstone to her career. Certainly it was a recognition of the social gospel notions which had always underpinned her public life.[41]

8

The Liberal Cause

The CIO, and through it her aim to bring social change to the South, was Lucy Mason's work and became her life. Most of her activities were carried out under its aegis. Yet she was connected to other institutions and groups, all of them aiming in some way to bring change to the South. To these she gave as much time as she could, sometimes reinforcing the work she was doing with the CIO but sometimes going beyond it. Through membership in these groups, too, she was able to take her place in the region's wider liberal community.

One such body was the Southern School for Women Workers. The Southern School was very much an outgrowth of the same impulse which led to the development of the YWCA's Industrial Department. It was founded by Louise Leonard McLaren and Lois McDonald, both former YWCA industrial secretaries for whom, in the words of Mary Frederickson, "the YWCA provided an arena within which they could glimpse a vision of the humane and co-operative society." From 1927 till 1951, a period during which it operated more or less continuously, the school offered short courses for female industrial workers, the vast majority of them tobacco or textile workers from the North Carolina piedmont. These courses were normally taught in the summer. The school sessions were residential, and the curriculum stressed involvement with contemporary social and political issues. Increasingly the students came as representatives of their unions. Though, from 1938 onward, men were enrolled as well as women, it remained nevertheless in administration and in outlook primarily a women's organization, providing, in Frederickson's apt words,

"young workers from textile, garment and tobacco factories with the ana-
lytic tools for understanding the social context of their lives, the opportunities to develop solidarity with one another, and the confidence for full
participation in the emerging southern labor movement."[1]

Inevitably, given Mason's background, her attitudes, and her friendship
with both of its founders, she would be drawn toward the summer school's
activities. As early as 1933 she had been invited to become a member of
the school's advisory committee. Though she had felt unable to accept at
that time because of the "demanding and absorbing nature of her work
with the Consumers League," she nevertheless expressed her interest in
its activities.[2] Once she had moved to the CIO, she became much more
closely involved with it, giving courses entitled "Unions and Legislation
in the South" and participating, along with other representatives of labor,
in seminars and panel discussions. By July 1939 she had joined the
school's advisory committee and shortly afterward became a member of
its executive board, serving as treasurer in 1944. She remained on the
board until the school closed in 1951 and regularly attended board meetings.[3]

Her connection with the summer school became particularly close in
the years following Louise McLaren's retirement in 1944. McLaren was
replaced by none other than Brownie Lee Jones, with whom Lucy Mason
had worked years before at the Richmond YWCA, where Brownie Lee
had been industrial secretary. The two women had remained friends, and
through her Lucy was drawn closer to the work of the summer school.
Brownie wrote to Miss Lucy constantly about the school's policies and its
problems, and Mason always did her best to help. In the years after the
Second World War, the school fell on increasingly hard times, primarily
because more and more unions preferred to run their own worker education programs rather than send their members to places such as the summer school. Money became increasingly tight and the school's activities
became correspondingly restricted. Lucy Mason, therefore, early in 1948
"made a silent promise" to try to raise part of its budget. She wrote scores
of letters to college presidents, philanthropic agencies, and her liberal
friends, seeking financial support. That the school was able to survive for
another three years had much to do with her energetic fund-raising
activities.[4]

Miss Lucy was able to help, too, in another way. As the peace of 1945 was replaced by the tensions of the Cold War, fringe institutions such as the Southern Summer School were easy to tar with the Communist brush. Even presumed allies within the labor movement attacked them. Each time Miss Lucy vigorously defended the school. Thus she reacted angrily in December 1948 when W. A. Copeland, the CIO's Memphis director, reportedly called the school Communist. "When I recall the invaluable work Miss Jones did for PAC in Virginia in the last Presidential campaign," she reproached him, "and how she worked on registrations in Danville and elsewhere, it makes me pretty hot for some one to flippantly state that the school is left-wing. If you knew Miss Jones and the excellent board of directors, you would know this was false and very unjust." Copeland duly accepted the rebuke but countered some of her allegations. As far as possible, she worked extremely hard to protect the school and her friend Brownie Lee from such attacks. Mason stayed involved with the summer school until its demise in January 1951. She was saddened to see it close, although she saw that its end was inevitable, given the dwindling union support. It had brought together two of her longest and most deeply held concerns, the growth and development of labor unions and labor consciousness and the provision of opportunities for personal growth to southern working women. Small wonder that she mourned its passing.[5]

Miss Lucy still had an interest in worker education, however, through her long involvement with the Highlander Folk School in Monteagle, Tennessee. Highlander was probably the most important of the Left-liberal community schools to operate in the South, and certainly it was the most long lasting. Its founder and guiding light from 1932 until 1973 was Myles Horton. Horton, the son of Tennessee sharecroppers, had had a background in YMCA work and had attended Union Theological Seminary in 1929, where he was deeply influenced by Reinhold Niebuhr. In 1931, he traveled to Denmark to study its famous folk school system and returning to the United States, determined to open such a school of his own, where he could teach the poor people of the South what they needed to know to control their lives. The right opportunity came in 1932, when Lillian Johnson, the daughter of a Memphis banker who had turned her back on the lifestyle of a southern belle, asked him to take over a school she had established in Monteagle, Tennessee. The result was Highlander.[6]

From the start, Highlander's program was heavily labor oriented, and it

Miss Lucy during one of her frequent visits to the Highlander Folk
School. She is pictured here in 1948 discussing aspects of her work
with three young CIO local officials.

became even more so once the CIO had been formed. From the midthirties onward and throughout the war it was almost exclusively a labor school. Working primarily with the CIO, Highlander began to offer short courses and workshops sponsored by individual unions that wanted their members to absorb not only the general labor outlook found at Highlander but also specific skills such as grievance handling and organizational and administrative procedures. Its extension work was expanded to include full educational programs for unions in their home areas. It was, in short, an essential adjunct of the CIO's southern wing and indeed a focal point for southern liberals. Most of them—people like Aubrey Williams, Clifford and Virginia Durr, and James Dombrowski—had close connections with Highlander, and so, of course, did Lucy Randolph Mason.[7]

Lucy Mason's association with Highlander began almost as soon as she joined the CIO. No sooner had she taken up her new post than she had established an active liaison with the school. She sent promising young unionists there and addressed students as a guest lecturer. She was elected to the Highlander Executive Council in 1939, a position she held until her retirement. She rarely missed a meeting and participated actively in debates. She was particularly vocal on matters of fund raising. She constantly stressed the need to raise more money from other than labor circles, from "the outside, liberal non-union people. The leisure group," as she once termed them. She also insisted on the need for Highlander to cooperate closely with other bodies with similar aims, such as the Southern School for Women Workers, and on the need to maintain the closest of relationships with the CIO. Her own sense of commitment to Highlander was reflected in a motion she sponsored successfully at a council meeting in January 1948 to the effect that any member of the council who missed two consecutive meetings without adequate written explanations should be summarily dropped. People should not accept positions of responsibility and trust, she insisted, unless they were willing to take them seriously. She certainly took her involvement with Highlander very seriously indeed.[8]

In addition to serving on Highlander's Executive Council, Lucy Mason was also a frequent and popular participant in its workshops and seminars. "Your talk was very well received by our students," Dombrowski wrote her in 1939, after she had addressed a summer school colloquium. Her statement in 1952 that she had participated "in many of the CIO schools in Monteagle," was probably as accurate an assessment as she could make of her involvement in Highlander's program. She had spoken there so often that she could not recall every particular instance with precision. She loved going to Highlander, not only for the company and the reinforcement, but also because of its physical beauty and its peacefulness. The school was set high in the Tennessee mountains. As Miss Lucy grew older, she was sorry to find that for health reasons she could visit it less frequently, particularly in the colder weather. "It makes me sad to say so," she wrote Josephine Wilkins in 1952, "but my times for staying at Highlander in cold weather are over—reason, arthritis and other physical liabilities—and I hate to think this." Highlander, the place and its people, was a very important part of her life.[9]

Lucy Mason was one of Highlander's most assiduous fund raisers. She wrote lengthy letters to wealthy liberals, her "leisure group," extolling its virtues and asking for financial support. "I think the School deserves the support of all of us who have a concern for a strong and responsible labor movement. More and more it has become a real workers' education center," she told Florina Lasker in 1943, in one such appeal. Many responded, including Mrs. Roosevelt, who created a scholarship fund there and joined Highlander's national sponsoring committee. Anthony Dunbar argues that her support was due in large part to her affection for Lucy Mason. Certainly Miss Lucy was assiduous in keeping the First Lady fully aware of the school's activities. "You will remember asking me to keep you informed about Highlander Folk School," read one such report. "I have just come back from a week-end conference there of the School's Executive Committee, and can make a report with the utmost enthusiasm." There followed a detailed account of the school's activities and tribulations, political and otherwise. "Some day I hope you can visit the School and see for yourself what is being done. It is undoubtedly one of the most useful institutions in the South and I hope its work will be progressively broadened and strengthened as the years go on."[10]

Given her enthusiasm for Highlander and its work, her distress when the CIO and the school parted company was intense. As in the case of the Southern School for Women Workers, the issue had to do with Cold War tensions. By 1949, the CIO, itself becoming increasingly anti-Communist, insisted on a statement from Highlander opposing communism as a condition of further union involvement with it. This statement the executive council refused to provide, stating that it wished to retain a positive policy embracing all democratic organizations. Not satisfied, the CIO severed its relations with the school, thus depriving it of the main source of students. The rupture came as a bitter blow.[11]

Miss Lucy worked hard to avoid the split. At the crucial council meeting of November 1949, when the matter came to a head, she desperately sought a compromise, proposing that the school support an amended statement that "we oppose totalitarianism in any form, whether communist or fascist." She spoke vigorously in support of this position, warning her fellow council members that the school would have difficulty surviving a CIO withdrawal but to no avail. Her amendment was lost. The council refused to condemn communism, because, as Horton said, our position "has always been a positive, democratic one," and the CIO and Highlander severed relations. It was a trying time for Miss Lucy, but unlike other CIO members of the council, such as Paul Christopher, she did not sever her personal connection with the school and remained involved with it until her retirement in 1953. It had become too important a part of her life for her to give it up.[12]

The fact that so many of the institutions and bodies with which she was connected, and in which she so deeply believed, were dividing internally on the Communist issue made her sad. Lucy Mason was scarcely a friend of the Communists. Politically poles apart from them, she was, she once said, also "a bit gun shy" of them "because I have suffered several times from the unconscionable tactics such persons can follow in the mad pursuit of their own ends." She disliked, too, their preference for secrecy, which, she thought, often brought suspicion on innocent people. If she ever became a Communist, she said, "which is something I will *not do*," she would wear a "large button with the word Communist on it" to make it clear where she stood. She was no red-baiter either, however, and did not approve of the CIO's distancing itself from the Southern Summer School or from Highlander because of fancied Communist connections. She knew that was not the case, and it distressed her that, at a time when liberals needed unity in the South as never before, they were instead dividing.[13]

Nowhere was this fragmentary tendency more apparent than in the last years of the life of the Southern Conference for Human Welfare, another liberal organization with which Lucy Mason was closely connected and to which she devoted an extraordinary amount of time, effort, and emotional energy. George Tindall called the SCHW "the one regional group that ever effected a broad coalition of liberals and radicals." Its origins are still shrouded in a certain degree of mystery, but it is generally thought to have stemmed from twin roots. One was Franklin D. Roosevelt, who in March 1938 seemed to presage a major liberal drive in the region when, in a speech in Gainesville, Georgia, he attacked anti–New Deal southern politicians, blaming them for the South's economic and cultural backwardness. Thereafter the National Emergency Council investigated the South. Lucy Mason was an adviser and in the report characterized the region as the nation's "number 1 economic problem." Roosevelt endorsed the report, advocating legislation to rectify the inequalities it cited. These activities greatly encouraged the region's liberals, both within and outside the administration. Mason wrote to FDR after the Gainesville speech to say how much it had meant to her just to feel that he understood her frustrations and supported her efforts. She was particularly thrilled that he had quoted her two relatives George Mason and Edmund Randolph in the address. Liberals, then, stood ready to respond to the president's call.[14]

The second original base of support for the SCHW came from a more radical source. In 1936 Joseph Gelders, southern secretary of the National Committee for the Defense of Political Prisoners, and a man very close to the Communist party, if not a member of it, was kidnapped and brutally beaten in Birmingham, Alabama, during an organizing drive among the ironworkers there. This outrage brought Gelders a certain degree of national attention and a substantial amount of sympathy from the region's liberals, including Lucy Randolph Mason. Thomas Krueger, the SCHW's historian, says that early in 1938 Gelders discussed the idea of a regional conference on civil liberties violations with Lucy Mason and that she subsequently arranged for him to meet Mrs. Roosevelt and, through her, the president. Both Roosevelts, it is said, encouraged Gelders to press ahead with such a conference, and he returned to the South determined to arrange one.[15]

Krueger's version of the sequence of events, including Miss Lucy's role in arranging a crucial meeting with the White House, has become generally accepted. Lucy Mason may well have played such a part; certainly

Virginia Durr believed that she had. Gelders and Miss Lucy had become
friendly as a result of working together in a strike in Tupelo, Mississippi,
she recalled, and Lucy subsequently went to see Mrs. Roosevelt on his
behalf. Indeed, Mrs. Durr claimed, Lucy Mason was extremely important in uniting the two groups, "the New Dealers and the labor people
together," in what was to become the SCHW.[16] Oddly, nowhere does
Miss Lucy mention such a role, not even in her autobiography, and there
is absolutely no trace of it in her files. She did, however, have lunch with
Mrs. Roosevelt on April 23, 1938, and this could well have been the occasion on which she pressed Gelder's case. Whatever happened, it is known
that Gelders did meet with the president, that FDR endorsed the idea of
a conference on civil liberties, and that he urged Gelders to conduct a
campaign against the poll tax. Gelders returned south, consulted with a
number of the region's liberals, including members of the Alabama Policy
Committee, and arrangements were completed for a meeting. Meanwhile
the Emergency Council's *Report on Economic Conditions of the South*
appeared, and it was decided to broaden the agenda even further to include discussion of the South's "economic colonialism."[17]

On November 20, 1938, the first meeting of the Southern Conference
for Human Welfare was formally convened in the municipal auditorium in
Birmingham, Alabama. The list of sponsors and participants was impressive. Mrs. Roosevelt addressed the meeting; so did NYA director
Aubrey Williams and Supreme Court Justice Hugo Black. Senators Lister
Hill, John Bankhead, and Claude Pepper were associated with it, as were
such newspapermen as Ralph McGill, Mark Ethridge, and Virginius
Dabney. Mary McLeod Bethune and other prominent blacks were also
present. Frank Graham, already the region's most important liberal edu-
cator, was elected its first president after the inevitable decision to institu-
tionalize the conference had been taken. Many of these distinguished
southerners would soon cool to the SCHW, and some would actively oppose it, often because of one of its earliest decisions, namely a resolve that,
having complied reluctantly with Birmingham's segregation ordinance, it
would hold no further segregated meetings. Initially, however, the atmosphere was one of unity, even of euphoria. As Gunnar Myrdal was later to
write, "For the first time in the history of the region . . . , the lonely
Southern liberals met in great numbers—actually more than twelve hundred, they experienced a foretaste of the freedom and power which large-
scale political organization and concerted action give." Lucy Mason was

present and delighted in the sense of solidarity which the meeting produced. Present, too, were those who, even more than the Negro issue, were to bring about the SCHW's decline, a scattering of members of the American Communist party. Almost unnoticed in 1938, their connection, however tangential, with the organization was eventually to cost it dearly in terms of outside support and internal unity.[18]

These tensions and divisions were in the future, however. Lucy Mason, like many others, was enthusiastic about what had happened in Birmingham and was determined to make the conference a vital force in the South. "For years I have known that the South cannot be saved by its middle class liberals alone," she wrote Frank Graham, "that they must make common cause with labor, the dispossessed on the land and the Negro. At last we have had a southern conference considering human welfare which combined all of these elements. Some liberals may find it too shocking to have the other three groups so articulate about their needs. But this is the basis of progress in democracy, economic justice and social values in the South." In time, Lucy Mason, too, would find it impossible to work with some of the representatives of these "other groups," but in 1938, having been elected to the SCHW Executive Council, she was determined to do all she could to make it a positive force for change in the region.[19]

One of her concerns was to place the conference on a sound administrative footing. To this end she supported the appointment of a permanent executive secretary. A decision was taken in 1939 to appoint one. The man selected for the job was Howard Lee, son of an Arkansas sharecropper, a former theological student—and a man of whom many of the SCHW's liberal members were deeply suspicious because of his alleged closeness to the Communist party. His political affiliations were carefully scrutinized before he was hired, and eventually it was decided to take the risk. Miss Lucy was one of his supporters. Having had several discussions with him, she had formed the opinion that he was not too close to the Communists and that he would be an efficient secretary. Without such a position, she thought, the conference would collapse. Most liberals eventually supported Lee's appointment, yet the disquiet it caused was symptomatic of the tensions between right and left that would shortly limit the SCHW's effectiveness within its region and its credibility outside it.[20]

Lee's appointment having been confirmed, Mason spent much of the

next three months working with him on the organization of the next
SCHW regional conference, to be held in Chattanooga in April 1940. In
the early months of 1940 she was in constant contact with Frank Graham
about a whole range of conference matters, from program formation to
fund raising. She was particularly concerned to keep liberals like publishers Mark Ethridge and Barry Bingham, those most concerned at any
perceived left-wing drift, fully involved. She also worked tirelessly to ensure that black delegates would not be embarrassed, as they had been in
Birmingham; that seating would be on an integrated basis; and that the
city of Chattanooga would accept this arrangement. To this end she was in
continuous touch with the city's liberals. She arranged sponsors, she
raised money, and, most important of all, largely because of her insistence, Mrs. Roosevelt agreed to interrupt her schedule to appear at the
conference for one day. Indeed, as Clark Foreman admitted, Lucy Mason
more than anyone else was responsible for launching the conference in
1940. Her administrative and persuasive skills were stretched to the utmost.

Given the effort she had put into the organization of the 1940 conference, she must have been deeply disappointed by its results. The
meeting had its high points, notably Mrs. Roosevelt's appearance, but
there was also much bitterness, most of it engendered by a resolution
from William T. Couch, of the University of North Carolina Press, condemning Soviet aggression against Finland and favoring aid to the Western
democracies. There was a violent reaction from some delegates, and
Couch was even knocked away from the microphone as he attempted to
speak to his proposal. The resolution, in effect, tore the conference apart.
Liberals supported it; the CIO and Mine Worker delegates were willing
to deplore Russian aggression but were less happy about aiding the Allies;
the Socialists were wildly enthusiastic about condemning the Soviet
Union but stood equally vehemently against aid to the Allies. Only the
Communists and their supporters opposed the resolution totally. The
problems of the South were temporarily forgotten as tempers flared over a
clearly symbolic issue, one which laid bare profound ideological differences. Eventually a compromise that satisfied all but the Communists
passed overwhelmingly. It condemned all forms of aggression, Communist, fascist, and imperialist, but dropped all mention of aid to the Allies.
The conference turned back to other business, but the bitterness and

division remained. It was not possible to elect a new SCHW chairman at the meeting, so deeply divided were its members. Graham, who wanted to resign, was persuaded to stay in office for a few more months until a replacement acceptable to all factions could be found.[21]

Lucy Mason was deeply disturbed by these events. Hearing of the Couch resolution in advance, she had anticipated the worst. "Our friends from right, left and middle should have some patience about what they try to do to this gathering if they want it to become a permanent thing," she had told Lee in March. She was also most disturbed, however, at the behavior and attitudes of some of the left-wing participants at the conference. Writing to Frank Graham soon after it had ended, she suggested that Lee be replaced as executive secretary by Will Alexander in order to make the SCHW more acceptable generally in the South. Frank Mc-Callister, a Socialist SCHW member, told Graham soon afterward that Lucy Mason now believed both Lee and Gelders to be Communists. Graham agreed that Lucy Mason had been seriously disturbed by some aspects of Gelders's behavior in particular.[22]

By this time, Lucy was no longer a member of SCHW's Executive Council. Whether she had wanted to stand again is difficult to determine. She claimed she chose not to; she "had worked so hard on getting the conference to live that I thought it best to eliminate myself from any office lest it be thought I was trying to dominate too much.[23] This was, in fact, not the case. As George C. Stoney, an Executive Council member, explained, given the decision to have all groups and interests represented there, the nominating committee was unable to find a place for her: labor already had a delegate. Stoney was most unhappy at this outcome. "Think what would have happened had Miss Mason been absent from our meetings last year," he wrote Graham. "Now she will have no official position and will feel hesitant about coming. We need her badly. Also, she represents more than labor. She represents the awakened women in the South—YWCA, welfare workers, church workers—who have the courage to buck the status quo."[24]

Whatever the reason, Lucy Mason was not part of the SCHW's official structure during the next two years, years of continued internal dissension for the organizaton. Frank Graham, Clark Foreman, and others desperately sought an acceptable liberal to take over as conference chairman but to no avail. Will Alexander, though interested in the secretaryship, chose to go to the Rosenwald Fund, which offered a higher salary. He also declined to accept the chairmanship. Eventually the conference's board, in the absence of any other candidate, chose Reverend John B. Thompson to succeed Graham. Thompson, like Lee, was a man suspected by some of Communist leanings. Certainly at the same time that he became SCHW chairman he also accepted the presidency of the American Peace Mobilization, a body closely connected with the American Communist party. Prominent liberal members of the SCHW, including some of its biggest financial supporters, promptly resigned or otherwise severed their connections with it. Barry Bingham, for example, had told Graham he would leave if Thompson took over. Bingham did so, and many went with him.[25]

As Thomas Krueger writes, "During Thompson's chairmanship, the Conference remained nearly inactive, beset with financial malnutrition and obsessed with the several humors within it," its primary purposes subordinated to the desire of Thompson, Lee, and Gelders, through the American Peace Mobilization, to oppose America's growing involvement with the Allied cause in the war now raging in Europe. Meanwhile, liberals chafed and fretted, and the SCHW became hopelessly divided between isolationists and interventionists.[26]

In March 1941 the issue came to a head. Thompson and Lee cosigned a letter on SCHW stationery on behalf of the American Peace Mobilization. Though they did insist that they were doing so in their private capacities, the use of the SCHW letterhead seemed to indicate that the organization endorsed the letter. The response from those liberals remaining in SCHW was vehement. Graham was particularly outraged. In an angry exchange of letters he accused Thompson and Lee of supporting Communist causes and of risking the credibility of the SCHW in so doing. Thompson and Lee both responded equally heatedly.[27]

The dispute was eventually taken to a council meeting in May, where the interventionists clearly had the upper hand. Thompson formally apologized for having used SCHW stationery on American Peace Mobilization business. Lee concurred and offered to go on leave without pay for two months. This offer was accepted, and shortly afterward he resigned. Gelders, too, soon quit all formal association with the SCHW, while Thompson remained a figurehead chairman for the rest of his term. Admitting that he had been a poor performer, he would have preferred to quit as well, but as he told Virginia Durr, he could not "figure out any

graceful way to fade out of the picture until my successor is elected" and
therefore had to wait until the next full conference. So ended, igno-
miniously for the radicals and their allies, their period of greatest involvement in the SCHW power structure. Henceforth the liberals were to remain firmly in control.[28]

With Lee's resignation, the SCHW once again had to find an executive
secretary. Eventually the job went to James A. Dombrowski. The son of a
Tampa jeweler, he had been educated at Emory and Harvard universities
and at Berkeley and had taken a doctorate under Niebuhr at Union Theological Seminary. His dissertation, "The Early Days of Christian Socialism in America," was later published. A convinced Christian socialist
himself, he had been staff director at Highlander Folk School for ten years
before coming to the SCHW. There he had met Lucy Mason, who liked
him and was sure that, though he was on the Left, he was no Communist.
With his appointment she began to involve herself fully in SCHW activities again. She was particularly helpful in the organization of the 1942
conference, which was to be held in Nashville, and spent two weeks there
in April, assisting Dombrowski with various arrangements. "Things are
running smoothly," she reported to Graham, "the panels are well filled,
mail goes out promptly, some memberships come in, and registrations are
growing." Whatever Communist influence there had been in the organization had now been eliminated, she said, and things were on the move.[29]

Though Mason was right in her assessment of the decline in Communist influence in SCHW, not all its members were similarly convinced. In
particular, Frank McCallister, leader of its Socialist faction, came to the
Nashville conference determined to remove all traces of Communist influence from within its ranks. His views were shared by Roger Baldwin of
the Robert Marshall Civil Liberties Trust Fund, which had helped finance
the Nashville meeting. Once again there was bitterness and acrimony
over the fellow-traveler issue, both on the conference floor and in the
weeks that followed. Lucy Mason, who was now back on the board, was
particularly.incensed at McCallister's accusations, which, she said, were
completely unproven.[30]

Privately, however, she acknowledged that such allegations were not
totally without foundation. Gelders was too close to the Party for comfort,
she admitted to Dombrowski. "You will remember that I was uneasy (as
was Mrs. Roosevelt and Frank Graham) about certain people speaking at

the conference or continuing on the Board because of the opportunity given our opponents to bring charges of left-wing dominance." That had happened anyway, and all that SCHW could do now was to "look for a way to assure donors and liberals like Baldwin that Party politics do not dominate the conference, the board or the executive committee." That was never possible. Baldwin and others like him withdrew their support, convinced that the SCHW leadership did "not appreciate the risks they [ran] in collaborating closely with fellow-travellers identified with Communist Party movements." The Communist issue was the SCHW's constant cross until its disbandment in 1948.[31]

One of the positive results of the Nashville conference was the replacement of Thompson as chairman by Clark Foreman, who was to hold the office for the rest of the SCHW's existence. Foreman, born into a distinguished Georgia family, had studied at both Harvard University and the London School of Economics, had joined Will Alexander and his Commission on Interracial Cooperation, and from 1933 had worked for the New Deal as Harold Ickes's special adviser on Negro matters. With Lowell Mellett of the National Emergency Council, he had helped produce the report on the South's economic conditions which had provided part of the impetus for SCHW's first meeting in 1938. Foreman had attended this meeting and had subsequently served the organization as treasurer and as a member of its finance committee before assuming the chairmanship. A quick, aggressive, decisive man, Foreman brought a dynamism to the leadership which Thompson had manifestly lacked. Eventually, these qualities were to produce friction with the slower, more deliberate Dombrowski and tension with other council members, including Lucy Mason. In 1942, however, after the travail of the previous two years, Foreman's energy was clearly necessary.[32]

The SCHW kept a fairly low profile for the next two years. It held no major conferences or conventions save a "Win the War" rally in Raleigh in July 1942. Finance continued to be a pressing problem, despite Dombrowski's careful housekeeping, and increasingly the body depended for its survival on subsidies from the CIO. For this reason as well as because of her continued commitment to SCHW Miss Lucy once again became closely involved in its operation. She and Dombrowski were in constant touch. She performed a variety of administrative tasks for him, from redesigning the organization's nomination forms to persuading CIO people to serve on the various committees and councils. And then there was fund raising. She worked tirelessly, convinced of the need to raise money within the region. Here she was eventually to disagree sharply with Foreman, who was coming to rely more and more on the wealthy liberals of Washington and New York for financial support. Though she often regretted that she could not do more for SCHW at this time because of the pressure of her other duties, Dombrowski was in no doubt as to the value of her work. "You are the one person that I can always count on to do a job," he once wrote in appreciation.[33]

In early 1945, victory over fascism was assured, and there was a world to reconstruct. Having forged a close alliance with the CIO, which, at its annual convention in 1944 had pledged it "all positive and constructive support," including increased financial assistance, the SCHW prepared for peace in a mood of optimism. An early decision was made to set up state committees, and by the end of 1945 eleven had been created, the most active being in Alabama, North Carolina, and Georgia. The Committee for Georgia was established in January 1945. During the meeting, Lucy Mason, according to Margaret Fisher "looking precisely like an angel," disarmed critics of the move in her most southern of ways. It is scarcely surprising that, given her long commitment to SCHW, she would also become deeply involved in the Committee for Georgia, particularly with Margaret Fisher as its executive secretary. Under Margaret's energetic direction, the committee plunged into the fight for a number of liberal causes, including repeal of the poll tax, a permanent FEPC, and opposition to the state's white primary. By the end of the year, it was well established as the SCHW's most effective state organization.[34]

Miss Lucy was delighted with the committee's initial success and proud of Margaret's accomplishments within it. A letter to Philip Murray describing in detail events at the organizational meeting reverberated with joy at her friend's triumph.[35] Some aspects of the SCHW's general administration, however, were beginning to bother her. In particular she was worried by Foreman's tendency to take crucial executive decisions without adequate board discussion and sometimes without even referring them to the board. "We founder at each board meeting," she complained to Dombrowski, "trying to think out weighty and complex problems in half an hour. If the Conference is *really* to be a *membership* organization, sound and hard thinking is needed as to how to make it that way in deed and truth." Board members were often ignorant of what the issues were, and then in a short space of time had "to consider and vote on weighty matters of enormous importance to the future of the conference," she told Foreman at the same time. She was particularly bothered by his action in establishing large committees in Washington and New York and diverting funds there, without proper reference to SCHW's southern members. "I have a deep, uneasy feeling that plans are being made with too little reference to their effect on Southern membership," she warned him. She cared a great deal about the Southern Conference, she went on to say, and wanted to see it "live and grow and become greatly effective." It could not do so, however, "unless its roots are in Southern soil. Not the finest superstructure in Washington and the North can be of permanent value unless its foundations are in the every-day people down in the Southern states. It is these people that I keep thinking about and want to take along with us."[36]

Foreman was inclined to ignore her criticisms. He should have taken them more seriously. They were symbolic of widening divisions within the SCHW structure regarding future directions and also reflected growing dissatisfaction with his style of leadership, fissures which in the next two years were fatally to weaken the organization. Lucy Mason was to become a leader of the anti-Foreman group within it.[37]

Miss Lucy's growing uneasiness toward Foreman's leadership was heightened by the tension between him and the Committee for Georgia. Margaret Fisher had a strong, somewhat aggressive personality. Given Foreman's own forceful character, they were bound to clash. "We never got along too well together," he recalled later. "Margaret was very dominating, and I guess I'm very dominating." Throughout 1946 the two of them niggled over the degree of influence the SCHW executive should have in local affairs. Fisher was insistent that the Committee for Georgia should remain a decentralized, grass-roots organization. Foreman was equally insistent that he had the right to intervene in matters of local policy if he chose to do so. He was particularly critical of the committee's activities in the 1946 Georgia gubernatorial primary, believing that it should have stated publicly its opposition to the forces of Eugene Talmadge rather than working quietly in support of his opponent, J. V. Carmichael. "During the whole campaign against Carmichael," he complained to Aubrey Williams, "the Committee for Georgia was merely a

sponsoring list for the political activity of Margaret Fisher." Her reluc-
tance to involve herself in the day-to-day business of organization had
caused the committee to wither on the vine and had necessitated his intervention. The committee, he said, was being sacrificed to "the egotism
of one person." He wanted Margaret "out of the picture."[38]

Margaret responded to such criticism by resigning. Though she was
persuaded to withdraw her resignation pending an inquiry into the roots
of the disagreement, the committee, in an atmosphere of considerable
bitterness, decided in 1947 to disband. It had little choice, given Foreman's decision to withhold funds from it in the future. Lucy Mason, of
course, supported her friend Margaret throughout the disputes, and relations between Foreman and herself became correspondingly cooler.[39]

It is possible that a compromise could have been reached in the disagreement over Georgia had it not been for a much bigger dispute which
rocked the conference at the end of 1946, one in which Mason and Foreman again found themselves very much on opposite sides of the fence. It
concerned the position of James Dombrowski. In January 1946, principally because its political activities were endangering its tax-exempt status, the SCHW decided to separate its educational and political work.
The Southern Conference Educational Fund (SCEF) was created to direct
all educational activities, and the SCHW became purely a political action
organization. Foreman headed both bodies, but to all intents and purposes they were separate.[40]

The aggressive Foreman and the quiet, self-effacing, cautious Dombrowski were quite different in personality. Increasingly, Foreman had
become irritated at what he considered to be the executive secretary's
lack of drive and initiative and blamed this deficiency in particular for
SCHW's disastrous financial state at the end of 1946. Accordingly, he resolved to use the split in the SCHW's activities to remove Dombrowski.
On December 1, 1946, he suddenly presented to a board meeting from
which more than half the members were absent a plan to move Dombrowski full time to SCEF, replacing him at SCHW with Miss Branson
Price, the executive secretary of the New York Committee. The plan was
presented as necessary because the administrative work of the conference
had simply become too great for one man. Moreover, Dombrowski, it was
alleged, favored the move. The rump board, including Miss Lucy, taken
by surprise, accordingly ratified the plan unanimously.[41]

The trouble was that Dombrowski did not approve of the shift. In fact, he bitterly opposed it. He thought that Foreman had dealt with the whole matter in an underhanded way and said so. Others became similarly convinced, none more so than Lucy Mason. "The more I have thought about this during the past week, the more firmly I am convinced that a terrible mistake has been made," she wrote Foreman. "If the Conference is to continue as a useful agency in the South, I believe we must undo the wrong we have done." Arguing that both the decision and the manner in which it was taken were unsound, and accepting culpability for her part in its ratification, she nevertheless protested that "it was a great mistake to propose action on such a fundamental matter without giving the Board advance knowledge of what was contemplated and opportunity to think it through." She pointed out that the decision was taken at a board meeting with only a bare quorum present and urged that it be set aside, pending a general meeting of the board to review the situation. She sent a copy of this letter to all SCHW board members.[42]

At first Foreman was not inclined to accede to her request. "I wonder if you have forgotten how many times you and Margaret have told me that Jim was a good man but not an administrator," he reminded her in declining to review the decision. Branson Price had accepted her new position. It was just too late to do anything more. Miss Lucy would not let the matter drop, however. Her sense of justice had been deeply offended. She contacted every member of the board personally, urging them to put pressure on Foreman and keeping up her own attack on him. To Dombrowski, she wrote encouragingly of her commitment "to trying to make a little bit of democracy work. I shall not turn back from this endeavor, cost what it may."[43]

Her persistence and her pressure were successful. Foreman was eventually forced to call a special board meeting, which met in Greensboro, North Carolina, on January 5, 1947, and which reinstated Dombrowski as administrator of the SCHW. Miss Lucy's sense of justice had been vindicated but at the expense of further deterioration in relations between herself and Foreman. He had laid "the whole revolt at my door," she told Dombrowski, and was bitterly resentful of her activities, which she found sad but unavoidable. The one thing she could not forgive herself for was her "dumbness" at the board meeting when the scheme was initially proposed. Foreman remained bitter for a long time. Years later he alleged that Lucy Mason had only taken the stand she had because of her obsession to further the career of Margaret Fisher. Had he offered the job of SCHW administrator to Margaret instead of Branson Price, matters would have been different. "I think the main thing was that she felt Margaret Fisher was a superhuman person. She felt that Margaret Fisher was the person to do the job and she really felt that Margaret Fisher should have the job," he claimed. There is no evidence, however, that Lucy ever promoted Margaret for the position. It seems likely that her actions arose more from a conviction that Dombrowski had been treated extremely shabbily than from the desire to advance the career of her young friend.[44]

Whatever the reason, the tension between Foreman and Lucy Mason, who distrusted his style of leadership and the direction in which he was leading the SCHW, was one reason for her gradual dissociation from an institution to which she had devoted so much time. Another reason was a change in the CIO's attitude. The SCHW had hoped to be a crucial component in Operation Dixie. Instead, on April 18, 1946, Van Bittner bitterly denounced it, along with Communists and Socialists, as an "organization living off the CIO." Partly this criticism reflected CIO irritation at accusations from some SCHW members that the organization was equivocating on the race issue; partly it resulted from renewed CIO concern that SCHW was tainted by Communists, but mainly it was due to a recognition that the CIO did not need the SCHW. In the changed situation, with a major organizing drive concentrated in the southern states, continued financial support of the SCHW was a luxury the CIO could no longer afford. Within a year or so most CIO representatives, including Miss Lucy, had quietly withdrawn from SCHW activities, and financial support had been terminated. The SCHW's demise was of course hastened by the withdrawal of its main source of funds.[45]

For Miss Lucy, the growing estrangement between the SCHW and the CIO and the divided loyalties it engendered within her simply compounded her problems with Foreman and his style of leadership. At a board meeting on April 19, 1947, she brought matters to a head in an impassioned speech calling for a radical change in SCHW's direction. "The Conference is facing slow death at its Southern roots," she claimed. State committees were starved of funds, the whole financial structure was chaotic, and the conference was promising things it simply could not deliver. Too much control had moved from the South. The administrative

structure was top-heavy and divorced from real southern problems. The
conference could never be a mass organization, she argued; rather, its
function was as "a small, militant, standard-bearing organization in the
South." It should be indigenous to the South—"with no question about
that fact." All its officers should reside there, should serve without salary,
and should be solely responsible for policy and direction. "In fact its entire operation must be controlled within the region," she asserted. "The
charge of outside financial assistance can be offset if there is no question of
the policy control resting in the South." She went on to make certain
specific suggestions as to how the direction of SCHW could be altered in
line with her ideas and concluded by moving that her statement be included in the minutes of the meeting. She withdrew the motion after
discussion, with the privilege of bringing it up again.[46]

Nothing came of her program, which marked her last attempt to influence the course of SCHW policy. She immediately ended her actual involvement with the organization and formally resigned in October 1947,
ostensibly because, given her age and health, she needed to concentrate
her energies on her CIO work. In reality her reasons were more complex.
She disagreed so fundamentally with Foreman's policies and saw so little
chance of altering them that there seemed no point in remaining a member of the SCHW. Thus she terminated her connection with a body which
she had helped start and with which she had been closely connected for
nearly ten years. It was a sad time for her and for many people still in the
SCHW. The organization limped along for only a few more months before
quietly disbanding in November 1948, its race well and truly run. Virginia
Durr claimed that Miss Lucy left the SCHW because of the Communist
issue—she had become "nervous about Communism." There was little
truth in this assertion. Certainly Miss Lucy did not trust Communists (a
view bolstered, incidentally, by her work with them in the SCHW), yet
her fundamental disagreement with Foreman, not any fear of being tarred
with the Communist brush, caused her to quit the organization she had
served so long and so well.[47]

It was rare, during her years with the CIO, for Miss Lucy to be able to
direct her energies specifically toward women's issues, as she had during
her years with the Consumers League, for example. The nature of the job
really precluded doing so, though her work with the Southern School for
Women Workers clearly reflected her perennial feminism. Occasionally,

however, she had another chance to wave the social feminist banner. In February 1944, for example, she took vice president Henry A. Wallace severely to task for writing to the National Woman's party, endorsing the "so-called Equal Rights Amendment." Telling him of the damage such an amendment would do to "vast numbers of wage-earning women," and claiming that the Woman's party was "willing to throw out the baby with the bath and to jeopardize the welfare of countless numbers of working women," she urged him to withdraw his endorsement. To Mrs. Roosevelt she wrote of her distress at Wallace's action and asked Eleanor to make her own concern known to the vice president. Miss Lucy's views had certainly not changed, though her opportunities for expressing them had been curtailed in her new position.[48]

The various bodies with which Lucy Mason became involved outside her CIO work, of which the Southern School for Women Workers, Highlander, and SCHW are the most important examples, all complemented her activity with the unions. In their various ways, they too sought to change the South, to make it a more just, a more democratic, a more tolerant society. Her work with them and her work with the CIO were inseparable, part of the same particular dedication.

9

Last Days

Lucy Mason retired officially from the CIO on February 1, 1953, not long before her seventy-first birthday. It was her decision, she said. Her health was such that she was "not fit to go on working." She had no intention of giving up all her public activities, however, and continued to attend Highlander Executive Council meetings whenever she could. In April she even traveled to Cincinnati for the National Religion and Labor Foundation Convention, where she was a group leader. In June she was keynote speaker at the twentieth anniversary of the Michigan Consumers League, which she had helped found, and gave a speech entitled "The Consumer's League—Our Heritage." She was extremely well received. People wrote, telling her how much they had enjoyed her address, which pleased her. She found the experience extremely tiring, however, and indeed, she almost collapsed after she had finished her talk. Afterward she decided to make no more public appearances. She broke this vow only once, to take part in a Tuskegee Institute symposium called "The New South and Higher Education" in October, where again, her contribution was much appreciated.[1]

The CIO people still drew on her skills from time to time. Cary Haigler, the acting national director of the CIO Organizing Committee, wrote to her in August 1953, seeking her assistance in a dispute with the Gray Lumber Company in Waverley, Virginia. The company, which was refusing to sign a contract with the Woodworkers Union, was represented in negotiations by Collins Denny. Haigler believed him to be the son of Bishop Collins Denny, of Richmond, whom, he presumed, Miss Lucy must have known at some time or other. Was there anything she could do, therefore, to persuade his son to change his mind "and work out an amicable agreement with the Woodworkers Union?" No, she replied, much as she would have wished to, she simply was not up to it. "I at last recognise that my dream of doing much volunteer work when my paid work was over is fading out, for each time I go on a trip I am more limp and useless afterwards." "I guess the last two or three years 'got me,'" she continued. "I might be called 'an occupational hazard.' Between near heat prostration, some bad blows to my right knee, which led to arthritis, and an aversion to close reading, I am compelled [sic] much of my life in one place and without work." She hated to turn down his request, she told Haigler, but she really was, "generally speaking out of the running."[2]

Indeed, by the end of the year she was no longer even able to drive her own car. She had earlier been appointed a member of the Warm Springs Memorial Commission, an honor she valued highly. She regularly attended commission meetings, as Warm Springs was easily accessible by car from Atlanta. She would find it harder to do so in the future, she told the commission's secretary, J. E. Smessner, early in 1954, as she could no longer drive. If they wanted her, she would need to be taken down, as public transport was also out of the question.[3]

All too soon, the question of attending meetings became irrelevant. She succumbed to advanced senility. Family and friends who saw her during the 1953 Christmas season were worried by her confused state, and it rapidly worsened during early 1954. One of the last letters she ever wrote, concerning the paranormal, mirrors this state of mind. In it she discussed séances she had attended when she had talked to her dead brother, Ranny, and claimed to have "witnessed" his death in battle. The letter also indicated that she was under the impression that her father had been dead for but a few months. It must certainly have caused her nephew, to whom it was addressed, great concern.[4]

By April Miss Lucy could clearly no longer live on her own. She had little sense of where she was and spent much of her time talking long distance to Margaret, under the impression that she, too, was in North Carolina. Accordingly, her doctor, distant cousin, and friend L. Minor Blackford arranged for her to be admitted to a private nursing home. She furiously accused him of "interfering with her constitutional rights." After a week there she escaped by taxi, claiming that the gentle, middle-aged woman who ran the place was trying to murder her.

Yet she clearly needed more surveillance than the nursing home was able to provide. She needed constant care, and at times she needed to be restrained. Blackford, using his Atlanta medical connections, had her admitted to Brawners, a private mental hospital, where she was to remain for the rest of her life. He visited her regularly. Indeed, his devotion to his elderly cousin, whose politics he barely understood and certainly abhorred, impressively reflected the strength of family ties.[5]

In regular letters to family and friends Blackford chronicled Lucy Mason's swift decline. Increasingly unable to recognize anyone and completely "out of touch with reality," she was, he said in May 1954, "the most woebegone spectacle I have ever seen. My prime responsibility now is to keep her in physical comfort as long as she lives." This he managed to do. He had himself appointed her legal guardian. Margaret Fisher disposed of her friend's personal effects, for Margaret "a hauntingly painful experience." She saw it through as much as possible in accordance with Miss Lucy's wishes and also carefully went through the few files that remained in Lucy's apartment. Most of them had already been sent to Duke University. In a letter to Taylor Burke, Margaret paid tribute to Blackford's concern and devotion. "It is a merciful blessing he is in Atlanta," she wrote. "He is a distinguished doctor and a very busy one, but nothing has been too much for him to do for Lucy. There have been no limitations on time, patience or understanding. I have no words which are adequate with which to pay tribute to Minor Blackford." Lucy Mason spent her last years surrounded by love and concern.[6]

Soon she could not always recognize even Blackford, and though, as he said "her phrases and the construction of individual sentences sounded just exactly like her . . . , no one sentence had the remotest connection with the sentence that had just gone before." By the end of 1955 she was completely helpless, bedridden, and in need of constant care. Occasionally she still recognized people—she knew Margaret when she came for a Christmas visit—but usually only fleetingly. The nurses in the hospital loved her, Margaret said. Indeed they washed "out her negligees themselves rather than entrust them to the laundry." Unlike many of the other patients, she was rarely irritable, remaining, wrote Blackford, "almost all of the time in a wonderful humor" and "chuckling constantly."[7]

Soon, however, even limited awareness vanished. "Why our beloved kinsman continues to live I do not know," Blackford stated early in 1958. For several weeks she had been in a state of semi-consciousness, eating no

solid food and uttering only an occasional monosyllable. Death was imminent, he wrote Burke three weeks later. Indeed, "everything about her is
already dead," he said.[8]

Lucy Mason's constitution, however, was strong. She continued to
breathe for more than another year. She finally died peacefully and without pain on March 6, 1959, at the age of seventy-six. A week later, after a
simple memorial service held at the Ivy Hill Cemetery in Alexandria, it
was decided to institute a small fund in her memory that would enable
theological students to become acquainted with labor leaders. In particular, the money would be used to help the students attend union conventions. Given her own lifelong Christian witness, and her equal commitment to the CIO, she would have wanted no greater memorial.[9]

Epilogue

I n his foreword to *To Win These Rights*, George S. Mitchell told "the best of all the stories about Lucy Mason." It concerned her visit to a Virginia textile town, far up the James River, where she had been sent to investigate the harassment of union organizers. During the visit, she found herself arguing about civil rights with a local cattle farmer. He was far from impressed with her message. "Lady," he rudely interrupted her at one point, "I would like to ask you some questions. What's back of you? Who sent you here, and what salary do you make? And by what right do you come into the State of Virginia talking all this about civil rights?" Drawing herself up to her full height, which was not very great, Miss Lucy told him exactly who she was. Starting with George Mason, she included everyone. John Marshall, James Murray Mason, Robert E. Lee. The young man listened, now very impressed. "Madam," he said when she had finished. "I don't know what the CIO pays you, but I am sure you are worth it."[1]

Myles Horton made the same point. Recalling for an interviewer his days as an organizer, he started to talk about Lucy Mason and her lineage. "You can't get more kosher than that in Virginia," he remarked, "but she kind of had an interest in working people that most people of that kind of background don't have." He was in no doubt as to the value of her work. "When anybody would get into trouble, she would move in and help out." He went on to describe how "she could just barge in on the bishops and newspaper editors. . . . you know, she had a name that she could use. She had a way of talking to anybody that she wanted to and she would go in and pull this prestige thing and use it, just beat them over the head with it and she kind of shamed them, this white haired old lady, into stopping all their indecencies. Boy, she was a power. We would all yell for Lucy anytime that we needed help and she would come into the toughest situation and was great. She played a tremendous role, a tremendous role."[2]

The labor organizers who worked with her in the South all had their Miss Lucy stories, and there were hundreds of them: Miss Lucy trailing a gang of thugs around a Georgia mill town because she feared for the safety of a union official and believed "the mob would think twice about attacking him if an old lady was there as a witness"; Miss Lucy solemnly warning a Mississippi police chief that she was going to report him to the Justice Department; Miss Lucy driving some women organizers, threatened with floggings, around the mill village, scorning the threats and warnings of its inhabitants. The cumulative weight of such testimony is clear. Lucy Mason was regarded by those with whom she worked as an important, effective, and courageous member of the CIO's southern team. For this aspect of her work she was most remembered and deservedly so.[3]

Still, concern for labor's cause was but one of the interrelated themes that imbued and unified her public life. The others were feminist concerns and the South. Lucy Mason clearly epitomized the social feminist. From her earliest involvement with the suffrage movement, she was enlisted in the struggle to enable women to participate more fully and equally in the public life of the USA while at the same time protecting them from exploitation in a male-dominated world. Throughout her life she was constant in her advocacy of women's issues, her determination to secure protection for women less fortunate than she, and her insistence that women and men should participate equally.

It is possible that her concern for the cause of women, her consistent advocacy of their basic equality, may help explain her support for the blacks. Sara Evans has brilliantly explored the connections between feminism and a concern for racial justice. "Twice in the history of the United States the struggle for racial equality has been midwife to a feminist movement," she writes. In the abolition movement, and in the civil rights revolution more than a century later, women who began by working for racial justice ended up claiming equality for themselves. Moreover, she notes, "in each case . . . , the complex web of racial and sexual oppression embedded in Southern culture projected a handful of white Southern women into the forefront of those who connected one cause with the other."[4]

Evans observes that in both the 1830s and the 1960s southern white women first explicitly and publicly linked racial and sexual oppression. Furthermore, there were, even before the civil rights movement, a few isolated women in the twentieth-century South who transcended the constraints of class and caste and began actively to oppose their region's segregated culture. Evans names the most prominent: Virginia Durr, Anne Braden, Lillian Smith, and Paula Snelling. Smith is singled out as particularly significant for her "pioneering analysis of the intertwined racial and sexual repression in the South," especially in *Killers of the Dream*.[5] All of these women were friends of Lucy Mason's. They had worked together in various capacities, particularly in the SCHW. They shared similar values and convictions. Sara Evans could easily have added Lucy Mason to her list of twentieth-century southern women who, in opposing the dominant political culture of their region, explicitly linked racial and sexual repression.

Lucy Mason's feminism did have its limits. She never supported the Equal Rights Amendment, partly because of her commitment to protective legislation and partly because she disapproved of the strident anti-male attitudes of some of the more extreme feminists. Lucy Mason liked men. She always had men friends, and she worked well and easily with her many male colleagues in the CIO. Indeed, she may well have related more easily to them than to the female organizers. The evidence is sparse, but Eula McGill, an organizer with the TWOC and then with the Amalgamated Clothing Workers Union, was almost alone in criticizing Mason's importance in the CIO. She had had little effect on the labor movement, McGill said. "You ain't going to reach bosses that way" but through bargaining strength. Yet even McGill did not resent Lucy Mason's presence in the movement. Her work could not have "hurt us," she explained, and may even have been of some help.[6]

Lucy Mason's moderate social feminist attitudes had been forged long before she joined the CIO. Nevertheless the positive experiences she had with such men as Steve Nance, Paul Christopher, Buck Borah, and John Ramsay must surely have reinforced them. Her opposition to the extreme feminist perspective as much reflected her positive experiences with men as her fears of the consequences of abandoning protective legislation.

It may also have arisen in part from her southernness, from her easy acceptance of much of the traditions of the southern lady. In a moving obituary, Ralph McGill described her as "a very kind sweet lady, characterized, too, by all the graces of the old Virginia of plantations and the gentry." She was small, he said. Her hair was prematurely gray, she wore gold-rimmed glasses, and she blushed easily. Above all, she was "a born lady. She never had to act like one. She was one," even though she was "so sweetly unconscious of this fact." Others confirmed this judgment. A woman so obviously feminine, in some ways so much a part of her class, her region, and her heritage, would have had real problems appreciating the attitudes and perspectives of the National Woman's party activists.[7]

There were times when this southernness may have been a hindrance rather than a help to her. Erma Angevine, once president of the National Consumers League, thought that some of Miss Lucy's problems with Emily Marconnier arose from her inability to understand the viewpoint of northern women. Southern ladies like Lucy Mason, Erma said, abhorred aggression, stridency, and taking a dominant role. Miss Lucy got what she wanted all right, but she got it by "using a woman's wiles," a southern woman's wiles, not by frontal attack. Her style, Erma Angevine believed, was very difficult for people like Marconnier, accustomed to the quite different social milieu of New York City, to deal with.

There may be some truth in this view, although it was not shared by others who worked with Lucy Mason during her days in the Consumers League. Esther Peterson, former consumer advocate to the White House, who first became involved with the league in 1932, about the time Miss Lucy took over as general secretary, remembered her as a "strong" and "terrific" person. She doubted that Miss Lucy's southernness had much to do with any tension between her and Marconnier. It was more likely simply to have resulted from personal friction, she believed, something not uncommon during a period which considerably broadened the career opportunities available to women but also increased the competition between women for these positions.[8]

One thing is certain. Whether it caused resentments or not, the National Consumers League under Lucy Mason's direction was transformed from an organization that had responded principally to the concerns of the industrialized, urbanized Northeast into one that devoted more and more time to the problems of the rural, industrially backward South. Miss Lucy had accepted the position on the condition that she be permitted to effect this change in emphasis, and she consistently made it her prime concern. In her letter of resignation to Nicholas Kelley in 1937, she thanked him for providing her with "the opportunity to extend to new areas the principles and ideas to which Mrs. Kelley and the League under her leadership were devoted."[9] Lucy Mason was always a southerner. Even when she held a national office her main concern was to bring needed reforms to her region. Throughout her life, whether she was with the YWCA, the NCL, the CIO, the Southern School, or the SCHW, her aim was always to help change the South, to make its structures more democratic, more responsive to the needs and desires of ordinary southern people, black and white, and more in conformity with the ideals espoused by the southerners she admired most, Thomas Jefferson, Robert E. Lee, and, above all, George Mason. Unlike many of her regional contemporaries, Lucy Mason rarely spoke or wrote about her love for the South, about the region's tragic history, or about what it meant to be southern. She did not have to do so. Her region was part of the very fabric of her life, part of how she looked, how she spoke, part of everything she said and did.

If this driving concern to create a more democratic and decent South took her into the CIO, it also led her to support the aspirations of its black citizens for a better life. While she was with the CIO, she could say relatively little publicly about the race issue because of the prejudices of the white labor force she was trying to organize. The CIO, Miss Lucy included, was often forced to sacrifice egalitarian ideals to the realities of local custom. Yet she took quiet pride in the gains in racial understanding that the CIO had been able to promote. Indeed, in 1947 she felt justified in claiming that it had "done more to raise the economic and civil status of the Negro in the South and to improve race relations than any other organization." In states where the white primary had denied blacks access to the effective poll, the CIO unions had pressed consistently for primaries open to both races and had even led registration drives. "Many church people," she claimed, wished "that organized religion would be as aggressive and realistic as the CIO in promoting justice, citizenship and economic opportunity for Negroes." In expressing solidarity with black aspirations, she was expressing a principle to which she adhered throughout her life.[10]

Lucy Mason rarely attacked southern segregation directly, yet there is little doubt as to where she stood on the issue. Throughout her years with the SCHW, for example, she was always on the side of those who argued consistently for the fullest possible involvement for blacks in the organization. In the preparations for the 1940 conference she was insistent that blacks be included on all the discussion panels; indeed her initial enthusiasm for the SCHW arose in part from her belief that black southerners would be able to participate fully within it.[11]

Such beliefs indicate not only her solidarity with black aspirations but also one of the characteristics which impelled her throughout her public life. Lucy Mason had a deep, abiding faith in democracy and in the potential of the American system of government. In 1940, as she told Ralph McGill, this faith caused her finally to abandon her long pacifist commitment. In view of the threat confronting the world, she saw nothing else to do. Nevertheless, even the exigencies of wartime emergency should not prevent the continuance of efforts to make American democracy better. "We have got to make democracy real to make it work," she wrote, "not leave huge masses shut out of it, unable to function." She commended to McGill the maxim "Never let the lesser absorb the greater; always let the greater absorb the lesser." It had always been a guide to her. If Americans as a people could absorb this message, she believed, "we will hold to the great and real values" and survive the ordeal of war, with the nation's democratic ideals strengthened rather than set at risk.[12]

Because of this abiding faith in the eventual triumph of American democracy she embraced the New Deal enthusiastically and came to idolize the Roosevelts, for she saw them and the movement they led as having both saved and advanced the great cause, of having provided, in a time of darkness and terror, a real "light on the hill." For Mrs. Roosevelt her love and admiration verged on the adulatory. When in 1951 Miss Lucy called it "a blessing under the providence of God that you were a President's wife, and then became " 'the first lady of the world,' when he was gone," she may have been indulging in hyperbole, but she was also clearly expressing her opinion regarding Mrs. Roosevelt's contribution to the furtherance of democratic ideals in America and on the world stage.[13]

She had similar views about FDR's importance. Writing to him in 1939, after his Jackson Day address, she spoke of him as one of only five democratic national leaders who had "striven to keep the traditional faith of the Democratic party." The others were Jefferson, Jackson, Bryan, and

Wilson. She had placed him in exalted company indeed. Her "joy and gratitude" at his reelection in 1940 was, with that of millions of others, the more profound because of her conviction that it meant that the march toward a more just society which had begun in 1933 would not be terminated. In her faith in the Roosevelts, in her belief that they embodied the best of America's democratic and egalitarian heritage, in her determination to act on the ideals she perceived them as espousing, Lucy Mason was very much both a product of and a protagonist for, the New Deal's social democratic aspect. [14]

If her abiding faith in a democratic future was one of the sustaining props to her public commitments, without doubt the single most important force in her life as a whole was her Christian faith. Her own accounts of her development make this point quite explicit. Born into a profoundly Christian home, she embraced Christianity as a young child, and throughout her life her faith never wavered. She often told how, having forsworn her earliest dreams of serving God on foreign mission fields, she had decided to be a missionary for social action at home. Christianity gave her work its meaning and her life its unity.

Christianity, she said, the social gospel, both drew her to her fellow men and linked her to eternity. She realized early that, as she put it, "personal goodness is not enough. There must be a passion for social justice." Her Christian belief impelled her to fight the fights she fought, to espouse the causes she espoused, and to hold the social beliefs she held. "I cannot separate the ideal of loving God with all my being from loving my brother as myself," she once wrote, and her whole life was witness to this conjuncture. Asked to speak on a radio worship service in 1948, she took as her text the words of the prophet Micah, "What doth the Lord require of thee, but to do justly, and to love mercy, and to walk humbly with God." There could be no better exemplar of the prophet's dictum than Miss Mason herself. At times, especially during her days with the CIO, Lucy Mason doubtless despaired at the obtuseness and intransigence of some of those charged with preaching the word of God, but she never ever doubted the word itself. She was always a deeply committed Christian lady. [15]

In addition to linking her with her fellow men, Christianity gave her a perception of eternity. One of the strongest aspects of her spiritual belief was her conviction that physical death could be transcended, that the barrier it seemed to create was a false one. "In every great emotional experience, whether of joy or sorrow," she wrote in 1947, "the barriers separating me from God and man have seemed to dissolve and I have known what the words *identity* and *unity* can mean in the soul's experience. Conjoined with this experience, there is a perception of eternity, and even in the here and now I sense immortality." Twenty years earlier, in the agony of the loss of Katherine, she had jotted down these words:

> There is no Death—one Life continuing immortal, whole. Oh joy indestructible, oh happiness inviolable for those who know there is no death. . . . There is no separation, but immortal presence for those who love. There is no death, one Life, continuing, whole, eternal. Always I knew this was true, but when the door between time and eternity swing [sic] open to close again upon the Comrade of my soul, I knew it with fresh and energizing power.[16]

This belief in the essential unity of the soul's experience, in the impermanence of death, was something she carried with her all her life. Trying to explain it to the Gerwicks in 1930, she said it had originally been revealed to her by her mother. The death of little Anna, Mason's infant sister, had first drawn her mother into the spiritual world, Lucy Mason said, and in turn she too had become convinced of the immortality of the soul: "She had opened the door to me." When Katherine died ("when my Beloved left me") her mother's example "made it possible for me to accept it, and build something out of it." Throughout her life, she continued to believe that those who had died could still be reached, could still be talked with, and could still act in this world, "that life and love can pass the barriers of death." If this conviction led her into spiritualism, and even if it caused some people to consider her a little odd, it also sustained her through the crises of her life, in particular the death of Katherine, as well as helping her sustain others. The point need not be labored. It was, however, an essential component of her view of the world, and a vital aspect of her Christian belief.[17]

One other aspect of her life must be mentioned. Though Lucy Mason never married and for the greater part of her life lived alone, she was rarely lonely. She was sustained first by her family and then by her friends. There is little purpose in speculating further on the nature of her intense relationships with Katherine Gerwick and Margaret Fisher. Katherine was a life partner, even after her death. Margaret, for her part, became the daughter that Lucy Mason would otherwise never have had. There were other women friends too, however, and good ones: Josephine Wilkins, Carrie and Hermine Moore, Clara Beyer, Brownie Lee Jones, and others. Then, too, there were the men with whom Miss Lucy worked in the CIO and in the South generally: Paul Christopher, Buck Borah, Steve Nance, George Mitchell, and John Ramsay. With these men she shared both triumph and defeat, camaraderie and tragedy. Her life was filled with people, and human relationships helped give it shape and meaning.

When Lucy Mason died, Ralph McGill wrote: "It did not occur to her to be fearful. . . . She was a genuine person without guile or any deceit. And she was a great lady in the full meaning of the word." A few years later, in discussing her work with the CIO, McGill asserted that she symbolized "an awakening of Southern women to the basic problems of their communities." Moreover, when it came to ancestors, she "made all the others seem parvenus." Lucy Mason, he concluded, "was one of those symbols of conscience which the South continually has produced in time of need."[18] His words have in them much truth. Through her work, through her life and its example, the region, and indeed, the United States, can learn much about its recent past—and its best self.

Notes

Preface

1. *Charlotte* (North Carolina) *News*, August 15, 1946.

1. A Virginia Girlhood

1. Lucy Randolph Mason Papers, Perkins Library, Duke University (hereinafter cited as Mason Papers). Drafts of autobiography (hereinafter cited as Drafts).

2. Ibid. See also Lucy R. Mason, *To Win These Rights* (New York: Harper and Row, 1952), introduction; *St. Louis Post Dispatch*, June 27, 1946; *Week in Greater Miami*, December 13, 1945; Ralph McGill, *The South and the Southerner* (Boston: Little Brown, 1963), p. 192.

3. Mason Papers, Drafts; *Richmond Times Dispatch*, June 21, 22, 1923.

4. Lucy R. Mason, "I Turned to Social Action Right at Home," *Labor's Relation to Church and Community* (New York: Harpers, 1947), pp. 145ff. Memorandum on Lucy Randolph Mason and Work in the CIO, April 1947, Mason Papers, Memoranda, 1937–53; Drafts; Lucy R. Mason, "Why I Joined Labor," *Witness*, January 25, 1945, p. 9; *Richmond Times Dispatch*, September 6, 1936; Reverend Sam Higginbotham to Mason, March 23, 1951, Mason Papers, Box 7, Folder 3.

5. See Anne Firor Scott, *The Southern Lady: From Pedestal to Politics* (Chicago: University of Chicago Press, 1970), especially chapter 6.

6. John P. McDowell, *The Social Gospel in the South: The Woman's Home Mission Movement in the Methodist Episcopal Church, South, 1886–1939* (Baton Rouge: Louisiana State University Press, 1982), pp. 2–5, 144–48.

7. Mason Papers, Drafts, memoranda, 1937–53.

8. Mason Papers, Drafts.

9. Mason, "I Turned to Social Action," p. 145.

10. Mason Papers, Drafts.

11. Michael B. Chesson, *Richmond After the War, 1865–1890* (Richmond: Virginia State Library, 1981), p. 210.

12. Chesson, *Richmond After the War*, esp. pp. 148, 171, 190–210; Ellen Glasgow, *The Woman Within* (New York: Harcourt Brace, 1954), pp. 80–90. For a slightly more positive view of Richmond's economic and social position at the turn of the century, see Christopher Silver, *Twentieth Century Richmond: Planning Politics and Race* (Knoxville: University of Tennessee Press, 1984), pp. 17–22.

13. Peter J. Rachleff, *Black Labor in the South: Richmond, Virginia, 1865–1890* (Philadelphia: Temple University Press, 1984), pp. 195–201 (I have quoted pp. 197 and 199).

14. Rachleff, *Black Labor*, pp. 143–56; Leon Fink, *Workingmen's Democracy: The Knights of Labor and American Politics* (Urbana: University of Illinois Press, 1983), pp. 149–77.

15. Glasgow, *The Woman Within*, pp. 80–90.

16. Mason to Miss Natalie Bunting, March 5, 1949, Mason Papers, Box 6, Folder 2.

17. Mason Papers, Drafts; *Memphis Press Scimitar*, March 2, 1943. The "Powell's School" was the name for the Richmond Female Seminary, which had been founded by John Henry Powell. See Virginius Dabney, *Richmond: The Story of a City* (Garden City: Doubleday, 1976), pp. 230–31.

18. Nancy Schrom Dye, *As Equals and as Sisters: Feminism, the Labor Movement, and the Women's Trade Union League of New York* (Columbia: University of Missouri Press, 1980), pp. 1–3, 162–66. See also Clark A. Chambers, *Seedtime of Reform: American Social Service and Social Action, 1918–1933* (Minneapolis: University of Minnesota Press, 1963), pp. 1–12.

19. See McDowell, *Social Gospel*, p. 20.

20. Mason, "I Turned to Social Action," pp. 146–47.

21. For Braxton, see Raymond H. Pulley, *Old Virginia Restored: An Interpretation of the Progressive Impulse, 1870–1930* (Charlottesville: University Press of Virginia, 1968), pp. 94–104.

22. Mason, "I Turned to Social Action," pp. 146–47; *St. Louis Post Dispatch*, June 27, 1946.

23. Mason, "I Turned to Social Action," pp. 146–47; Lawrence Lader, "The Lady and the Sheriff," *New Republic*, January 5, 1948, pp. 17–19; *St. Louis Post Dispatch*, June 27, 1946; Silver, *Twentieth Century Richmond*, pp. 46–48. The strike eventually resulted in a decisive defeat for the operators.

24. William L. O'Neill, *Everyone Was Brave: A History of Feminism in America* (Chicago: Quadrangle Books, 1969), pp. 122–25, 147. See too Aileen S. Kra-

ditor, *The Ideas of the Woman Suffrage Movement, 1890–1920* (New York: Columbia University Press, 1965), pp. 1–13; Southern Oral History Collection (hereinafter cited as SOHC), University of North Carolina at Chapel Hill, Adele Clark, interviews with W. Broadfoot, February 28, 1964, July 12, 1964. See also list of those present at the inaugural meeting of the Virginia Equal Suffrage League, November 20, 1909, in Adele Clark Papers, James Branch Cabell Library, Virginia Commonwealth University, Richmond, Virginia (hereinafter cited as Clark Papers), Box 128.

25. Lucy Cary, *The Religious and Social Aspect of the Suffrage Movement* (Richmond: Equal Suffrage League of Virginia, 1912), unpaginated, in Mason Papers, Printed Material, 1912–45, Folder 1.

26. McDowell, *Social Gospel*, pp. 57–59. See also Jacquelyn Dowd Hall, *Revolt Against Chivalry: Jessie Daniel Ames and the Women's Campaign Against Lynching* (New York: Columbia University Press, 1979), pp. 19–56.

27. Lucy Randolph Mason, *The Divine Discontent* (Richmond: Equal Suffrage League of Virginia, 1912), pp. 2–9, in Mason Papers, Printed Material, Folder 1.

28. Typescript, Clark Papers, Box 128.

29. Mason Papers, Drafts; notes in Clark Papers, Carton 130.

30. *Richmond Times Dispatch*, March 23, 1914, Mason Papers, Drafts.

2. Social Work and Suffrage

1. Mary Frederickson, "A Place to Speak Our Minds: The Southern School for Woman Workers" (Ph.D. diss., University of North Carolina, 1981), p. 16.

2. Mary Frederickson, "Citizens for Democracy: The Industrial Programs of the YWCA," in Joyce L. Kornbluh and Mary Frederickson, eds., *Sisterhood and Solidarity: Workers' Education for Women* (Philadelphia: Temple University Press, 1984), pp. 77–79, 94 (quotation on p. 79); Frederickson, "A Place to Speak Our Minds," pp. 16–38; Katharine du Pre Lumpkin, interview with J. Hall, August 4, 1974, SOHC.

3. Susan B. Ware, *Beyond Suffrage: Women in the New Deal* (Cambridge, Mass.: Harvard University Press, 1981); Frederickson, "A Place to Speak Our Minds," pp. 16–38; Lumpkin interview.

4. Mason to Miss Anne Pridmore, March 26, 1940, Mason Papers, Box 1, Folder 4.

5. Mason to Florence Simms, September 10, 19, 1917, Records of the National Board of the YWCA, Local Files, Richmond (hereinafter cited as YWCA Local Records, Richmond), YWCA Archives, New York.

6. Mason to Simms, October 18, 1917, ibid. She did not name the union.

7. Mason to Miss Anne Pridmore, March 26, 1940, Mason Papers, Box 1, Folder 4; Mason, *To Win These Rights*, p. 5.

8. Mason Papers, Drafts; YWCA Scrapbooks, Records of the Richmond YWCA, Richmond, Virginia; *Richmond Times Dispatch*, September 6, 1916.

9. Lucy Mason, "Changing Industrial Conditions," *Messenger*, vol. 111, no. 2 (November 1917), in Mason Papers, Printed Material, 1912–39.

10. Mason, *To Win These Rights*, p. 6; Mason to Simms, October 18, December 24, 1917 (quoted), YWCA Local Records, Richmond.

11. Mason, *To Win These Rights*, p. 5.

12. Mason Papers, Drafts (first quotation); Mason to Ralph McGill, May 23, 1940 (second quotation), Mason Papers, Box 2, Folder 1.

13. Mason to Ida Burke, August 27, 1918 (second quotation), Mason Papers, Box 1, Folder 1; Mason to Ralph McGill, May 23, 1940 (first quotation), Mason Papers, Box 2, Folder 1.

14. *Richmond Evening Journal*, January 6, 1919; *Richmond Times Dispatch*, January 15, 1919.

15. *Richmond News Leader*, July 2, 1919; Mason Papers, Miscellany, 1925–40.

16. J. Stanley Lemons, *The Woman Citizen: Social Feminism in the 1920's* (Urbana: University of Illinois, 1973), pp. 49ff., 118–20; Susan D. Becker, *The Origins of the Equal Rights Amendment: American Feminism Between the Wars* (Westport, Conn.: Greenwood Press, 1981).

17. *Richmond Times Dispatch*, January 28, February 4, 1922; Alice Kessler-Harris, *Out to Work: A History of Wage Earning Women in the United States* (New York: Oxford University Press, 1982), pp. 206–11; Chambers, *Seedtime of Reform*, pp. 77–79.

18. *Richmond Times Dispatch*, December 1, 1920, January 8, 1922, March 23, 1922, October 3, 1923; Minutes of the Second Convention of the Virginia League of Women Voters, January 24–26, 1923, Clark Papers, Carton 136.

19. Mason to Edith Clark Cowles, September 3, 21, 1920, Adele Clark Papers, Carton 130; to Adele Clark, July 12, August 3, 9, September 4, 18, 1922, all in Adele Clark Papers, Carton 149.

20. Mason to Edith Clark Cowles, September 13, 1921, Adele Clark Papers, Carton 149.

21. League of Women Voters Papers, Library of Congress (hereinafter cited as LWV Papers), Series 1, Box 2; *Newsletter of Committee on Women in Industry*, No. 3, December 28, 1922; Edward Costigan to Mason, December 26, 1922, Mason Papers, Box 1, Folder 1.

22. Mason to Adele Clark, July 12, 1922 (quoted), Clark Papers, Carton 149; Belle Sherwin to Mason, July 17, 1922, Mason Papers, Box 1, Folder 1.

23. LWV Papers, Series 1, Box 2; *Newsletter of Committee on Women in Industry*, No. 4, January 20, 1923; *Richmond Times Dispatch*, January 28 (first quotation), February 25 (second quotation), 1923; Mason Papers, Clippings, 1910s–1930s, Box 1; Mason to Adele Clark, July 12, 1922, Clark Papers, Carton 149.

24. *Richmond Times Dispatch*, April 9, 1922, June 25, 1922, February 11, 1923.

25. Silver, *Twentieth Century Richmond*, pp. 120–29.

26. *Richmond News Leader*, May 25, 1923; *Richmond Times Dispatch*, January 5, 1923; Adele Clark, interview with B. Friedman, SOHC. The "latent capacity" statement is quoted from the *Richmond Times Dispatch*; the other quoted statements appeared in the *Richmond News Leader*.

27. Mason to Gordon Hancock, March 6, 1932, Mason Papers, Box 1, Folder 2; *Richmond Planet*, July 4, 23, 1932.

28. McDowell, *The Social Gospel in the South*, pp. 88–115; Hall, *Revolt Against Chivalry*, pp. 82–106.

29. Frances S. Taylor, "On the Edge of Tomorrow: Southern Women, the Student YWCA, and Race, 1920–1944" (Ph.D. diss., Stanford University, 1944); Hall, *Revolt Against Chivalry*, pp. 82–106.

30. *Richmond Times Dispatch*, January 26, 1922, January 28, February 4, 1923.

31. *Richmond Times Dispatch*, April 23, 30, May 1, 2, 3, 1922.

32. Mason to Edith Clark Cowles, September 18, 1922, Adele Clark Papers, Carton 149. Why Lucy Mason did not marry we do not know. Her papers yield no clues as to any romantic attachment with a man. It may simply be that she was never asked.

33. Florence Kelley to Mason, September 5, 1923, Mason Papers, Box 1, Folder 1; *Richmond Times Dispatch*, May 30, October 3, 1923; Mason, *To Win These Rights*, pp. 6–7.

3. At the Richmond YWCA

1. Frederickson, *A Place to Speak*, pp. 16–24 (the quoted statement appears on p. 24).

2. Frederickson, *A Place to Speak*, pp. 16–24 (quoted statement on pp. 21–22); Lemons, *The Woman Citizen*, pp. 137–39; Eleanor Copenhaver Anderson, interview with M. Frederickson, November 5, 1974, SOHC.

3. Myron McLaren, interview with M. Frederickson, November 4, 1974, Brownie Lee Jones, interview with M. Frederickson, April 20, 1976, both in SOHC; Frederickson, *A Place to Speak*, pp. 34–36; Alleyne Y. Stokes to Mrs. Speer, undated, 1921, YWCA Local Records, Richmond.

4. Brownie Lee Jones interview, SOHC.

5. Mason to William S. Ryland, Vice President, State and City Bank and Trust Company, December 12, 1924, Mason to Mary Sims, December 17, 24, 1927, January 6, 1928, December 16, 23, 1929, Sims to Mason, December 20, 1929, all in YWCA Local Records, Richmond; Mason to Rufus, April 6, 1931, Mason Papers, Box 1, Folder 1; *Richmond Times Dispatch*, October 16, 22, 1925, October 26, 1927.

6. Mason to Helen Schuyler, July 28, 1928, Mason to Mildred Corbett, September 4 (first quotation), 7 (remaining quotations), 1928; Transcript of discussion between Richmond YMCA and YWCA, September 6, 1928, all in YWCA Local Records, Richmond.

7. Mason, *The Divine Discontent*, pp. 5–9.

8. *Richmond Times Dispatch*, November 1, 1927.

9. Lucy Mason, "Is the Secretary a Dweller or a Sojourner in her Community?" Mason Papers, Printed Material, no date; Evaluation of Richmond Program, March 1930, YWCA Local Records, Richmond.

10. *Richmond Times Dispatch*, July 2, 1925, November 14, 21, 1926, December 15, 1927, January 15, 1928, February 2, 1929; *Richmond News Leader*, February 18, 1926, October 7, 8, 1929, January 14, 1930.

11. Lawrence S. Wittner, *Rebels Against War: The American Peace Movement, 1941–1960* (New York: Columbia University Press, 1969), pp. 1–11. See also Charles Chatfield, *For Peace and Justice: Pacifism in America, 1914–1941* (Knoxville: University of Tennessee Press, 1971).

12 C. Roland Marchand, *The American Peace Movement and Social Reform, 1898–1918* (Princeton: Princeton University Press, 1972), especially chapters 6 and 7.

13. McDowell, *The Social Gospel in the South*, pp. 71–82.

14. Jean Grigsby Paxton, " 'The Dream Was Too Cheap for Her': A Study of the Life and Service of Katherine S. Gerwick," *Womens Press*, September 1927, pp. 607–10.

15. Ibid.; *Richmond Times Dispatch*, September 22, 1925; Alice Tullis Lord Parsons, "The Exquisite Gift," *Womens Press* (September 1927), pp. 610–11. The copies of the *Womens Press* which I consulted were located in the Archives of the National Board of the YWCA of the United States of America, New York City.

16. Ware, *Beyond Suffrage*, p. 26.

17. Obituary from *Zanesville Sunday Times Signal*, May 22, 1927, in Archives of the General Board of the YWCA (henceforth YWCA Archives) New York City; Mason, Notes on Death, August 1927, Mason Papers, Miscellany, 1920–40.

18. Mason to Cecil Scott, October 1930, Mason Papers, Box 1, Folder 1.

19. Mason to Katherine, January 25, 1931, Mason Papers, Box 1, Folder 1.

20. Brownie Lee Jones interview, SOHC.

21. R. Laurence Moore, *In Search of White Crows: Spiritualism, Parapsychology, and American Culture* (New York: Oxford University Press, 1977). See also Howard Kerr, *Mediums and Spirit Rappers and Roaring Radicals: Spiritualism in American Literature, 1850–1900* (Urbana: University of Illinois Press, 1972).

22. *Richmond Times Dispatch,* November 1, 1927; Mason Papers, Drafts; Raymond Gavins, *The Perils and Prospects of Southern Black Leadership: Gordon Blaine Hancock, 1884–1970* (Durham: Duke University Press, 1977), pp. 48–49.

23. Silver, *Twentieth Century Richmond,* pp. 109–26.

24. *Richmond Times Dispatch,* January 15, February 1, 5, 12, 1929; G. H. Harris to Mason, February 2, 1929, Mason Papers, Box 1, Folder 1.

25. *Richmond Planet,* July 4, 23, 1932. On Hancock, see Gavins, *Perils and Prospects.*

26. *Richmond Planet,* July 4, 23, 1932.

27. L. R. Reynolds to Mason, September 6, 1932, Mason Papers, Box 1, Folder 1.

28. See *Virginia Pilot,* June 13, 1926.

29. See Mason Papers, Miscellany, 1920–40, "Notes on Effigies and Crucifixes," 1929.

30. Mason, *To Win These Rights,* pp. 8–9; Mason to Rufus, Mason Papers, April 6, 1931, Box 1, Folder 1.

31. Mason, *To Win These Rights,* pp. 8–10.

32. Mason to W. M. McLauren, February 14, 17, 1931, Mason to Donald Comer, January 23, 1931, Feburary 14, 1931, Mason Papers, Box 1, Folder 1.

33. Florence Kelley to Mason, March 23, 1931, Mason Papers, Box 1, Folder 1.

34. Mason to Miss Emily S. Thomason, March 23, 1931, Mason Papers, Box 1, Folder 1; Mrs. James Clarence Farr to Mason, March 31, 1931, Bernard Cocke Nash to Mason, March 1931, Mason Papers, Box 1, Folder 2.

35. Mason to Rufus, Mason Papers, April 26, 1931, Box 1, Folder 1.

36. Lucy R. Mason, *Standards for Workers in Southern Industry* (New York: National Consumers League, 1931); Mason, *To Win These Rights,* pp. 10–11.

37. Mason Papers, "An Appreciation by Her Friends," bound volume.

38. Mason, *To Win These Rights,* p. 11.

39. Mary Dewson to Emily Marconnier, October 16, 1931, Mason Papers, Box 1, Folder 1; to Lucy Mason, March 27, 1951, Mason Papers, Box 7, Folder 3.

40. Minutes of the Forty-fifth Meeting of the Board of Directors of the National Consumers League, May 23, 1932, Records of the National Consumers League, Library of Congress (hereinafter cited as NCL Records), Group A, Carton 2 (here-

inafter group and carton will be indicated as A/2).

41. Louise Catterall to Mason, May 28, 1932, Mason to the President and Board of Directors of the YWCA, Richmond, June 14, 1932, Mason Papers, Box 1, Folder 2; Mason, *To Win These Rights*, pp. 11–12.

4. Turning on the Light: The National Consumers League

1. O'Neill, *Everyone Was Brave*, pp. 47, 153. On the history of the league, see also Chambers, *Seedtime of Reform*, esp. pp. 4–7, 61–83; Kessler-Harris, *Out to Work*, esp. pp. 166–71; Allis Rosenburg Wolfe, "Women, Consumerism, and the National Consumers' League in the Progressive Era, 1900–1923," *Labor History*, vol. 16, no. 3 (Summer 1975), pp. 378–92.

2. O'Neill, *Everyone Was Brave*, pp. 95–96, 238.

3. Ibid., 97–98. See also Minutes of Thirty-fourth Annual Meeting of the NCL, December 13, 1933, NCL Records, A/9.

4. O'Neill, *Everyone Was Brave*, p. 152; Chambers, *Seedtime of Reform*, pp. 4–14.

5. Ware, *Beyond Suffrage*, p. 36.

6. O'Neill, *Everyone Was Brave*, pp. 232–40; Lemons, *The Woman Citizen*, pp. 189–90; Chambers, *Seedtime of Reform*, p. 78.

7. O'Neill, *Everyone Was Brave*, pp. 237–40.

8. Mason to Mrs. Anne O'Hare McCormick, September 24, 1932, Records of the National Consumers League, NCL Records, B/20.

9. William E. Leuchtenburg, *The Perils of Prosperity, 1914–1932* (Chicago: University of Chicago Press, 1958), pp. 254–57; Mason, *To Win These Rights*, pp. 13–14.

10. Excerpts from the discussion at the Conference on the Breakdown of Industrial Standards, December 12, 1932, NCL Records, G/6 (unpaginated typescript); Lucy Randolph Mason, "Progress and Administration of Minimum Wage Laws in 1933," NCL Records, D/4.

11. Mason to Emma Zanzinger, April 21, 1933, NCL Records, C/54; Ware, *Beyond Suffrage*, p. 36.

12. Mason, *To Win These Rights*, p. 15.

13. "Proposed Principles for Labor Provisions of NRA Codes," NCL Records, C/7; Lucy Randolph Mason, "Objections to Minimum Wage Discriminations Against Negro Workers," August 29, 1933, NCL Records, D/4.

14. Mason to Mrs. Mary A. Gardner, July 13, 1933, NCL Records, B/9; Mason to Mrs. Martha Adamson, September 4, 1933, NCL Records, C/7.

15. Minutes of the Fifty-third and Fifty-fourth Meetings of the NCL Board, April 4, May 17, 1934, NCL Records, A/3.

16. Mason, *To Win These Rights*, p. 15; Mason to Eleanor Roosevelt, December 6, 1933, Eleanor Roosevelt Papers, Franklin D. Roosevelt Library, Hyde Park, New York, Box 1270.

17. Report of Second Annual Meeting of the Labor Standards Conference, December 12, 1933, NCL Records, G/6.

18. Ware, *Beyond Suffrage;* Mason to Beyer, November 1, 1935, Beyer to Mason, November 12, 1935, NCL Records, B/24.

19. For the charts, see NCL Records, G/6.

20. "Report of Southern Trip, from January 22 to March 25, 1934," NCL Records, A/9.

21. Ibid.

22. Mason to Beyer, November 17, 1935, NCL Records, B/24.

23. Mason to Beyer, January 11, 1936, NCL Records, B/24; Minutes of the Fifty-ninth Meeting of the NCL Board, October 28, 1935, NCL Records, A/3.

24. Mason to Mrs. George T. Settle, June 26, 1935, March 30, 1936, NCL Records, B/1; NCL Newsletter, January 17, 1936, March 4, 1936, NCL Records, B/3; Minutes of the Sixtieth Meeting of the NCL Board, February 18, 1936, NCL Records, A/3.

25. Mason to Mrs. Olivia C. Fuller, August 14, 1936, NCL Records, C/55; Mason to Mrs. C. R. Mueller, December 14, 1936, NCL Records, B/3.

26. Mason to Mrs. Mueller, February 10, 1937, NCL Records, B/3; Memo of Secretary's Conference on Minimum Wage, April 8, 1937, NCL Records, C/52.

27. Mason to Louise Stitt, February 19, 1937, Stitt to Mason, February 23, 1937, NCL Papers, B/24.

28. Mason to Emma Zanzinger, April 25, 1934, NCL Records, C/54; Report on Standard Minimum Wage Bill for Women and Minors, February 6, 1935, NCL Records, C/51; Memorandum to State Leagues, May 24, 1934, NCL Records, B/3.

29. Mason to Frank Graham, October 25, 1932, Graham to Mason, October 27, 1932, Frank P. Graham Papers, Southern Historical Collection, Wilson Library, University of North Carolina at Chapel Hill.

30. File of letters on Southern Committees, NCL Records, F/2; Mason to Mrs. Olivia C. Fuller, Houston, Texas, August 14, 1936, NCL Records, C/55; Mason to Graham, May 15, 1937, Graham Papers.

31. Marconnier to Mrs. Lowell J. Herbert, June 10, 1936, NCL Records, B/8; Dewson to Mrs. Roosevelt, April 10, 1935, NCL Records, B/21.

32. Perkins to Mason, May 5, 1933, November 2, 1934, NCL Records, B/20; Dewson to Mrs. Roosevelt, April 10, 1935, NCL Records, B/21.

33. Mason to Mrs. Roosevelt, February 10, 1937, File on the organization of the Second Southern Regional Conference on Labor Standards, NCL Records, B/21.

34. Mason to Anderson, May 3, 1935, NCL Records, B/24; Anderson to Mason, August 3, 1936, Mason to Anderson, August 5, 1936, NCL Records, C/51; Mason to Anderson, April 18, 1935, June 6, 1936, May 4, 1937, Anderson to Mason, May 6, 1937, all in Women's Bureau Papers, National Archives, Washington, D.C., Box 843.

35. Becker, *Origins of the Equal Rights Amendment*, pp. 277–79; Anderson to Mason, September 16, 1936, Mason to Anderson, September 23, 1936, NCL Records, C/7; Anderson to Mason, May 13, 1935, Mason to Anderson, May 14, 1935, Women's Bureau Papers, Box 843.

36. Draft Charter attached to Anderson and Mason, September 16, 1936, preamble, NCL Records, C/7.

37. Draft Charter, passim.

38. Draft Charter, Explanatory Notes.

39. Mary Anderson to Mason, October 23, 1936, NCL Records, C/7.

40. *New York Times*, December 29, 1936.

41. Mason to Anderson, January 27, 1937, to Mrs. Edith Houghton Hooker, March 1, 1937, NCL Records, C/7.

42. Mason to Elizabeth Magee, March 30, 1937, NCL Records, B/9, to Margaret Hook, February 5, 1937, NCL Records, B/8.

43. Mason to Mrs. C. R. Mueller, August 7, 1935, NCL Records, B/3; Mason to Mary Anderson, July 6, 1936 (quoted), NCL Records, B/24; Mason to Molly Dewson, January 15, 1934, NCL Records, C/1.

44. Statement by Paul Kellog, April 30, 1934, Minutes of luncheon meeting of the Social Policy Committee, both in NCL Records, C/50.

45. Mason to Mrs. C. R. Mueller, December 14, 1936, February 10, 1937, NCL Records, B/3.

46. Mason to Mrs. R. B. Halleck, May 14, 1937, NCL Records, B/1; Mason to Mrs. Roosevelt, February 10, 1937, Mrs. Roosevelt to Mason, February 15, 1937, NCL Records, B/21.

47. Mason to Frank Graham, May 15, 1937, Graham Papers, Marconnier to Mary King, July 16, 1937, NCL Papers, B/25; Marconnier to Nicholas Kelley, May 28, 1937, Mason to Nicholas Kelley, May 28, 1937, NCL Records, A/1. Mason was to remain on the Consumers League's council, however, for the rest of her life.

48. Mason, *To Win These Rights*, pp. 16–17.

49. Virginia Durr, interview with author, December 9, 1981, La Trobe University; Mason to Frank P. Graham, June 10, 1937, Graham Papers.

5. The CIO: The First Years

1. Jacquelyn Dowd Hall, Robert Korstad, and James Leloudis, "Cotton Mill People: Work, Community, and Protest in the Textile South, 1880–1940," *American Historical Review*, vol. 91, no. 2 (April 1986), p. 245.

2. George F. Tindall, *The Emergence of the New South, 1913–1945* (Baton Rouge: Louisiana State University Press, 1967), p. 318.

3. Ibid.

4. Hall, Korstad, and Leloudis, "Cotton Mill People," p. 259.

5. Liston Pope, *Millhands and Preachers: A Study of Gastonia* (New Haven: Yale University Press, 1942); Hall, Korstad, and Leloudis, "Cotton Mill People," p. 271.

6. Tindall, *Emergence of the New South*, pp. 351–53.

7. Ibid., pp. 509ff. See also Ray Marshall, *Labor in the South* (Cambridge, Mass.: Harvard University Press, 1967), pp. 166–69; Irving Bernstein, *Turbulent Years: A History of the American Worker, 1933–1941* (Boston: Houghton Mifflin, 1970), pp. 301–15.

8. Bernstein, *Turbulent Years;* Tindall, *Emergence of the New South*, pp. 512–13.

9. Mason to Graham, June 10, 1937, Graham Papers.

10. Mason to Lewis, September 11, 1937, Mason Papers, Box 1, Folder 2.

11. Mason to Hillman, September 11, 1937, Mason Papers, Box 1, Folder 2.

12. Mason to FDR, August 12, 1937, Mason Papers, Box 1, Folder 2.

13. Mason to Molly Dewson, September 6, 1937, Mason Papers, Box 1, Folder 2.

14. Mason to Hillman, September 11, 1937, Mason Papers, Box 1, Folder 2; Mason, *To Win These Rights*, pp. 22–25.

15. Mason, *To Win These Rights*, pp. 145–47, 158–59; Borah to Mason, April 22, 1944, Mason Papers, Box 3, Folder 3.

16. Jonathan Daniels to Mason, September 9, 1937, Mason to Jonathan Daniels, September 11, 1937, Mason Papers, Box 1, Folder 2.

17. Mason to Editors, October 5, December 18, 1937; Mason to John Temple Graves, *Birmingham Age Herald*, March 9, 1938, Mason Papers, Box 1, Folder 2.

18. Grover Hall to Mason, January 8, 1938, Mason to Hall, January 19, 1938, Mason Papers, Box 1, Folder 2.

19. Mason to Ministers, August 25, 1937, Mason Papers, Box 1, Folder 2.

20. Reverend Arthur J. Barton, Wilmington, North Carolina, to Mason, September 7, 1937, Reverend William W. Lumpkin, Charleston, South Carolina, to Mason, September 16, 1937, Mason to Hillman, January 21, 1938, Mason Papers, Box 1, Folder 2.

21. Mason to James Dombrowski, December 16, 18, 1937. Papers of the High-lander Research and Education Center (hereinafter cited as Highlander Papers), State Historical Society of Wisconsin, Box 41, Folder 12; Mason to Claude Clayton, Mason to Governor Hugh White, Mason to Congressman John F. Rankin, Mason to Franklin Delano Roosevelt, all April 14, 1938, Mason to Eleanor Roosevelt, April 16, 1938, all in Mason Papers, Box 1, Folder 2.

22. Mason to FDR, March 25, 1938, Mason Papers, Box 1, Folder 2.

23. Mason to James Roosevelt, April 19, 1938, FDR Papers, OF 407-B.

24. Mason to editors, November 16, 1938, Mason Papers, Box 1, Folder 3; Carroll Kilpatrick to Mason, April 20, 1938, Mason to Kilpatrick, April 21, 1938, Mason Papers, Box 1, Folder 2.

25. Tindall, *Emergence of the New South,* p. 627; Lowell Mellett to Mason, June 25, 1938, Mason Papers, Box 1, Folder 3.

26. Mason to Mrs. Roosevelt, November 30, 1938, Roosevelt to Jesse Jones, December 10, 1938, Jesse Jones to FDR, February 24, 1939, all in Roosevelt Papers, OF 643.

27. Memorandum on visit to Milan (Tennessee), March 3, 1938, Papers of John G. Ramsay, Southern Labor Archive, Georgia State University, Atlanta, Georgia.

28. Ibid.

29. Mason to Jonathan Daniels, August 6, 1938, Mason Papers, Box 1, Folder 3.

30. Ibid. See also James Price to Mason, July 9, 1938, Mason to Price, July 12, 1938, LeRoy Hodge to Mason, July 14, 19, 1938, all in Mason Papers, Box 1, Folder 3.

31. Molly Dewson to Mason, June 27, 1938, Mason Papers, Box 1, Folder 3.

32. Mason to Marvin McIntyre, May 21, 1938, Roosevelt Papers, OF 3853, Mason to McIntyre, July 15, 1938, Roosevelt Papers, OF 200C.

33. Mason to Mrs. Roosevelt, February 24, 1939, Eleanor Roosevelt Papers, Box 756.

34. Mrs. Roosevelt to Mason, March 3, 1939, Mason to Franklin Roosevelt, June 1, 1939, Mason to Eleanor Roosevelt, June 1, 1939, all in Eleanor Roosevelt Papers, Box 756.

35. Mason to Allan S. Haywood, October 15, 1940, Mason Papers, Box 2, Folder 1.

36. Lewis to Mason, November 24, 1939, Mason Papers, Box 1, Folder 4; Mason to Lewis, August 21, 1940, Mason Papers, Box 2, Folder 1.

37. Mason to Lewis, October 27, 1940, Mason Papers, Box 2, Folder 1; Lewis to Mason, October 31, 1940, Mason Papers, Box 2, Folder 1; Mason to Lewis, November 4, 1940, Mason Papers, Box 2, Folder 2.

38. Mason to Murray, November 24, 1940, Mason to Lewis, December 10, 1940, January 8, 1941, Mason Papers, Box 2, Folder 2.

39. Horace R. Cayton and George S. Mitchell, *Black Workers and the New Unions* (Westport, Conn.: Negro Universities Press, 1970), pp. 190–224. For statistics on the increase in black union membership, see the tables on pp. 446ff.

40. George S. Mitchell, "The Negro in Southern Trade Unionism," *Southern Economic Journal,* vol. 2, no. 3 (January 1936), pp. 26–33.

41. Mason to Mrs. Roosevelt, January 9, 1941, Mason Papers, Box 2, Folder 2; Mrs. Roosevelt to Robert H. Jackson, January 14, 1941, Eleanor Roosevelt Papers, Box 808.

42. Mason to Mrs. Roosevelt, May 2, 1941, Eleanor Roosevelt Papers, Box 813.

43. Mason to Allan Haywood, April 14, 1941, Mason Papers, Box 2, Folder 2.

44. Ibid.

45. Mason to Allan Haywood, to Miss Augusta Roberts, National Student Council, YWCA, both April 14, 1941, Mason Papers, Box 2, Folder 2.

46. Mason to Dabney, May 1, 1941, Dabney to Mason, May 3, 1941, Mason Papers, Box 2, Folder 2; Morton Sosna, *In Search of the Silent South: Southern Liberals and the Race Issue* (New York: Columbia University Press, 1977), pp. 121–39.

47. Mason to Albert Quinn, October 1, 1941, 12, to Dabney, September 30, 1941, June 16, 1942, Dabney to Mason, October 6, 12, 1941, all in Virginius Dabney Papers, Manuscripts Department, University of Virginia Library. I thank Mr. Dabney for permitting me to use this collection.

48. Mason to Mrs. Roosevelt, January 29, 1941, Mason Papers, Box 2, Folder 2.

49. Ibid.

50. Mason to Eleanor Roosevelt, November 12, 1941, Eleanor Roosevelt to Franklin Roosevelt, November 17, 1941, Franklin Roosevelt to Eleanor Roosevelt, November 19, 1941, all in Eleanor Roosevelt Papers, Box 813.

51. *Richmond Times Dispatch,* June 23, 1940, *Raleigh News and Observer,* July 21, 1940, *Memphis Commercial Appeal,* July 14, 1940, Mason Papers, Addresses, 1931–49, Folder 1.

52. Lillian Smith to Mason, April 19, 1939, Mason Papers, Box 1, Folder 3; Lucy R. Mason, "Southerners Look at the South," *North Georgia Review* (Fall and Winter 1938–39), pp. 17ff.

53. Mason to Burnett Maybank, October 21, 1939; Mrs. Carlton Barnwell to Mason, November 13, 1939, Mason Papers, Box 1, Folder 4; Mason to Reverend Walker, March 24, 1940, Mason Papers, Box 1, Folder 4.

54. Mason to Reverend Walker, March 24, 1940, Mason Papers, Box 1, Folder 4; Mason to Margaret Fisher, November 20, 1940, Mason Papers, Box 2, Folder 2.

6. The CIO at War

1. *Richmond Times Dispatch*, November 21, 1926, December 8, 1929; Mason to Eleanor Roosevelt, January 9, 1941, Eleanor Roosevelt Papers, Box 813; Mason to Samuel Chiles Mitchell, September 26, 1940, Samuel Chiles Mitchell Papers, Southern Historical Collection, University of North Carolina, Folder 102.

2. For the above, and for much of what follows in the next few pages, I am greatly indebted to Nelson Lichtenstein's superb recent study *Labor's War at Home: The CIO in World War II* (New York: Cambridge University Press, 1982).

3. Lichtenstein, *Labor's War*, pp. 32–43 (pp. 32 and 43 are quoted).

4. Ibid., pp. 44–66.

5. Richard Polenberg, *War and Society: The United States, 1941–1945* (New York: Lippincott, 1972); Marshall, *Labor in the South*, pp. 227–30.

6. Tindall, *The Emergence of the New South*, pp. 695ff.; Marshall, *Labor in the South*, pp. 225–45.

7. Tindall, *The Emergence of the New South*, pp. 713–15 (Rankin is quoted on p. 715).

8. Mason to Philip Murray, to Philip H. Van Gelder, Secretary-Treasurer, Industrial Union of Marine and Shipbuilding Workers of America, December 7, 1942, Mason Papers, Box 3, Folder 1.

9. Mason to Mrs. Roosevelt, May 29, 1943, Mason Papers, Box 3, Folder 2.

10. Mason to Mrs. Roosevelt, December 8, 1942, Eleanor Roosevelt Papers, Box 841.

11. Mason to Mrs. Roosevelt, May 7, 1942, Eleanor Roosevelt Papers, Box 841; Mason to Mrs. Roosevelt, January 22, 1944, to Thompson, January 28, 1944, Eleanor Roosevelt Papers, Box 920; Mason to Paul Christopher, September 17, 1943, Records of the CIO Organizing Committee, Tennessee, Perkins Library, Duke University, Folder 313, Mason.

12. Lichtenstein, *Labor's War*, pp. 172ff. For the PAC, see James C. Foster, *The Union Politic: The CIO Political Action Committee* (Columbia: University of Missouri Press, 1975).

13. Foster, *The Union Politic*, pp. 41–48, 61; Lichtenstein, *Labor's War*, pp. 174–76. On Hillman and the developing links between union officials and government policy, see Steve Fraser, "From the 'New Unionism' to the New Deal," *Labor History*, vol. 25, no. 3 (Summer 1984), pp. 406–30.

14. Mason to Allan Haywood, February 3, 1944, Mason Papers, Box 3, Folder 2, to Haywood, April 29, May 4, July 28, September 15, 1944, all in Mason Papers, Box 3, Folder 3; Foster, *The Union Politic*, pp. 64–65.

15. Mason to Philip Murray, October 30, 1944, Mason Papers, Box 4, Folder 1.

16. Mason to Victor Rotnem, Chief, Civil Rights Section, Department of Justice, July 20, 1944, Mason Papers, Box 3, Folder 3.

17. R. E. Starnes and Mason to Philip Murray, August 21, 1944, Mason to Mrs. Roosevelt, September 2, 1944, Mason Papers, Box 3, Folder 3.

18. Mason to Rotnem, September 5, 1944, Mason Papers, Box 3, Folder 3, Ralph A. Bard to Mrs. Roosevelt, October 1944, Mason Papers, Box 4, Folder 1.

19. Mason to Rotnem, March 10, 1944, Mason Papers, Box 3, Folder 2.

20. Mason to Rotnem, March 10, 31, 1944, Mason Papers, Box 3, Folder 2.

21. Toxey Hall to Mason, May 17, 1944, Mason Papers, Box 3, Folder 3.

22. George Brown to Mason, May 17, 1944, Mason to Toxey Hall, May 24, 1944, to Eleanor Bontecou, May 24, 1944, both in Mason Papers, Box 3, Folder 3.

23. Mason to Rotnem, May 9, 1943, Neil Andrews to Mason, June 10, 1943, Mason to Davis, March 30, 1944, all in Mason Papers, Box 3, Folder 2; Davis to Mason, April 5, 1944, Mason to Davis, July 23, 1944, Mason Papers, Box 3, Folder 3.

24. Mason to Haywood, October 19, 1943, Mason Papers, Box 3, Folder 2, Mason to Haywood, March 28, 1945, Mason Papers, Box 4, Folder 1; Mason to Henry G. Hart, Student Christian Association, Vanderbilt University, January 29, 1943 (first quotation); *Vanderbilt Hustler,* January 31, 1943 (second quotation); telegram, *Nashville Tennessean* to Mason, January 30, 1943, *Nashville Tennessean,* January 30 (third quotation), February 1, 1943, all in Mason Papers, Box 3, Folder 1.

25. George N. Mayhew to Mason, February 1, 1943, Mason to *Nashville Tennessean,* January 30, 1943, Mason Papers, Box 3, Folder 1.

26. George N. Mayhew to Mason, February 1, 1943, Mason to *Nashville Tennessean,* January 30, 1943, Mason to Mayhew, February 9, 1943, to Charles Houk, Student Pastor, Westminster Foundation of the Synod of Tennessee, February 23, 1943, all in Mason Papers, Box 3, Folder 1.

27. Script of radio talk, Greensboro, North Carolina, May 11, 1943. See also scripts, Suffolk, Virginia, March 18, 1943, Winston-Salem, N.C., July 20, 1943, Charlotte, N.C., January 24, 1944, Mason Papers, Addresses, 1931–49, Folder 2.

28. Lucy R. Mason, "The CIO in the South," *South and World Affairs,* vol. 6, no. 4 (April 1944).

29. McDowell, *The Social Gospel in the South,* pp. 51–54.

30. Mason to Mrs. Roosevelt, September 23, 1942, to Allan Haywood, September 28, 1942, to Philip Murray, October 9, 1942, Murray to Margaret Fisher, October 12, 1942, all in Mason Papers, Box 3, Folder 1.

31. Mason to Ellis Arnall, February 6, 1945, Arnall to Mason, February 19,

1945, Mason to Allan Haywood, March 28, 1945, all in Mason Papers, Box 4, Folder 1.

32. Mason to Arnall, August 14, 1942, Mason Papers, Box 3, Folder 1.

33. Mason to Arnall, August 14, 1942, Arnall to Mason, August 18, 1942, both in Mason Papers, Box 3, Folder 1.

34. Mason to Haywood, July 7, 1942, Mason Papers, Box 3, Folder 1.

35. Mason to Murray, October 31, 1944, Mason to Haywood, January 14, both in Mason Papers, Box 4, Folder 1.

36. Mason to Mrs. Roosevelt, March 20, 1942, Eleanor Roosevelt Papers, Box 841; Mason to Philip Murray, November 5, 1942, Mason to Malvina Thompson, May 9, 1943, both in Mason Papers, Box 3, Folder 2.

37. Durr interview, December 9, 1981; Mason to Mrs. Roosevelt, March 10, 1944, Mason Papers, Box 3, Folder 2; Mason to Mrs. Roosevelt, June 8, 1944, Mason Papers, Box 3, Folder 3; Mason to Philip Murray, January 14, 1945, Mason Papers, Box 4, Folder 1.

38. Mason to Mrs. Roosevelt, January 3, 1943, Mason Papers, Box 3, Folder 1; Mason to Roosevelt, August 18, 24, 1943, Mason to Sidney Hillman, August 17, 1943, Mason to Ralph McGill, September 3, 1943, Mason to Borah, August 18, September 3, 1943, Borah to Mason, August 14, September 14, November 16, December 28, 1943, all in Mason Papers, Box 3, Folder 2; Borah to Mason, May 9, 1944, Mason Papers, Box 3, Folder 3.

39. Borah to Mason, June 2, August 22, 1944, Mason Papers, Box 3, Folder 3.

40. Mason to Mrs. Roosevelt, September 4, 1944, Mrs. Roosevelt to Mason, September 14, 1944, Mason Papers, Box 3, Folder 3.

41. Landon Burke to Mason, August 27, 1943, Mason Papers, Box 3, Folder 2; Charles Burke to Mason, September 23, 1944, Major L. M. Blackford to Mason, June 13, June 16, 1944, Mason Papers, Box 3, Folder 3.

7. Operation Dixie

1. Lichtenstein, *Labor's War at Home*, pp. 80–81, 182.

2. Lichtenstein, *Labor's War at Home*, pp. 203–32.

3. Marshall, *Labor in the South*, pp. 246–69 (quotation on p. 254). The best study of Operation Dixie is Barbara S. Griffith, "The Crisis of American Labor: Operation Dixie and the Defeat of the CIO" (Ph.D. diss., Duke University, 1986).

4. Marshall, *Labor in the South*, p. 269.

5. Griffith, "The Crisis of American Labor," pp. 216–17.

6. Marshall, *Labor in the South*, p. 266; Griffith, "The Crisis of American Labor," p. 243.

7. Griffith, "The Crisis of American Labor," p. 243.

8. George Bentley, International Woodworkers of America, to Turner Smith, Civil Rights Section, Department of Justice, May 9, 1946, Mason to Theron Caudle, May 15, 1946, Smith to Mason, May 28, 1946, all in Mason Papers, Box 4, Folder 2.

9. William Smith to Van Bittner, August 27, 1946, Mason Papers, Box 4, Folder 3.

10. William Smith to Van Bittner, August 27, 1946, Paul Christopher to Mason, January 24, 1947, Mason Papers, Box 4, Folder 3; Ernest Pugh to Mason, April 17, 1947, Mason to Pugh, April 22, 1947, Mason Papers, Box 5, Folder 1.

11. Mason to Abbot Rosen, May 3, 1948, Mason Papers, Box 5, Folder 3.

12. Mason to Abbot Rosen, May 3, 5, 1948, Mason Papers, Box 5, Folder 3; Mason, *To Win These Rights*, pp. 114–17.

13. Van Bittner to Mason, January 10, 1947, Mason Papers, Box 4, Folder 3; *Week in Greater Miami*, December 15, 1946; *Business Week*, February 15, 1947; Lawrence Lader, "The Lady and the Sheriff," *New Republic*, January 5, 1948, pp. 17–19; Milton Mackaye, "The CIO Invades Dixie," *Saturday Evening Post*, July 20, 1946, p. 12ff.

14. Mason to Molly Dewson, May 10, 1947, Mason Papers, Box 5, Folder 1; Mason to Paul Christopher, October 9, 1947, Mason Papers, Box 5, Folder 2.

15. Mason to Christopher, August 19, 1948, Mason Papers, Box 6, Folder 1; Mason to Robert Parker, High Point, N.C., April 16, 1952, Mason to Franz Daniel, April 16, 1952, Report on Thomasville, North Carolina, April 24, 1952, all in Mason Papers, Box 8, Folder 2.

16. Marshall, *Labor in the South*, p. 254; John G. Ramsay to author, August 12, 1983.

17. Ramsay to author, August 12, 1983; Ramsay to Mason, January 16, 1946, Mason to Ramsay, January 21, 1946, Mason Papers, Box 4, Folder 2.

18. Memorandum for John Ramsay on visit to Staunton, Virginia, October 11–15, 1948, Ramsay Papers.

19. Mason to Ramsay, January 24, 1949, Mason to Carey Haigler, Alabama Director, CIO Organizing Committee, February 16, May 13, 1949 (quoted), all in Ramsay Papers.

20. *The Churches and Labor Unions* (unpaginated), in Mason Papers, Printed Material.

21. Ibid.

22. Mason to Executive Council, Church of God, June 26, 1948, Mason Pa-

pers, Box 5, Folder 3; Mason to John C. Jernegan, General Overseer, Church of God, August 13, 1948, Mason Papers, Box 6, Folder 1.

23. Mason to Allan Haywood, March 28, 1945, Mason Papers, Box 4, Folder 1, to Earl Taylor, September 14, 1946, Mason Papers, Box 4, Folder 3. Copies of both papers can be found in Mason Papers, Clippings, 1940s. See also *CIO News*, vol. 12, no. 14 (April 1949), for a discussion of them both; clipping on Parson Jack in the John Ramsay Papers.

24. Mason to Gladys Dickson, November 9, 1950, Mason Papers, Box 7, Folder 2; Mason to Paul W. Harding, CIO Organizing Committee, Charlotte, North Carolina, October 24, 1950, Mason to Lloyd Vaughan, CIO Organizing Committee, Columbia, South Carolina, November 25, 1950, Harding to Tom Stokes, November 2, 1950, John Ramsay to Maxie Garner, May 10, 1955, Alan L. Swim, "Southern Industrialists Attack Churches by Fanning Race, Religious Prejudice," *Alabama News Digest,* March 14, 1947, all in John Ramsay Papers.

25. "The Churches and Brotherhood" (1951), in Mason Papers, Printed Material.

26. Mason to friends, March 9, 1951, Mason Papers, Box 7, Folder 3.

27. Mason to Mrs. Roosevelt, August 31, 1951, Mason to Paul Christopher, September 18, 1951, Mason Papers, Box 8, Folder 1; George S. Mitchell to Mason, January 10, 1952, Mason Papers, Box 8, Folder 2.

28. Mason to Lawrence Lader, January 28, 1952, to Aubrey Williams, February 28, 1952, to Ethel Stanley, March 6, 1952, all in Mason Papers, Box 8, Folder 2.

29. See *To Win These Rights; Atlanta Constitution,* November 16, 1952; *Christian Science Monitor,* November 8, 1952; *Richmond News Leader,* August 5, 1953; *Steel Labor,* February 1953; clippings in Mason Papers, Clippings, 1950s; Mason to Eleanor Roosevelt, September 21, 1952, Mason Papers, Box 8, Folder 2; Mason to Carey Haigler, January 26, 1953, Mason Papers, Box 8, Folder 3.

30. Mason to Congressman Robert Ramspeck, November 28, 1945, Mason Papers, Box 4, Folder 2.

31. Lorraine Nelson Spritzer, *The Belle of Ashby Street: Helen Douglas Mankin and Georgia Politics* (Athens: University of Georgia Press, 1982), pp. 62–65.

32. Spritzer, *The Belle of Ashby Street.*

33. Spritzer, *The Belle of Ashby Street,* pp. 69–72; Mason to James B. Carey, March 16, 1946, Mason Papers, Box 4, Folder 2.

34. Spritzer, *The Belle of Ashby Street,* pp. 105–30, Mason to Mrs. Marshall Field, September 21, 1946, Mason Papers, Box 4, Folder 3.

35. Mason to Natalie Bunting, March 5, 1949, Mason Papers, Box 6, Folder 2; Lader, "The Lady and the Sheriff," *New Republic,* January 5, 1948, p. 18.

36. Mason to Eleanor Roosevelt, September 8, 24, 1946, Mason Papers, Box 4, Folder 3.

37. Mason to Reverend Armstead Bowdman, Cleveland, Tennessee, October 18, 1947, to Frank Spenser, January 18, 1948, Mason Papers, Box 5, Folder 2; Mason to Bruce Hunt, August 25, 1949, Mason Papers, Box 6, Folder 3; Mason to Brownie Lee Jones, July 24, 1950, Mason Papers, Box 7, Folder 1.

38. Mason to Brownie Lee Jones, January 5, 1951, Mason Papers, Box 7, Folder 3.

39. Dewson to Mason, September 9, 1946, Mason Papers, Box 4, Folder 3, March 27, 1951, Mason Papers, Box 7, Folder 3.

40. Mason to Eleanor Roosevelt, September 20, 1949, Mason Papers, Box 6, Folder 3, September 12, 1951, Mason Papers, Box 8, Folder 1; Eleanor Roosevelt to Mason, November 20, 1945, Mason Papers, Box 4, Folder 2; Mason to Molly Dewson, April 21, 1951, Mary W. Dewson Collection, Franklin D. Roosevelt Library, Hyde Park, New York, Container 3.

41. *Proceedings of the 1952 Annual Convention of the National Religion and Labor Foundation*, in Mason Papers, Miscellany, 1950–53. A copy of the citation can be found in the John Ramsay Papers.

8. The Liberal Cause

1. Frederickson, "A Place to Speak," introduction, p. 204. Frederickson's excellent dissertation is easily the best study of the school's activities.

2. Mason to Mary C. Barker, April 26, 1933, Mary C. Barker Papers, Robert Woodruff Library for Advanced Studies, Emory University.

3. Records of the American Labor Education Services (hereinafter cited as ALES records), Martin P. Catherwood Library, New York State School of Industrial and Labor Relations, Cornell University, Box 27, Reports of the Director, Southern Summer School for Workers.

4. Brownie Lee Jones to Mason, August 13, 1948, Mason to Jones, August 17, 1948, Mason Papers, Box 6, Folder 1; Mason to Dr. Sarah Blanding, President, Vassar College, January 17, 1948, Mason Papers, Box 5, Folder 2; Brownie Lee Jones to Mason, January 24, 1949, Mason Papers, Box 6, Folder 2.

5. Mason to W. A. Copeland, November 11, December 14, 1948, Copeland to Mason, December 20, 1948, all in Mason Papers, Box 6, Folder 1; Mason to Jones, June 11, 1950, Mason Papers, Box 7, Folder 1.

6. For background material on Highlander, and on Myles Horton, see Anthony P. Dunbar, *Against the Grain: Southern Radicals and Prophets, 1929–1959* (Charlottesville: University Press of Virginia, 1981), pp. 42–45. See also Frank Adams

with Myles Horton, *Unearthing Seeds of Fire: The Idea of Highlander* (Winston-Salem: Blair Publishing, 1977).

7. Adams, *Unearthing Seeds;* John A. Salmond, *A Southern Rebel: The Life and Times of Aubrey Willis Williams* (Chapel Hill: University of North Carolina Press, 1983), p. 239.

8. Lucy Mason to James Dombrowski, December 16, 18, 1937, Highlander Papers, Box 41, Folder 12; Mason to Myles Horton, January 15, February 13, 1938, to John Gass Bratton, July 14, 1952, Horton to Mason, February 21, 1938, all in Highlander Papers, Box 20, Folder 32; Minutes of Highlander Executive Council, Highlander Papers, Box 1, Folder 8.

9. Dombrowski to Mason, August 1, 1939, Mason to John Gass Bratton, July 14, 1952, to Josephine Williams, October 13, 1952, all in Highlander Papers, Box 20, Folder 32.

10. Dunbar, *Against the Grain,* pp. 219–20; Mason to Florina Lasker, January 8, 1943, Highlander Papers, Box 20, Folder 32; Mason to Eleanor Roosevelt, January 13, 1942. Eleanor Roosevelt Papers, Box 841.

11. Dunbar, *Against the Grain,* p. 240.

12. Minutes of Meeting of Highlander Council, November 29–30, 1949, Highlander Papers, Box 1, Folder 8.

13. Mason to Brownie Lee Jones, November 6, 1948, Mason Papers, Box 6, Folder 1; to Bruce Hunt, March 5, 1950, Mason Papers, Box 7, Folder 1. I have quoted both letters.

14. Tindall, *The Emergence of the New South,* p. 636; Sosna, *In Search of the Silent South,* pp. 88–89; Mason to FDR, March 25, 1938, Mason Papers, Box 1, Folder 2, to Eleanor Roosevelt, March 27, 1938, Eleanor Roosevelt Papers, Container 733.

15. Thomas A. Krueger, *And Promises to Keep: The Southern Conference for Human Welfare* (Nashville: Vanderbilt University Press, 1967), pp. 4–17. Virginia Durr, who knew Gelders well, said that he "never carried a CP card" (Durr interview, December 9, 1981).

16. See Tindall, *The Emergence of the New South,* p. 636; Dunbar, *Against the Grain,* pp. 187–88; Sosna, *In Search of the Silent South,* pp. 88–90; Durr interview, December 9, 1981.

17. Malvina Schneider to Mason, April 18, 1938, Mason Papers, Box 1, Folder 2; Krueger, *And Promises to Keep,* pp. 17–26; Tindall, *The Emergence of the New South,* p. 636.

18. Tindall, *The Emergence of the New South,* pp. 635–37 (quotation on p. 637); Myrdal is quoted by Tindall (p. 637).

19. Mason to Frank Graham, December 6, 1938, Graham Papers.

20. Mason to Graham, November 10, 11, 1939, Graham Papers; Krueger, *And Promises to Keep,* pp. 78–80.

21. Mason to Graham, January 22, 24, March 4, 1940, to Clark Foreman, February 10, 1940, Lee to Graham, January 22, 1940, Foreman to Graham, March 20, 1940, Lee to Barry Bingham, March 21, 1940, all in Graham Papers; Mrs. Roosevelt to Mason, February 26, 1940, Mason to Mrs. Roosevelt, March 2, 1940, Mason to Malvina Thompson, March 12, 1940, Thompson to Mason, March 19, 1940, all in Eleanor Roosevelt Papers, Container 783; Mason to Julian Harris, January 29, March 11, 1940, Julian L. Harris Papers, Robert H. Woodruff Library for Advanced Studies, Emory University, Atlanta, Georgia; Mason to Lee, January 24, February 19, March 23, 1940; Papers of the Southern Conference for Human Welfare (hereinafter cited as SCHW Papers), Tuskegee Institute Archives; Krueger, *And Promises to Keep*, pp. 61–64, 84.

22. Mason to Lee, March 23, 1940, SCHW Papers, Box 33, Graham to Mason, April 30, 1940, Mason to Graham, May 8, 1940, Frank McCallister to Graham, June 6, 1940, all in Graham Papers.

23. Mason to Julian Harris, April 26, 1940, Harris Papers.

24. George C. Stoney to Graham, April 29, 1940, Graham Papers.

25. Krueger, *And Promises to Keep*, pp. 80–84; Bingham to Graham, May 27, 1940, Graham Papers.

26. Krueger, *And Promises to Keep*, p. 84.

27. Graham to Thompson, January 31, 1941, to Lee, April 5, 1941, Thompson to Lee, March 29, 1941, to Graham, March 29, 1941, to Gelders, April 26, 1941, Lee to Graham, March 29, 1941, to Thompson, March 29, 1941, all in SCHW Papers, Box 29.

28. Krueger, *And Promises to Keep*, pp. 86–87; Thompson to Virginia Durr, April 7, 1942, SCHW Papers, Box 19.

29. Krueger, *And Promises to Keep*, pp. 104–6; Mason to Graham, April 10, 1942, Graham Papers.

30. Krueger, *And Promises to Keep*, pp. 89–92; Mason to Graham, May 5, 1942, Graham Papers.

31. Mason to Dombrowski, May 25, 1943, SCHW Papers, Box 34; Baldwin to Clark Foreman, May 1942, Graham Papers. I have quoted both letters.

32. Krueger, *And Promises to Keep*, pp. 103–4; Sosna, *In Search of the Silent South*, pp. 65–66.

33. Mason to Dombrowski, September 23, 29, 1942, October 24, 1942, January 8, 28, May 28, June 8, 10, July 1, 1943, Dombrowski to Mason, September 30, 1942, all in SCHW Papers, Box 34; Dunbar, *Against the Grain*, p. 218.

34. Krueger, *And Promises to Keep*, pp. 125–33; Margaret Fisher to James Dombrowski and Clark Foreman, undated, 1945, SCHW Papers, Box 27.

35. Mason to Philip Murray, January 14, 1945, Mason Papers, Box 4, Folder 3.

36. Mason to Dombrowski, April 18, 1945, Mason to Foreman, April 27, 1945, SCHW Papers, Box 34.

37. Foreman to Mason, April 21, 1945, SCHW Papers, Box 34.

38. Durr interview, December 9, 1981, Clark Foreman, interview with J. Hall, November 16, 1974, SOHC; Krueger, *And Promises to Keep,* p. 160; Foreman to Aubrey Williams, April 24, 1947, Carl and Anne Braden Papers, State Historical Society of Wisconsin, Box 18.

39. Fisher to Dombrowski, December 2, 1946, Foreman to Mason, October 7, 1946, Foreman to Dombrowski, April 9, 1947, all in Braden Papers, Box 18; Aubrey Williams to Foreman, April 28, 1947, Minutes of Special Meeting of the Committee for Georgia, July 26, 1947, SCHW Papers, Box 23.

40. Sosna, *In Search of the Silent South,* pp. 88–104, 140–49.

41. Krueger, *And Promises to Keep,* pp. 155–57.

42. Dombrowski to Foreman, December 6, 1946, Mason to Foreman, December 8, 1946, Mason Papers, Box 4, Folder 3.

43. Foreman to Mason, December 11, 1946, Mason Papers, Box 4, Folder 3; Mason to Dombrowski, December 19, 1946, Aubrey Williams to Mason, December 24, 1946, Braden Papers, Box 18.

44. Krueger, *And Promises to Keep,* p. 157; Mason to Dombrowski, December 19, 1946, Braden Papers, Box 18, Foreman interview, November 16, 1974, SOHC.

45. Krueger, *And Promises to Keep,* pp. 139–43.

46. Memorandum to Board of Directors, SCHW, April 19, 1947, Braden Papers, Box 18.

47. Krueger, *And Promises to Keep,* p. 199; Durr interview, December 9, 1981; Minutes of SCHW Board Meeting, October 16, 1947, Braden Papers, Box 18, Mason to Edmonia Grant, October 28, 1947, Mason Papers, Box 5, Folder 2.

48. Mason to Henry Wallace, February 9, 1944, Mason to Mrs. Roosevelt, February 11, 1944, in Eleanor Roosevelt Papers, Container 920.

9. Last Days

1. Mason to Olive Haskins, March 6, 1953, Joanna Willimetz to Mason, March 27, 1953, Carolina Davis, Director, Women's Bureau, UAW-CIO to members, June 8, Anne Little Brandeis to Mason, June 20, 1953, Florence C. Bowles to Mason, June 26, 1953, L. H. Foster, President, Tuskegee Institute, to Mason, November 2, 1953, all in Mason Papers, Box 8, Folder 3.

2. Cary Haigler to Mason, August 11, 1953, Mason to Haigler, August 12, 1953, Mason Papers, Box 8, Folder 3.

3. J. E. Smessner to Mason, January 13, February 26, March 17, 1954, Mason to Smessner, March 20, 1954, all in Mason Papers, Box 8, Folder 3.

4. Minor Blackford to Taylor Burke, April 13, 1954, Mason to Burke, March 6, 1954, both found in private papers held by Taylor Burke. I thank Mr. Burke for allowing me access to this collection.

5. Blackford to Burke, April 13, 15, 16, 20, 1954, Burke Papers.

6. Blackford to Burke, April 26, May 2, 7, 1954, Margaret Fisher to Burke, May 22, 1954, Burke Papers.

7. Blackford to Burke, July 12, 24, 1954, December 27, 1955, Fisher to Burke, December 11, 1955, Burke Papers.

8. Blackford to Burke, February 27, March 17, 1958, Burke Papers.

9. John Ramsay to the Friends of Lucy Randolph Mason, undated circular, Highlander Papers, Box 20, Folder 32.

Epilogue

1. *To Win These Rights*, pp. xi–xii.

2. Myles Horton, interview with M. Frederickson, SOHC.

3. See Lader, "The Lady and the Sheriff"; Ed Townsend, "Miss Lucy—A Very Real Legend," *Christian Science Monitor*, November 8, 1952.

4. Sara Evans, *Personal Politics: The Roots of Women's Liberation in the Civil Rights Movement and the New Left* (New York: Knopf, 1979), p. 24.

5. Ibid., p. 28.

6. Eula McGill, interview with J. Hall, September 5, 1976, SOHC.

7. Ralph McGill, "Miss Lucy Is Gone," undated clipping from *Atlanta Constitution*, in Highlander Papers, Box 20, Folder 32.

8. Erma Angevine, interview with Kerrie Newell, March 7, 1983, and Esther Peterson, interview with Kerrie Newell March 13, 1983, both at La Trobe University. I thank Ms. Newell for permitting me to use the transcripts of these interviews.

9. Mason to Nicholas Kelley, May 28, 1937, NCL Papers A/1.

10. Lucy Randolph Mason, "I Turned to Social Action Right at Home," in *Labor's Relation to Church and Community* (New York: Harpers, 1947), pp. 145–55.

11. Mason to Howard Lee, March 23, 30, 1940, SCHW Papers, Box 33.

12. Mason to Ralph McGill, May 23, 1940, Mason Papers, Box 2, Folder 1.

13. Mason to Eleanor Roosevelt, September 12, 1951, Mason Papers, Box 8, Folder 1.

14. Mason to Eleanor Roosevelt, September 12, 1951, Mason Papers, Box 8,

Folder 1, to Eleanor Roosevelt, November 6, 1940, Mason Papers, Box 2, Folder
2. Mason to FDR, January 12, 1939, Roosevelt Papers, PPF 200B.

15. Mason, *I Turned to Social Action*, pp. 145–47; Radio script of worship service, University of Oklahoma, February 25, 1948, Mason Papers, Addresses.

16. Mason, *I Turned to Social Action*, pp. 146–47; Notes on Death, August
1927, in Mason Papers, Miscellany, 1920–40.

17. Mason to Cecil Scott, October 31, 1930, Mason Papers, Box 1, Folder 1;
extract from Mason to Gerwicks, April 27, 1930, Mason Papers, Miscellany, 1920–
40.

18. Ralph McGill, "Miss Lucy Is Gone"; Ralph McGill, *The South and the
Southerner* (Boston: Little Brown, 1963), pp. 190–93.

Bibliography

The most important manuscript collection was the Lucy Randolph Mason Papers, held at the Perkins Library, Duke University. The bulk of this collection relates to her CIO work and documents her union activities in the South, but there is also a considerable amount of material dealing with the Southern Conference for Human Welfare and the Southern Summer School for Women Workers. There is also some material concerning her life in Richmond. In particular, the various drafts of *To Win These Rights* contain invaluable accounts, most of which were never published, of her girlhood. There are also a few family letters, and despite the fact that the collection was reportedly checked before deposit and almost all personal material removed, enough remains to give a picture of Mason's relationship with Katherine Gerwick. The various scrapbooks and testimonials presented to Lucy when she left Richmond in 1932 indicate her standing in the community, while there is a great deal of correspondence to do with her work in the South in 1931 under the auspices of the National Consumers League.

There is almost nothing in the Duke collection, however, of relevance to her years with the league as general secretary. Fortunately, the papers of the National Consumers League, in the Library of Congress, filled this particular gap. The Library of Congress collection is voluminous, and the years of Mason's general secretaryship are particularly well documented. Her letters from the field are there, as are her reports to the board and her correspondence with a vast array of public officials. There is also much material on the women's charter. Also at the Library of Congress, and illuminating regarding aspects of her early life, are the League of Women Voters Papers.

Perhaps the most important collection containing material to do with Mason's life in Richmond is the sprawling, uncataloged Adele Clark Collection at the James Branch Cabell Library, Virginia Commonwealth University. It is particularly helpful in regard to the Richmond Equal Suffrage League and the League of Women Voters. The Archives of the National Board of the YWCA, New York City, had a few items of interest pertaining to Miss Lucy's work in Richmond, as did the records of the Richmond YWCA, still held at the local YWCA office. The Richmond League of Women Voters Papers, at the Virginia State Library, contained little of value.

Three collections helped me unravel the complex story of Mason's work with the Southern Conference for Human Welfare. They were the Frank P. Graham Papers, Southern Historical Collection, University of North Carolina at Chapel Hill; the SCHW Papers, at the Tuskegee Institute Archives; and the Carl and Anne Braden Papers, at the Wisconsin State Historical Society. Also at Wisconsin, and of considerable value, were the Highlander Research and Education Center Papers. I could find nothing of relevance to Lucy Mason's life in either the John L. Lewis Papers or the Records of the Textile Workers Union of America.

At the Franklin D. Roosevelt Library, Hyde Park, the Franklin D. Roosevelt, Eleanor Roosevelt, and Mary Dewson collections all shed light on the interplay between the private and the public worlds during the New Deal period. The Eleanor Roosevelt collection was particularly helpful, containing as it does literally scores of letters from Lucy Mason, mainly to do with civil rights violations against CIO organizers. Some, however, were concerned with SCHW business, while a few dealt with political matters in Georgia. The Aubrey Williams Papers had a few items of interest, again mainly to do with the SCHW.

Other collections of value were the John Ramsay Papers at the Southern Labor Archive, Georgia State University, particularly for her last years with the CIO, the Virginius Dabney Papers at the Alderman Library, University of Virginia, and the privately held Taylor C. Burke Papers for her last sad years.

I made extensive use of the excellent Southern Oral History Collection at the University of North Carolina at Chapel Hill. The *Richmond Times Dispatch* gave me a sense of that city during the years when Lucy Mason lived there, and the *Atlanta Constitution* helped me in similar ways for her time in Georgia. I made more selective use of the *St. Louis Post Dispatch* and the *Memphis Press Scimitar*.

Like many other scholars I have leaned heavily on George F. Tindall's magisterial *The Emergence of the New South, 1913–1945* for the context of twentieth-century southern history. I also benefited from reading Ralph McGill's *The South and the Southerner*. F. Ray Marshall's *Labor in the South* remains the standard work in its field.

On southern liberals, Morton Sosna's *In Search of the Silent South* is still the best general study, though Anthony Dunbar's *Against the Grain: Southern Radicals and Prophets, 1929–1959* is a useful and lively complement. My own *A Southern Rebel* explores the life of one particular liberal figure, while Mary Frederickson's superb dissertation "A Place to Speak Our Minds" is an essential treatment of liberalism, labor, and the southern women's movement as they interrelate. Thomas Krueger's *And Promises to Keep* is still the only study of the SCHW.

Like many before me, I have used William O'Neill's *Everyone Was Brave* extensively. I have followed Stanley Lemons in *The Woman Citizen* in distinguishing between "social" and "egalitarian" feminists in the 1920s. Clark A. Chambers's *Seedtime of Reform* is invaluable on the women's reform network. Aileen S. Kraditor's *The Ideas of the Woman Suffrage Movement, 1890–1920* is still the standard work. Susan D. Becker's *The Origins of the Equal Rights Amendment* helped me understand the National Woman's party, while Susan B. Ware's *Beyond Suffrage* was invaluable in introducing me to the women's network and showed me how Lucy Mason fitted into it. Anne F. Scott's *The Southern Lady* helped me to understand southern women generally and Lucy's background. John P. McDowell's superb monograph *The Social Gospel in the South* enabled me to fit Lucy Mason within a particular religious context. Jacquelyn Dowd Hall's biography of Jessie Daniel Ames, *Revolt Against Chivalry*, also helped in this area and provided an impressive model. Lorraine N. Spritzer, *The Belle of Ashby Street*, taught me about the complexities of Atlanta's politics at the time Mason was living there.

Several books enabled me to glimpse something of the city in which Mason grew up and in which she worked. Michael B. Chesson's *Richmond After the War, 1865–1890* is a painstakingly documented and superbly written chronicle of a city in decline. Ellen Glasgow's memoir *The Women Within* includes some invaluable recollections of what it was like to be young in Richmond, while Virginius Dabney's *Richmond: The Story of a City* is a chatty, informed overview by one of Richmond's most illustrious insiders. Christopher Silver in *Twentieth Century Richmond* helped me understand the context of Lucy Mason's reform activities in the city during the 1920s; so from a rather different perspective did Raymond Gavins, *The Perils and Prospects of Southern Black Leadership*. Both Leon Fink, *Workingmen's Democracy*, and Peter Rachleff, *Black Labor in the South*, are valuable in fleshing out the picture of the city that formed her.

For the CIO's development during the years Miss Lucy worked for it, and especially during the war years, I have relied on Nelson Lichtenstein's brilliant synthesis *Labor's War at Home*, supplemented by Irving Bernstein's *Turbulent Years* and Barbara Griffith's recent dissertation, "The Crisis of American Labor." My most valuable source for these matters, and for much else, of course, was Lucy Mason's own book, *To Win These Rights*. It is a book rich in its detailed accounts of labor's struggles in the South during those years and infused with her own liberal Christian world view. As a key to understanding the CIO, the South, and Lucy Mason herself, I found it indispensable.

Manuscripts
Alderman Library, University of Virginia

Harry F. Byrd Papers
Virginius Dabney Papers
Dillard Family Papers

Catholic University, Washington, D.C.

Philip Murray Papers

James Branch Cabell Library, Virginia Commonwealth University

Adele Clark Papers

Library of Congress

League of Women Voters Papers
National Consumers League Papers
National Policy Committee Papers
Women's Joint Congressional Committee Papers

Martin P. Catherwood Library, New York State School of Industrial and Labor Relations, Cornell University

Records of the American Labor Education Service

National Archives

Women's Bureau Papers

National Board of the Archives of the YWCA, New York

National Board of the YWCA Papers

Perkins Library, Duke University

CIO Organizing Committee Papers
Lucy Randolph Mason Papers

Privately Held

Taylor C. Burke Papers

Richmond YWCA

Richmond YWCA Papers

Robert Woodruff Library, Emory University

Mary C. Barker Papers
Julian L. Harris Papers

Franklin D. Roosevelt Library

Mary W. Dewson Papers
Eleanor Roosevelt Papers
Franklin D. Roosevelt Papers
Aubrey W. Williams Papers

Schlesinger Library, Radcliffe College

Mary Anderson Papers
Mary W. Dewson Papers
Frances Perkins Papers

Sophia Smith Collection, Smith College, Northampton, Massachusetts

Mary Van Kleek Papers
YWCA Papers

Southern Historical Collection, University of North Carolina at Chapel Hill

Kenneth Douty Report on the Southern Conference for Human Welfare
Frank P. Graham Papers
Broadus Mitchell Papers
Samuel Chiles Mitchell Papers
Howard Odum Papers
Olive Matthews Stone Papers

Southern Labor Archive, Georgia State University

Paul Christopher Papers
John Ramsay Papers

Tuskegee Institute Archives

Southern Conference for Human Welfare Papers

Virginia State Library, Richmond, Virginia

Richmond League of Women Voters Papers

Wisconsin State Historical Society

Carl and Anne Braden Papers
James A. Dombrowski Papers
Highlander Research and Education Center Papers
John L. Lewis Papers
Textile Workers Union of America Papers

Interviews

Angevine, Erma. Interview with Kerrie Newell, March 1984. La Trobe University, Melbourne, Australia.
Durr, Virginia F. Interview with author. December 9, 1981. La Trobe University, Melbourne, Australia.
Peterson, Esther. Interview with Kerrie Newell. March 1984. La Trobe University, Melbourne, Australia.
Russell, Mattie C. Interviews with author. July–December 1981. La Trobe University, Melbourne, Australia.

Southern Oral History Collection, University of North Carolina at Chapel Hill

Adamson, Mary. Interview with M. Frederickson. April 19, 1976.
Ames, Jessie Daniel. Interview with P. Watters. 1965–66.
Anderson, Eleanor Copenhaver. Interview with M. Frederickson. November 5, 1974.

Camp, Miriam Bonner. Interview with M. Frederickson. April 15, 1976.

Clark, Adele. Interviews with W. Broadfoot. February 28, 1964. July 12, 1964.

———. Interview with B. Friedman. January 22, 1978.

Cook, Alice Hansen. Interview with M. Frederickson. October 31, 1974.

Coy, Mildred Price. Interview with M. Frederickson. April 26, 1976.

Creedy, Brooks Spivey. Interview with M. Frederickson. July 14, 1975.

Dabney, Virginius. Interview with J. Bass and W. DeVries. March 12, 1974.

Foreman, Clark. Interview with J. Hall. November 16, 1974.

Horton, Myles. Interview with W. Finger. December 6, 1974.

———. Interview with M. Frederickson. July 24, 1975.

———. Interview with D. Blanchard. April 12, 1984.

Jones, Brownie Lee. Interview with M. Frederickson. April 20, 1976.

Lumpkin, Katharine du Pre. Interview with J. Hall. August 4, 1974.

MacDonald, Lois. Interview with M. Roydhouse. June 24, 1975.

———. Interview with M. Frederickson. August 25, 1977.

McGill, Eula. Interview with L. Lipsitz. 1975.

———. Interview with J. Hall. February 3, 1976.

———. Interview with J. Hall. September 5, 1976.

McLaren, Myron. Interview with M. Frederickson. November 4, 1974.

Mitchell, Broadus. Interview with D. Singal. November 11, 1971.

———. Interview with M. Frederickson. August 14, 1977.

Raper, Arthur F. Interview with [?]. January 29, 1974.

———. Interview with J. Hall. January 30, 1974.

———. Interview with M. Sosna. April 23, 1971.

———. Interview with D. Singal. January 8, 1978.

Ribkin, Polly Hayden. Interview with M. Frederickson. June 12, 1974.

Smith, Hilda. Interview with M. Roydhouse. March 11, 1975.

Stone, Olive Mathews. Interview with S. Gluck. March 6, 1975. June 27, 1975. August 13, 1975. September 10, 1975. October 14, 1975. November 4, 1975. November 11, 1975.

Wilkins, Josephine. Interview with J. Hall. 1972.

Wright, Alice Spearman. Interviews with J. Hall. August 8, 1976. October 28, 1976.

Young, Louise. Interview with J. Hall. February 14, 1972.

Newspapers

Atlanta Constitution
Business Week

Christian Science Monitor
CIO News
St. Louis Post Dispatch
Memphis Press Scimitar
Raleigh News and Observer
Richmond Evening Journal
Richmond News Leader
Richmond Planet
Richmond Times Dispatch
Virginia Pilot
Week in Greater Miami
Witness

Books and Articles

Adams, Frank, with Horton, Myles. *Unearthing Seeds of Fire: The Idea of High-lander*. Winston-Salem: Blair Publishing, 1977.
Becker, Susan D. *The Origins of the Equal Rights Amendment: American Feminism Between the Wars*. Westport, Conn.: Greenwood Press, 1981.
Bernstein, Irving. *The Turbulent Years: A History of the American Worker, 1933–1941*. Boston: Houghton Mifflin, 1970.
Cayton, Horace R., and Mitchell, George S. *Black Workers and the New Unions*. Westport, Conn.: Negro Universities Press, 1970.
Chambers, Clark A. *Seedtime of Reform: American Social Service and Social Action*. Minneapolis: University of Minnesota Press, 1963.
Chatfield, Charles. *For Peace and Justice: Pacifism in America, 1914–1941*. Knoxville: University of Tennessee Press, 1971.
Chesson, Michael B. *Richmond After the War, 1865–1890*. Richmond: Virginia State Library, 1981.
Dabney, Virginius. *Richmond: The Story of a City*. Garden City: Doubleday, 1976.
Dunbar, Anthony P. *Against the Grain: Southern Radicals and Prophets, 1929–1959*. Charlottesville: University Press of Virginia, 1981.
Dye, Nancy Schrom. *As Equals and as Sisters: Feminism, the Labor Movement, and the Womens Trade Union League of New York*. Columbia: University of Missouri Press, 1980.
Evans, Sara. *Personal Politics: The Roots of Women's Liberation in the Civil Rights Movement and the New Left*. New York: Knopf, 1979.
Fink, Leon. *Workingmen's Democracy: The Knights of Labor and American Politics*. Urbana: University of Illinois Press, 1983.

Foster, James C. *The Union Politic: The CIO Political Action Committee.* Columbia: University of Missouri Press, 1975.

Fraser, Steve. "From the 'New Unionism' to the New Deal." *Labor History.* vol. 25, no.3 (Summer 1984): 406–30.

Gavins, Raymond. *The Perils and Prospects of Southern Black Leadership: Gordon Blaine Hancock, 1884–1970.* Durham: Duke University Press, 1977.

Glasgow, Ellen. *The Woman Within.* New York: Harcourt Brace, 1954.

Hall, Jacquelyn Dowd. *Revolt Against Chivalry: Jessie Daniel Ames and the Women's Campaign Against Lynching.* New York: Columbia University Press, 1979.

Hall, Jacquelyn Dowd, Korstad, Robert, and Leloudis, James. "Cotton Mill People: Work, Community, and Protest in the Textile South, 1880–1940." *American Historical Review,* vol. 91, no.2 (April 1986): 245–86.

Kerr, Howard. *Mediums and Spirit Rappers and Roaring Radicals: Spiritualism in American Literature, 1850–1900.* Urbana: University of Illinois Press, 1972.

Kessler-Harris, Alice. *Out to Work: A History of Wage-Earning Women in the United States.* New York: Oxford University Press, 1982.

Kornbluh, Joyce L., and Frederickson, Mary, eds. *Sisterhood and Solidarity: Workers' Education for Women.* Philadelphia: Temple University Press, 1984.

Kraditor, Aileen S. *The Ideas of the Woman Suffrage Movement, 1890–1920.* New York: Columbia University Press, 1965.

Krueger, Thomas A. *And Promises to Keep: The Southern Conference for Human Welfare.* Nashville: Vanderbilt University Press, 1967.

Labor's Relation to Church and Community. New York, Harpers, 1947.

Lader, Lawrence. "The Lady and the Sheriff." *New Republic,* January 5, 1948, pp. 17–19.

Lemons, J. Stanley. *The Woman Citizen: Social Feminism in the 1920's.* Urbana: University of Illinois Press, 1973.

Leuchtenburg, William E. *The Perils of Prosperity, 1914–1932.* Chicago: University of Chicago Press, 1958.

Lichtenstein, Nelson. *Labor's War at Home: The CIO in World War II.* New York: Cambridge University Press, 1982.

McDowell, John P. *The Social Gospel in the South: The Woman's Home Mission Movement in the Methodist Episcopal Church, South, 1886–1939.* Baton Rouge: Louisiana State University Press, 1982.

McGill, Ralph. *The South and the Southerner.* Boston: Little Brown, 1963.

Mackaye, Milton. "The CIO Invades Dixie." *Saturday Evening Post,* July 20, 1946, pp. 12, 94–99.

Marchand, C. Roland. *The American Peace Movement and Social Reform, 1898–1918.* Princeton: Princeton University Press, 1972.

Marshall, F. Ray. *Labor in the South.* Cambridge, Mass.: Harvard University Press, 1967.

Mason, Lucy Randolph. "The CIO in the South." *South and World Affairs,* vol. 6 (April 1944):4–8.

———. "Southerners Look at the South." *North Georgia Review* (Fall–Winter 1939):17–18, 40.

———. *Standards for Workers in Southern Industry.* New York: National Consumers League, 1931.

———. *To Win These Rights.* New York: Harpers, 1952.

Mitchell, George S. "The Negro in Southern Trade Unionism." *Southern Economic Journal,* vol. 2, no.3 (January 1936):26–33.

Moore, R. Lawrence. *In Search of White Crows: Spiritualism, Parapsychology, and American Culture.* New York: Oxford University Press, 1977.

O'Neill, William L. *Everyone Was Brave: A History of Feminism in America.* Chicago: Quadrangle Books, 1969.

Polenberg, Richard, *War and Society: The United States, 1941–1945.* New York, Lippincott, 1972.

Pope, Liston. *Millhands and Preachers: A Study of Gastonia.* New Haven: Yale University Press, 1942.

Pulley, Raymond H. *Old Virginia Restored: An Interpretation of the Progressive Impulse, 1870–1930.* Charlottesville: University of Virginia Press, 1968.

Rachleff, Peter J. *Black Labor in the South: Richmond Virginia, 1865–1890.* Philadelphia: Temple University Press, 1984.

Salmond, John A. *A Southern Rebel: The Life and Times of Aubrey Willis Williams, 1890–1965.* Chapel Hill: University of North Carolina Press, 1983.

Scott, Anne Firor. *The Southern Lady: From Pedestal to Politics.* Chicago: University of Chicago Press, 1970.

Silver, Christopher. *Twentieth Century Richmond: Planning, Politics, and Race.* Knoxville: University of Tennessee Press, 1984.

Sosna, Morton. *In Search of the Silent South: Southern Liberals and the Race Issue.* New York: Columbia University Press, 1977.

Spritzer, Lorraine N. *The Belle of Ashby Street: Helen Douglas Mankin and Georgia Politics.* Athens: University of Georgia Press, 1982.

Tindall, George F. *The Emergence of the New South, 1913–1945.* Baton Rouge: Louisiana State University Press, 1967.

Ware, Susan B. *Beyond Suffrage: Women in the New Deal.* Cambridge, Mass.: Harvard University Press, 1981.

Wittner, Lawrence S. *Rebels Against War: The American Peace Movement, 1941–1960.* New York: Columbia University Peace Press, 1969.

Wolfe, Allis Rosenberg. "Women, Consumerism, and the National Consumers' League in the Progressive Era, 1900–1923." *Labor History,* vol. 16, no.3 (Summer 1975):378–92.

Theses and Dissertations

Frederickson, Mary E. "'A Place to Speak Our Minds': The Southern School for Women Workers." Ph.D. dissertation, University of North Carolina, 1981.

Griffith, Barbara S. "The Crisis of American Labor: Operation Dixie and the Defeat of the CIO." Ph.D. dissertation, Duke University, 1986.

Taylor, Frances S. "On the Edge of Tomorrow: Southern Women, the Student YWCA and Race, 1920–1944." Ph.D. dissertation, Stanford University, 1984.

Index

Kamp, Joe, 136
Kelley, Florence, 22, 23, 28, 29, 46,
    49, 50–51, 53
Kelley, Nicholas, 176
Kellogg, Paul, 72
Kern, Mrs. G. T. W., 23
Killers of the Dream (Smith), 174
Kilpatrick, Carroll, 84
Kirchwey, Freda, 108
Kleek, Mary Van, 68
Knights of Labor, 7
Korstad, Robert, 75
Krueger, Thomas, 153, 158
Ku Klux Klan, 135

Labor activism: in post–Civil War
    Richmond, 7. *See also* CIO,
    National Consumers League
Lader, Lawrence, 130, 142
"The Lady and the Sheriff" (Lader),
    130
Langhorne, Nancy. *See* Astor, Lady
Lasker, Florina, 151
Lauder, A. Estelle, 49
League of Women Voters (LWV): Miss
    Lucy's involvement in, 22–24, 26,
    41, 119
Lee, Howard, 155–56, 157, 158, 159
Lee, Robert E., 2, 172
Legislation, wages-and-hours: Lucy
    Mason as advocate of, 51–65, 67
Leloudis, James, 75
Lemons, Stanley, 31
Leprosy: Lucy Ambler Mason's efforts
    to combat, 4
Leuchtenburg, William E., 53
Lewis, John L., 77, 96, 107; hires
    Lucy Mason for CIO, 73–74, 78; as
    supporter of Wendell Willkie,
    90–91, 97; Lucy Mason shows

support for, 97–98; as opponent of
    Roosevelt's foreign policy, 101–2
Lichtenstein, Nelson, 102, 124
Loray Mill, 76
Lowell, Josephine Shaw, 50
Lumpkin, Katharine, 15, 16
LWV. *See* League of Women Voters

McCallister, Frank, 157, 159
McCormick, Anne O'Hara, 53
McDonald, Lois, 146
McDowell, John P., 4, 12, 27, 37, 116
McGill, Eula, 174
McGill, Ralph, 2, 117, 154, 175, 177,
    180
McKaye, Milton, 130
McLaren, Louise Leonard, 146, 147
McLauren, W. M., 45–46
McNutt, Paul V., 103
Magee, Elizabeth, 49
Mankin, Helen Douglas, 141–42
Marchand, C. Roland, 37
Marconnier, Emily Simes, 65, 72–73,
    175
Marietta, Ga., 6
Marshall, John, 2, 172
Marshall, Roy, 125, 127
Marxism: as influence on social views,
    116–17
Mason, Anna, 3, 179
Mason, Anne Maria, 2
Mason, George, 1, 2, 44, 153, 172
Mason, Ida Oswald, 3, 20, 21, 29. *See
    also* Burke, Ida Mason
Mason, James Murray, 1, 96, 172
Mason, John Ambler, 3, 20
Mason, Landon Randolph (Lucy's
    father), 2; accepts post in
    Richmond, 6; differs with Lucy's
    feminist principles, 12, 13; Lucy